MICROSOFT® OFFICE 2007

Training Guide

(Visual Approach to Learning MS Office 2007 Package)

By

Satish Jain

B.S.c., B.E. (IISc), M.E. (IISc), M.Tech. (I.I.T. Kanpur)
Wing Commander (Retd.)
Professor of Information Technology,
Institute of Information Technology & Management,
GGS Indraprastha University, Delhi.

M. Geetha

Kratika

bpb

www.bpbonline.com

FIRST EDITION 2011
REPRINT 2025

ISBN: 978-81-8333-402-0

Distributors:

BPB PUBLICATIONS
20, Ansari Road, Darya Ganj
New Delhi-110002
Ph: 23254990/23254991

DECCAN AGENCIES
4-3-329, Bank Street,
Hyderabad-500195
Ph: 24756967/24756400

MICRO MEDIA
Shop No. 5, Mahendra Chambers,
150 DN Rd. Next to Capital Cinema,
V.T. (C.S.T.) Station, MUMBAI-400 001
Ph: 22078296/22078297

BPB BOOK CENTRE
376 Old Lajpat Rai Market,
Delhi-110006
Ph: 23861747

Published by Manish Jain for BPB Publications, 20 Ansari Road, Darya Ganj, New Delhi-110002 and Printed at Manipal Technologies Limited, Manipal

www.bpbonline.com

Dedicated to

Sri Raja Rajeshwari and Sai Baba

Who bless Immense Power of Knowledge

Preface

The objective of this training guide is to meet the growing need of different types of users who wish to explore the full capability of MS Office 2007 in a simple manner. It is observed that most of the books available in the market are written by foreign authors and such books do not explain MS Office 2007 from the first time user's point of view.

MS Office 2007 is a set of packages such as ***Word, Excel, PowerPoint, Access,*** and ***Outlook*** that enable you to work on complex jobs using PC in a very easy way. Most of the capabilities of these packages are explained in this guide with many screens.

A very useful feature of this guide is its visual approach showing steps on the screen and printed in the book as seen on the PC monitor. Buttons, Ribbons, Commands etc. are also explained in text, so as to enable a reader to understand subject matter without any outside help.

This guide covers all important features of MS Office 2007 packages. It may also serve as a useful reference guide for experienced users of earlier versions of MS Office.

We have made this guide user friendly by adding a comprehensive index at the end of the book. The index is very handy for locating page number of major topics discussed in this book.

A special feature throughout this book is that the salient and crucial information has been encapsulated within parallel and horizontal lines with a (✍) mark to draw the attention of the reader.

We shall feel obliged to the readers if they send us their critical opinion of the presentation, readability and coverage in this book and send us suggestions if any, in improving the subject matter.

20th October, 2010 Authors

Contents

Preface, v

MS OFFICE 2007

Training Guide

(Visual Approach to Learning Office 2007 Package)

Excel 2007 43

MS Word 2007

Notes:

To open All Office Packages you need to use the same method as explained in the following steps.

The keyboard shortcut to open a document is Ctrl + O.

When you open a file of another format, such as a file from a previous version of Word, it will automatically convert the file to current Word format.

Opening a file automatically creates in the current directory a temporary file, the name of which begins with a tilde (~). When the document is correctly closed, the temporary file is deleted.

Starting Word 2007

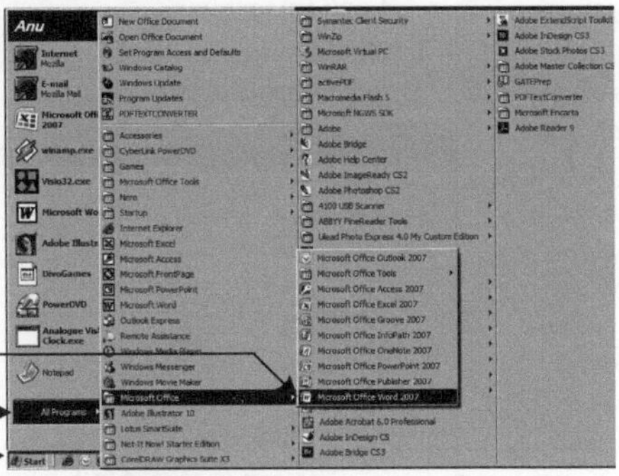

1. Click **Start** button.
2. Highlight **All Programs**. A sub menu appears, select **MS-Office.**
3. Select **MS-Office Word 2007**.

Open a Document

Word 2007 opens files in any of the several formats such as (doc, docx, docm, html, etc.)

1. Click **Office Button**, and then click **Open** command. The **Open** dialog box appears. Or you can click from **Quick Access Toolbar.**

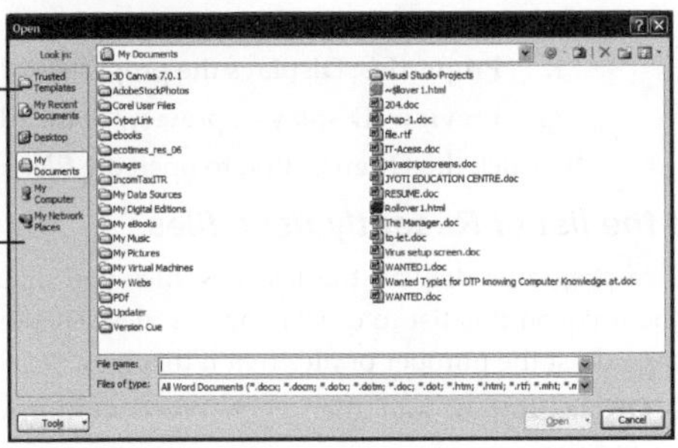

2. Click a folder button to change the file group displayed in the window.

Notes:

The Quick Access Toolbar is a customizable toolbar that contains a set of commands that are independent of the tab that is currently displayed. You can add buttons that represent commands to the Quick Access Toolbar. You can move the Quick Access Toolbar from one of the two possible locations.

3. Choose the desired folder:
   a. Click the **Up One Level** button to display the folders that are stored along with the folder currently displayed in the **Look in:** text box.
   b. Double click a folder icon in the list window to display the contents of that folder.

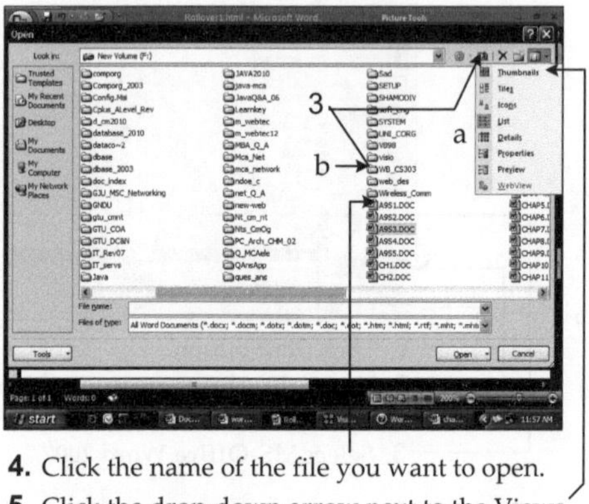

4. Click the name of the file you want to open.
5. Click the drop-down arrow next to the Views button to change the way the folder and file list is displayed.
   a. **Thumbnails:** It displays icon in Thumbnails. When you click a folder name, a thick highlighted border appears.
   b. **Tiles:** It displays icons in medium size.
   c. **Icons:** It displays icons in smaller size.
   d. **List:** Displays a list of commads.
   e. **Details:** Displays the details of the size type, last modifies, etc.
   f. **Properties:** Displays the properties of the file.
   g. **Preview:** Displays a preview of the file.
6. Click the **Open** button to open the file.

Customize the list of Recently used files

Many MS-Office programs display the last few files you opened in that program. You can use the links on this list to quickly access files. This feature is turned on by default. You can adjust the number of files that it displays.

1. Click the **Office Button**, and then click **Word Options.** The **Word Options** dialog box appears.
2. Click **Advanced**.
3. Under **Display**, in the **Show this number of Recent Documents** list, click the number of files that you want to display.

Notes:

Word gives you two methods to create new documents. The first is, to create a new document starting with a blank page. The second is, use a template to open a blank, preformatted document.

Creating a Document

:Office Button

1. Click **Office Button** and then select **New** button. A **New** document dialog box appears.

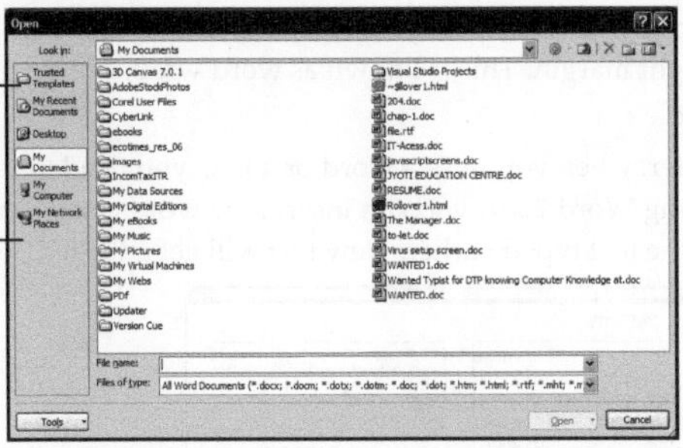

2. Click a folder button to change the file group displayed in the window.

What is Word Processing?

Word 2007 is a Word Processor that operates under Windows Operating System namely XP, Windows Vista and Windows 7. When you use a computer program to create, and edit text documents, you are using word processing power of this package. Word 2007 is one of the most sophisticated word processing program available to day. With Word 2007, it is easier than ever to efficiently create a wide range of business documents namely, a simple letter to a complex project report. Word 2007 includes many desktop features that you can use to enhance the appearance of documents so that they are easy to read.

Why use Word 2007?

Use Word 2007 as word processor for printing letters, preparing mailing lists, creating documents and reports. The speed of these operations is much faster and easier than what is possible on any other word processing package. You can even check the spellings in documents. You can get help to select appropriate words in a sentence. Moreover, you can add page numbers or change margins.

You can emphasize the selected words by printing them in boldface, italics or in bold italics.

Word 2007 can store very long documents in computer's hard disk. You can then modify such documents or print copies just by pressing a few keys from the keyboard. In case you have to make some changes in a letter, you can do so without retyping the whole letter.

> ✍ ***Word 2007 can be used to send the same letter to several different addressees using the Mail-Merge facility or using electronic mail facility on the Internet. You do not have to retype each individual letters for every person.***

Word Processing Terminologies

Word Wrap

A word processor automatically moves the text to the next line when you type beyond the right margin. This is known as word wrap.

Editing of Text

On a typewriter, when you miss a word or a line, you need to re-type the whole letter again. But using Word 2007, you can insert new words, new sentences or paragraphs anywhere in the text typed earlier. New text will get adjusted automatically.

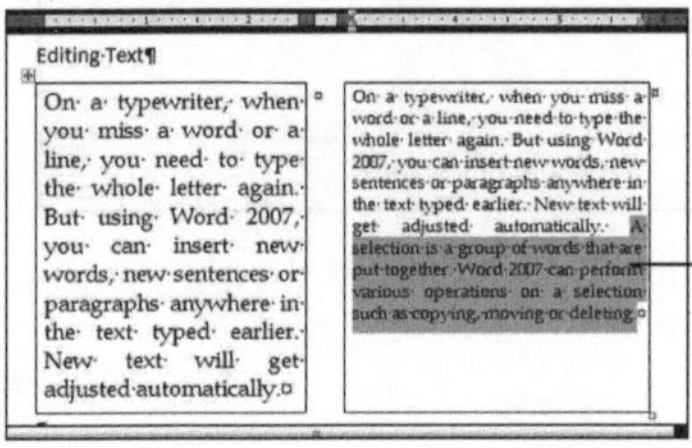

The highlighted text is being inserted

Selection

A selection is a group of words that are put together. Word 2007 can perform various operations on a selection such as copying, moving or deleting. The selection in Word 2007 gets highlighted. By giving the appropriate command, you can move or copy the selection to another place in the same document or to another document.

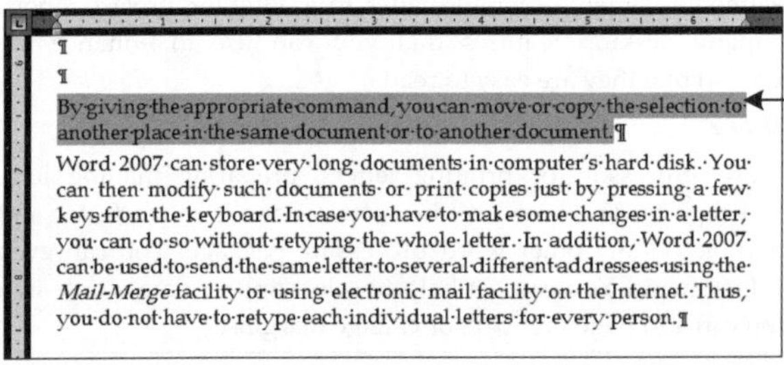

Text block highlighted

Moving/Copying Selected Block of Text

You can move a selected block of text to another location in the same document or copy the text at another location with the help of Word 2007. This saves the effort of retyping the text.

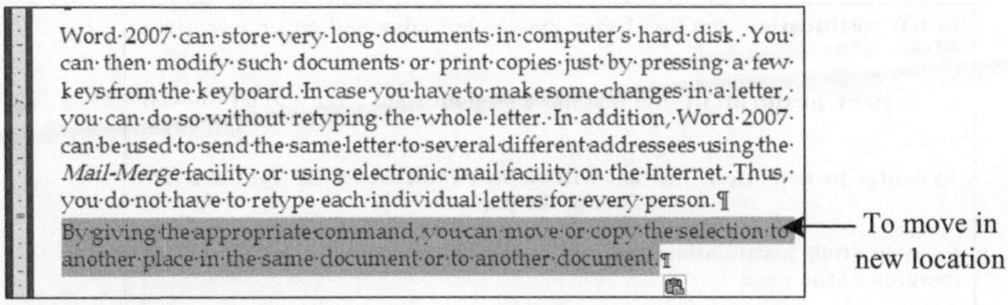

Search and Replace

Word 2007 can conduct a search for any specified word or character in a document and replace it with another word as desired. For example, suppose you have written Pencile in a document and you wish to replace it with Pencil throughout the document, then you can use search and replace feature of Word 2007 to do the same.

Dictionary/Grammar Check

You can check spellings and locate errors in your document using Word 2007. To check spelling in every word of the text you can use the dictionary available in Word 2007.

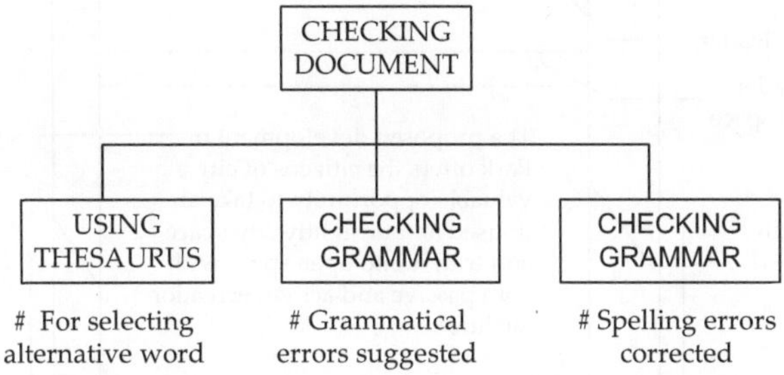

Character Styles and Sizes

You can change the type and the size of characters so that a printed document appears more attractive and professional. You can use bigger and bold letters for main headings. You can use italic characters to emphasize a word. Some examples of styles and sizes of characters are shown below:

Style	**Size**
Bold	12 Pt. Times New Roman
Italics	14 Pt. Arial
~~Strikeout~~	18 Pt. Arial Narrow
Underline	**24 Pt. Arial Bold**

Justification of the Text

Justification is the alignment of the text, typed within the given margins. The text can be *left, right, centre* or *even* justified. Various types of text justification are shown below:

In **left justification**, the text has a straight left edge and an uneven right edge.

In **right justification**, the text has a straight right edge and an uneven left edge.

In **center justification**, the text will be printed between the right and left edges of the paper.

In **even (full) justification**, the text is aligned on both the left and right margins of the page.

Header, Footer, Page Numbering and Margins

The document contains header, footer, page numbering and margins which, are shown below.

1. A header is a special text which is printed at the top of each page.

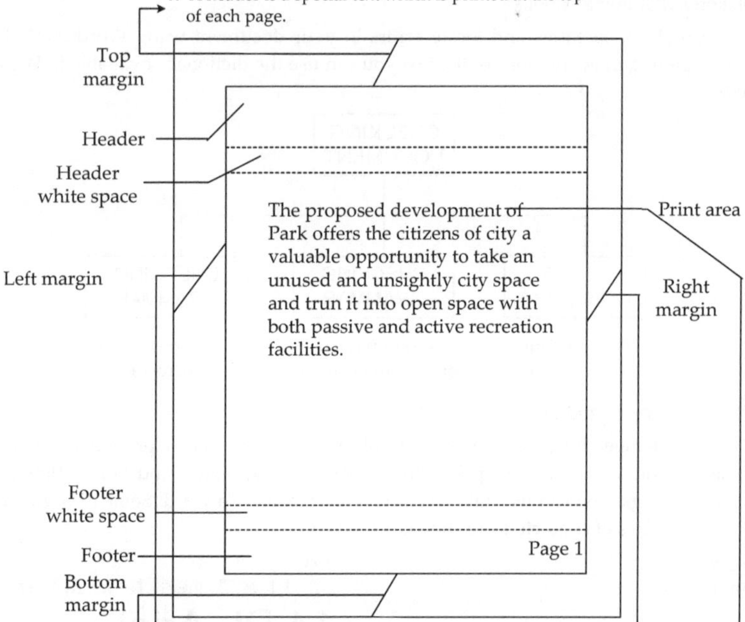

2. A footer is a special text which is printed at the bottom of each page.

3. The left and right margins are the distances between the text and left and right edges of the paper. It is normally one inch but you can adjust accordingly to your requirement.

4. The area which is document matter is printed.

Line Spacing

In Word 2007, the spacing between the lines can be adjusted. You can leave one or more blank lines between every two typed lines but the default line spacing is single line spacing. When one line is left blank between two typed lines, then it is known as double line spacing. Double line spacing is normally used for draft letters. Below figure shows a paragraph first typed in single line spacing and then made in double line spacing.

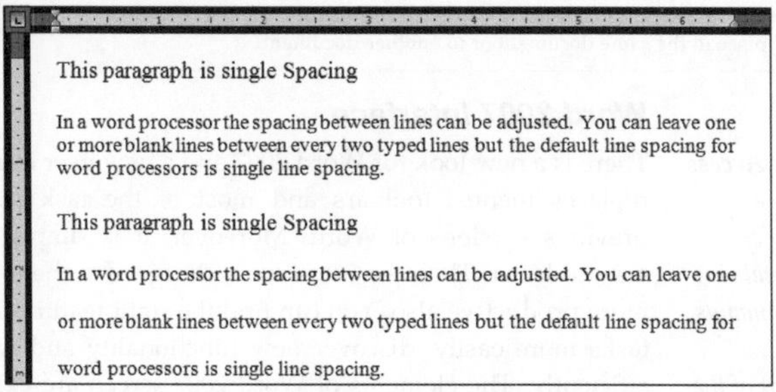

Tab Setting

You can set tabs in a Word 2007 for typing columns in a document as in the case of a typewriter. You may want to use the ruler to set Manual tab stops at the left side, middle and right side of your document as seen below:

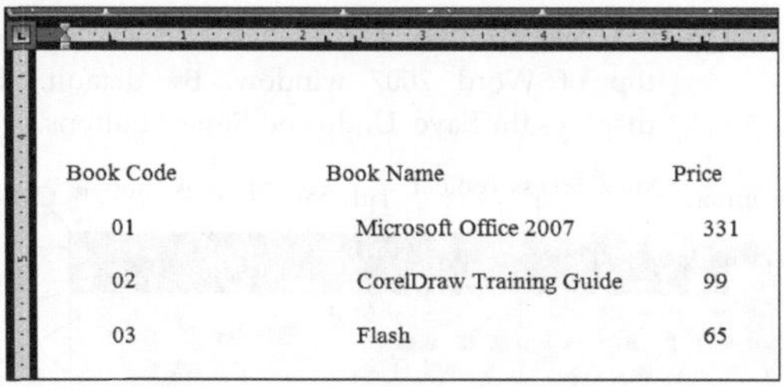

Table

A table is made up of rows and columns of cells that you can fill with text and graphics. You can use tables to align numbers in columns and then sort and perform calculations.

Hyphenating Documents

Hyphenation feature of Word 2007 can break or hyphenate words so that they may fit better on a line. It can hyphenate the words in a document automatically as you type a document or manually when you have finished typing.

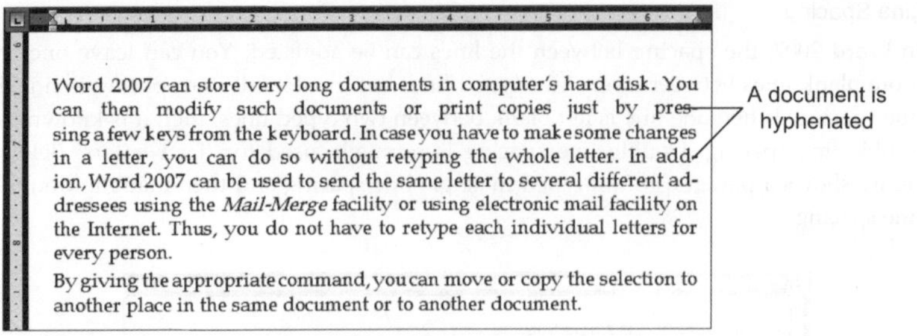
Word 2007 can store very long documents in computer's hard disk. You can then modify such documents or print copies just by pres-sing a few keys from the keyboard. In case you have to make some changes in a letter, you can do so without retyping the whole letter. In add-ion, Word 2007 can be used to send the same letter to several different ad-dressees using the *Mail-Merge* facility or using electronic mail facility on the Internet. Thus, you do not have to retype each individual letters for every person.

By giving the appropriate command, you can move or copy the selection to another place in the same document or to another document.

Notes:

*The **Quick Access Toolbar** is a customizable toolbar containing a set of commands that are independent of the tab that is currently displayed.*

Word 2007 Interface

There is a new look for Word 2007 and a new user interface that replaces menus, toolbars and most of the task panes from previous versions of Word. Moreover, it is simply and very easy to learn. The new interface is designed to help you to be more productive also. You can find the right features of various tasks more easily, discover new functionality and work more efficiently. The elements of Word 2007 screen are explained in detail as follows.

MS Office Button: This button is located in the upper-left corner of Word 2007 window. The command related to managing Word and Word documents are put together on a menu.

Quick Access Toolbar: This toolbar is located by default at the top of Word 2007 window. By default, this toolbar displays the Save, Undo and Repeat buttons.

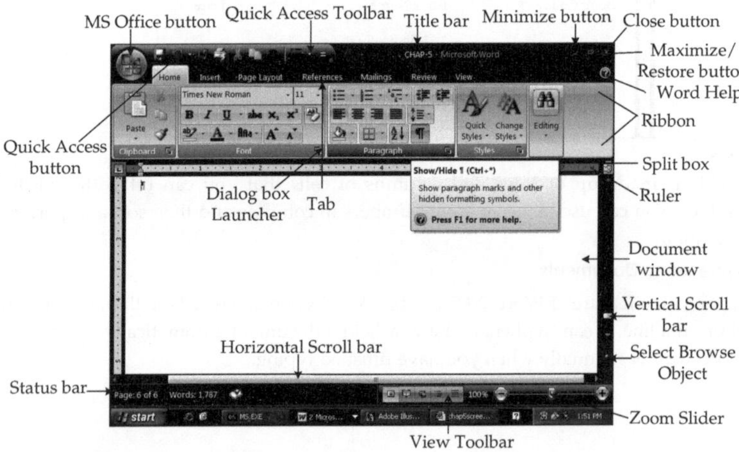

Home Tab: *This contains commands related to working with document such as clipboard, font, paragraph, styles and editing.*

Insert Tab: *This contains commands for related items you can insert such as tables, header, footer and symbols.*

Page Layout Tab: *This contains commands for items related to the appearance of your document such as Page Setup, Page Background, Paragraph, Themes and Arrangement of text.*

References Tab: *This contains the commands that are related to items you can add to long documents, such as Tables of Contents, Footnotes, Bibliography,* ***No table of contents entries found.****Index etc.*

Mailings Tab: *This contains commands related to creating mass mailings.*

Dialog box Launchers: The dialog box launchers are small icons that appear in some groups. Clicking a Dialog Box Launcher opens a related dialog box or task pane, providing more options related to that group.

Document window: You create a document in the document window. When more than one document is opened, each document has its own window.

Title bar: It is displayed at the top of the application window.

Minimize button: An underscore (_) at the right of a title bar which stores an application programme at the bottom of the screen.

Maximize button: A box at the right of a title bar that fills available space with the document or application.

Close button: A box at the right of a title bar (X) that closes the window or dialog box.

Restore button: A double box at the right of a title bar that restores an application or document into a sizable window.

Help button: It appears at the right end of the Ribbon. When the mouse pointer is over any button for a few seconds (called hovering), it displays a ScreenTip with not only the button's name but also its function.

Status bar: At the bottom of the window, the status bar gives you information about the current document. You can turn off the display of an item of information by right-clicking the status bar and then clicking that item.

View toolbar: At the right end of the status bar is the view toolbar. It provides tools for adjusting the size of document.

Mouse pointer: On-screen arrow, I-beam, or drawing button indicates the current location affected by your mouse actions.

Select Browse Object: The toolbar that enables you to browse through an active document by field, endnote, footnote, etc. Go To and Find functions are also part of this toolbar.

Ruler: A bar containing a scale that indicates *tabs, paragraph indents,* and margins in the paragraph where the insertion point (cursor) is located.

Split box: Light gray bar at the top of the vertical scroll bar that you can drag down to split a window into two different views of the same document.

Notes:

Review Tab: This button contains commands related to proofing, commenting and changing documents.

View Tab: This button contains commands related to changing the view or the display of documents.

Rulers helps you to control the margins, the paragraph indentation and the tab settings for a document

ScreenTips: Screentips show the name of the command button shown in ribbon. Screentips appear as soon as you position the mouse pointer on the toolbar button.

Ribbon: Ribbon is displayed just below the title bar. In Ribbon, Commands are organized in logical groups, which are collected together under tabs. You can hide the Ribbon by double-clicking the active tab. Different types of Tabs are available in Word 2007.

Displaying or Hiding Rulers

Word 2007 gives you the flexibility to hide or display ruler according to your working needs.

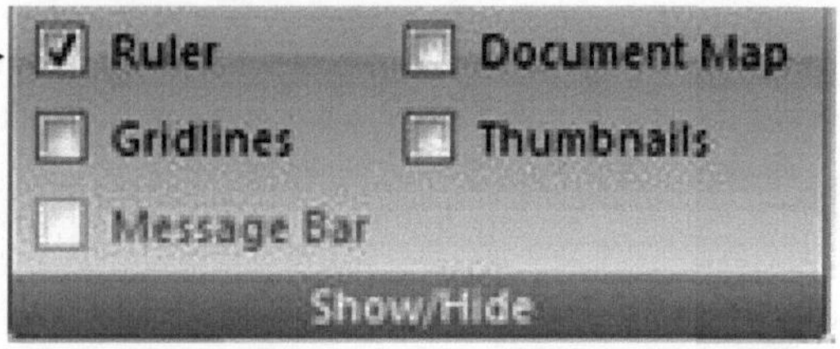

1. On the **View** tab, in the Show/Hide group, select the **Ruler** check box.

The Status Bar

The Status bar is, seen at the bottom of the Word 2007.

1. This is section number one of the document
2. This shows page 10 of 15 pages in the document. This page number is based on the actual number of pages in the document, not on the printed page number.
3. At 7.8" a line of text that is vertical position from the top of the page.
4. Beginning of the line character position within the line of the text.
5. Number of words in the document.

Mouse Terminology

The mouse terminology used in Word 2007.

Point: Position the mouse pointer on an item.

Single Click: If you Single-click the mouse, Word 2007 moves the cursor wherever you click.

Double-click: If you Double-click the mouse, Word 2007 selects a single word.

Using Undo and Redo command

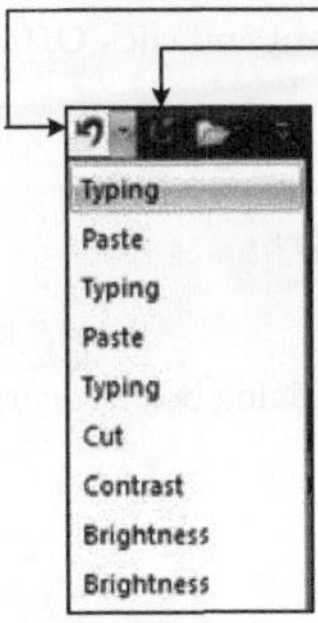

1. When you click the **Undo** button, the deleted sentence reappears. Clicking the Undo button reverses the last command or deletes the last entry you typed.

   Click the down-pointing arrow at the right side of the Undo button and a drop-down list displays containing changes made to the document.

2. Clicking the **Redo** button deletes the selected sentence. If you click the Undo button and then decide you do not want to reverse the original action, click the Redo button.

Saving a Document

The first time you save a file, you need to specify three items:

1. The drive and folder to store your file.
2. The name of your file.
3. The format to save your file.

 Office Button → 

1. Click the **Office Button**. A drop-down menu appears. Click **Save**. Or Alternatively, choose the save button on the **Quick Access toolbar**.
2. When you save a document for the first time, Word 2007 displays the Save As dialog box, so that, you can type a name for the document.

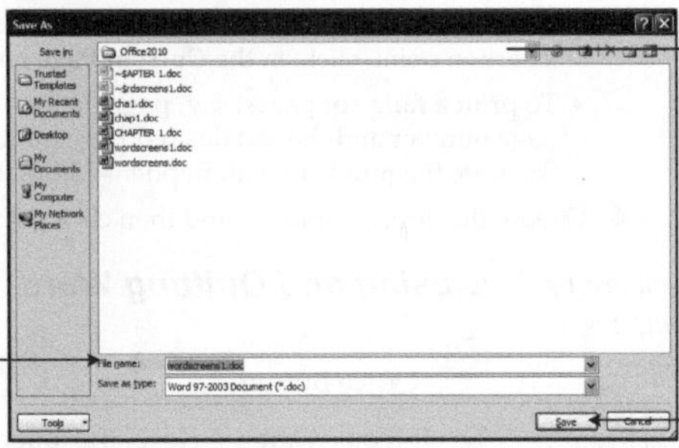

3. Click Save in: drop-down, to specify a drive and folder to save your file.
4. Click in the **File name:** text box and type a name for your file.
5. Click **Save** button.

Notes:

The keyboard shortcut to undo a task is Ctrl+Z; the shortcut to redo is Ctrl+Y.

The shortcut key to save a document is Ctrl + S.

The ***Save As*** *dialog box appears only when you are saving the document for the first time. Each additional save will save the most recent changes to the file you have already named. The Save As dialog box will not reappear unless you choose Save As.*

A document's temporary name (Document1, Document 2, etc.) can be changed when you save it.

Notes:

The keyboard shortcut to open a Print dialog box and press Ctrl+Shift+F12 keys together.

Printing a Document

The simplest way to print is to open a document and click **Office Button** and choose **Print**.

: Office Button → 

1. Click the **Office Button** and choose **Print**. The **Print** dialog box appears.

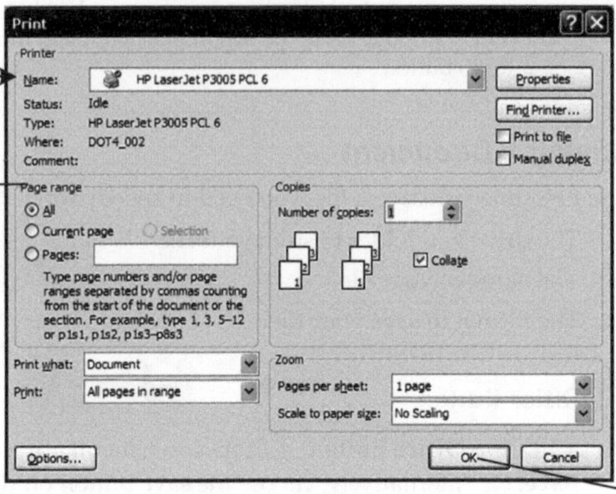

2. Select a printer from the **Name:** drop down list.
3. In the **Page range** options choose out of the following:
   - To print the entire document, click the **All** button.
   - To print just the page in your document currently containing the insertion point, click on the **Current Page** button.
   - To print a range of pages, say, pages 6-10 in a document, type the first page number and the last desired page number in the **Pages:** text box. Separate the numbers with hyphens like 6-10.
4. Choose the desired options, and then click **OK** button.

Before you print a document, it is necessary to preview it to check page breaks and the overall appearance of the document.

Closing and Quitting Word

: Office Button → 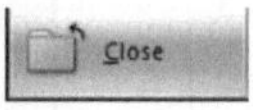

1. If you want to close the open documents, choose **Office Button** and then select **Close**.

: Office Button → 

2. To quit Word 2007 click **Office Button** and choose **Exit Word** button.

Getting Help in Word 2007

1. Click the Word 2007 Help button at the right corner of the window or press F1 key.
2. Type the word such as Alignment text in the Type words to search for box and press Enter key.

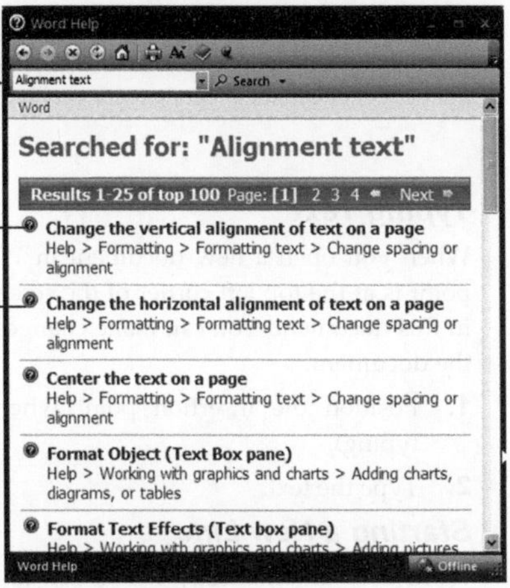

3. The help window display a list of topics, i.e searched for related topics. Choose the selected list topic you want.
4. The help window displays step-by-step explanations.
5. Click the Close button to close the Help window

Show or Hide ScreenTips

1. Click **Office** button and choose **Word Options**.

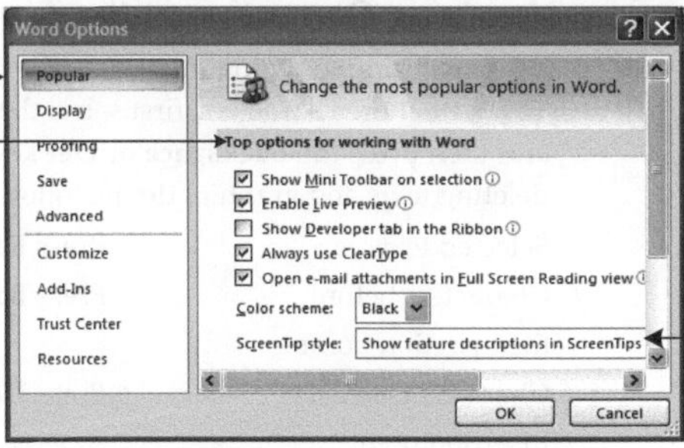

2. Click Popular
3. Under Top options working with Word options
4. In the ScreenTip Style: list, select the options that you want.

Notes:

ScreenTips are small windows that display descriptive text when you rest the pointer on a command or control.

Notes:

Enhanced ScreenTips are larger windows that display more descriptive text than a ScreenTip and can have a link to a Help topic. Enhanced ScreenTips are available in the following 2007-Office system programs: Access, Excel, PowerPoint, and Word. (see below icon)

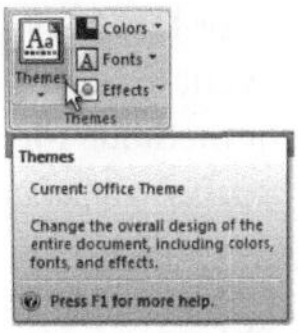

Notes:

*The **Quick Access Toolbar** is a customizable toolbar containing a set of commands that are independent of the tab that is currently displayed.*

*In Word Options dialog box, click Display. **Always show these formatting marks on the screen** options, you can display or hide all nonprinting characters such as paragraph marks, tab characters and spaces.*

To restore the deleted text, click Quick Access toolbar, click the Undo button. Or press Ctrl + Z keys together.

- **Show feature descriptions in ScreenTips** — This option turns on ScreenTips and Enhanced ScreenTips. This is the default setting.
- **Don't show feature descriptions in ScreenTips** This option turns off Enhanced ScreenTips. You still see ScreenTips.
- **Don't show ScreenTips**—This option turns off ScreenTips and Enhanced ScreenTips.

Typing Text

When you open a new document in Word 2007, the insertion point is at the top left corner of the screen. You can start typing in this document. You can make changes at any time by editing the document.

1. Position the insertion point where you want to begin typing.
2. Type the text.

Starting a New Line

Word 2007 automatically wraps text to the next line when the typed text reaches the end of the right margin.

1. Position the insertion point where you want to start the new line and then press **Shift + Enter** keys together.
2. Word inserts a line break character and moves the insertion point to the beginning of the next line.
3. To see the line breaks, click the Show/Hide command on the paragraph group of Home tab.

Applying Correction in the Typed Text

To correct simple typing mistakes, press **Backspace** or **Del** keys. To delete more characters, first select the text you want to delete and then press the **Backspace** or **Del** key. Different methods for deleting texts and graphics do the following.

Selected text	Press **Backspace** or **Del** key.
Characters before the insertion point	Press **Backspace** key.
Characters after the Insertion point	Press **Del** key.
A word after the insertion point	**Ctrl + Del** key.

Selecting Text

Notes:

While you are in Extend Selection mode, the word appears on the status bar at the bottom of the screen.

If the pointer touches the edge of the window as you are dragging, the window scrolls in that direction if more text exists.

Word 2007 works on the principle select, then do. If you want to delete a word in the text or move a sentence, you must first select what you want to change and then change. You can also use a mouse or a keyboard to select the text.

Selecting Text with a Mouse

You can select a piece of text, or a single character or an entire document. You can also combine mouse and keyboard selection techniques.

1. Click and hold the left mouse button at the beginning of the text you want to select.
2. Drag the pointer in any direction across the text you want to select.
3. Select text using mouse

Text to select	Mouse Action
A word	Double-click the word.
A line	Click selection bar (blank margin to left of a line of text).
Multiple lines	Click selection bar and drag up or down till the end of lines.
A paragraph	Double-click selection bar.
Document	Press **Ctrl** key and click in selection bar.
Rectangular block or column (not within a table)	Click the top left of the column to be selected and then hold **Alt** key while you drag to select the text.

Select Text with a Keyboard

The method for selecting text is to hold down the key as you move the insertion point. You can select text by using in combination with any move key. Some of these key combinations are listed below.

To select	Press
A word	**Shift + Ctrl** + ← or → arrow key
To the beginning of a line	**Shift + Home**
To the end of a line	**Shift + End**
To the end of a paragraph	**Ctrl + Shift** + ↓
To the beginning of a paragraph	**Ctrl + Shift** + ↑
One line at a time	**Shift** + ↑ or **Shift** + ↓
To the beginning of a document	**Shift + Ctrl + Home**
To the end of a document	**Shift + Ctrl + End**

Notes:

Full Screen Reading: *Full screen view displays as much of the typing area of the document as will fit on the screen at a size that is comfortable for reading. In this view, the Ribbon is replaced by a single toolbar at the top of the screen. You can print the document, highlight text and write comments.*

Web Layout View: *While creating a web page in Word 2007, you should work in Web Layout view. In Web Layout view, you can see that background text is wrapped to fit the window.*

Changing Document Views

The type of work that you do will help you to determine the best screen view as per your needs. There are different views available in Word 2007.

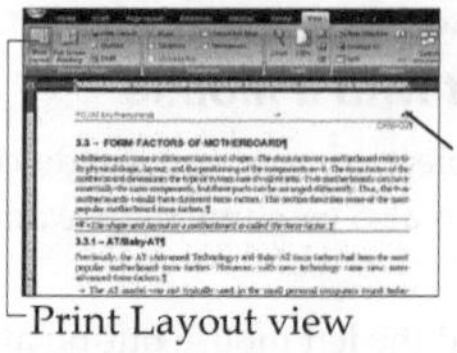

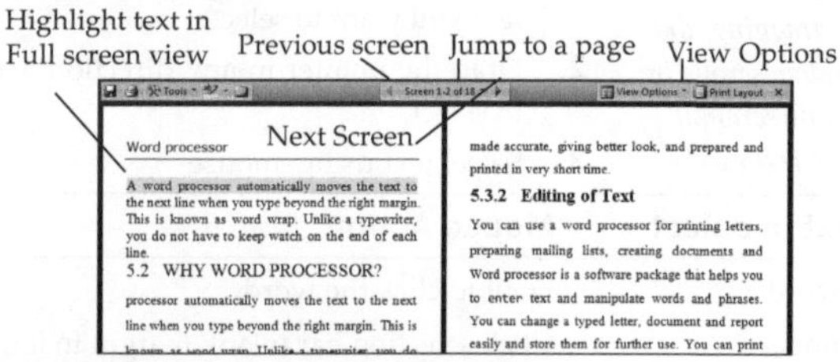

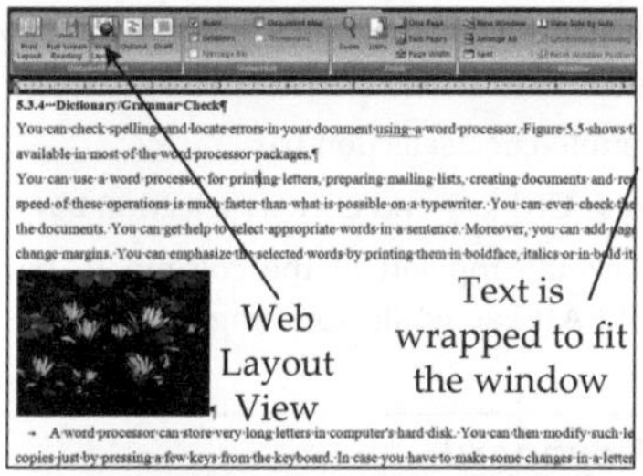

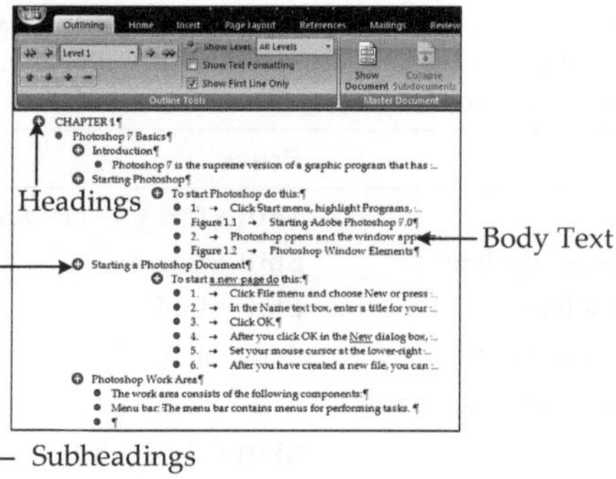

In the Outline view, you can collapse a document to see only the main headings or expand it to see the entire document.

Notes:

Document Map: *displays a list of headings and helps you navigate through large documents.*

The location of the scroll box in the vertical scroll bar shows the screen's location relative to the entire document's length and width.

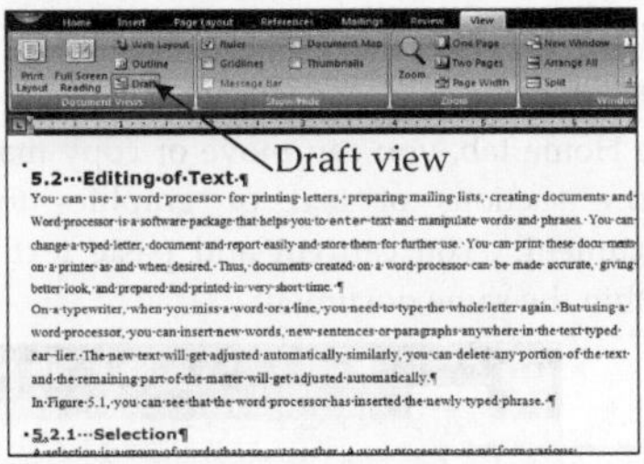

Draft view is the best view for most of your typing and editing. In this view, you can see character and paragraph formatting as the page will be printed. Line and page breaks, tab stops and alignments are accurate.

Moving or Scrolling with a Mouse

Directing the mouse pointer in the horizontal and vertical scroll bars allows you to scroll a document easily. Methods for scrolling Text using Mouse.

To move	Click
One line up or down	Click Once up or down scroll arrow for one line up or down.
One screen up or down	Click gray area above or below the scroll box in the vertical scroll bar.
One page up or down	Click next or previous page buttons.
Large vertical moves	Click drag vertical scroll box to a new location in the vertical scroll bar.
Horizontally	Click right or left scroll arrow and drag.

Moving or Scrolling with the keyboard

Using the keyboard you can also move or scroll in a document.

To move	Press
One character left	← arrow key
One character right	→ arrow key
One line up	↑ arrow key
One line down	↓ arrow key
One word to the left	**Ctrl + ←** keys
One word to the right	**Ctrl + →** keys
One paragraph up	**Ctrl + ↑**
One paragraph down	**Ctrl + ↓**
Up one window	**Pgup** key

Notes:

*The keyboard shortcut for cutting selected text is **Ctrl + X***

Word's Drag and Drop feature must be turned on in order to copy text using the drag and drop method. To turn it on, Click Office button, then click Word Options. In Word Options dialog box, click the Advanced options in the left pane. Click Allow text to be dragged and dropped

You must click the I-beam at the new location for typing. If you scroll to a new location and leave the insertion point at the old location, your typing or editing appears at the old location.

Cutting / Moving Text

With the Cut, Copy and Paste buttons in the Clipboard group in the Home tab, you can move or copy many words, sentences, or entire sections of text or graphics to other locations in a document. You can cut and paste text or copy and paste text within the same document.

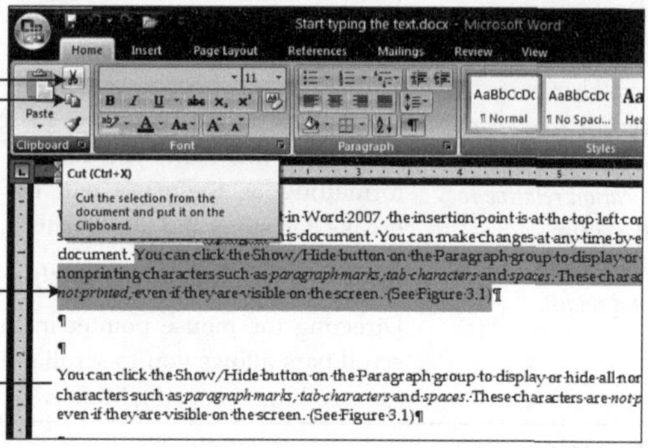

1. Select the text you want to cut from the text.
2. Click the **Cut** button in the **Clipboard** group in the **Home** tab.

   Clicking the **Cut** button places the text in a special location within Word called the clipboard.
3. Then, click the **Paste** button in the **Clipboard** group in the **Home** tab.
4. Position the insertion point where you want to paste the text. The selected text move into new location.

Cutting / Moving Text using Drag and Drop

1. Click and drag to select the text and graphics you want to copy.
2. Press and hold the **Ctrl** key, then click and drag the selected text to the new location (the insertion point will have a gray square with a plus sign (+) inside it to indicate that you are dragging a copy.
3. Release the mouse button at the spot where you want the copied information to appear.

Cutting / Moving Text using Pop-up menu

1. Click and drag to select the text and graphics you want to **Cut**.
2. Right-click and choose **Cut**. The selected portion gets removed. Select the new location where you want to paste.
3. Right click and choose **Paste** option.

Notes:

The keyboard shortcut for copying selected text is Ctrl + C.

Copying Text

Use the Copy command to copy text and graphics and place them elsewhere in the document, or in a different document. Because it is such a common word processing task, there are several ways to copy information.

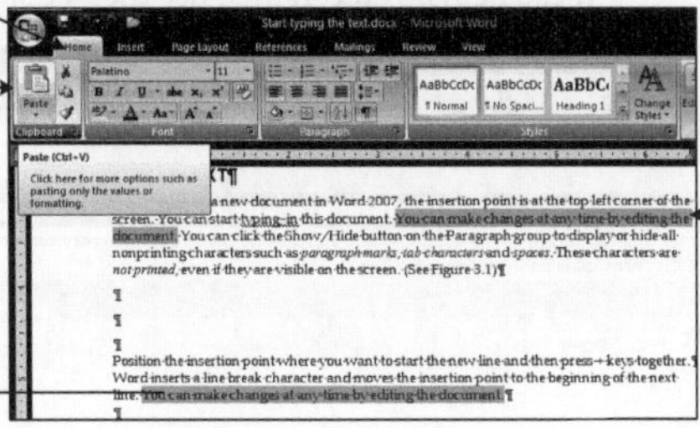

Copied information is placed on the Clipboard, where it remains until something new is copied or cut over it. (The Clipboard contents exist in RAM memory, and so it is not saved when the system is shut down)

1. Click and drag to select the text you want to copy.
2. Click the **Copy** button on the **Clipboard** group of **Home** tab.
3. Click the **Paste** button on the **Clipboard** group of **Home** tab.
4. From above selected portion gets copied, and then Paste it to the new location.

Copying Text using Drag and Drop

1. Select the text or the graphics you want to copy.
2. Press and hold down Ctrl key, point to the selected text or the graphics, and then press and hold down the left mouse button while you drag the dotted insertion point to the new location.

Copying Text using Pop-up menu

1. Click and drag to select the text and graphics you want to **Copy**.
2. Right-click and choose **Copy**. The selected portion gets copied. Select the new location where you want to paste.
3. Right click and choose **Paste** option.

Keyboards Shortcuts for moving and Copying Text or Graphics

Action	Key combination
Copy the selected text or the graphics to the Clipboard	**Ctrl + C** keys pressed together.
Move the selected text or the graphics to the Clipboard	**Ctrl + X** or **Shift + Del** keys pressed together
Paste Clipboard contents into a document	**Ctrl + V**, or **Shift + Ins** keys pressed together.
Move a paragraph Up	**Alt + Shift +** ↑ arrow keys pressed together

Using Find and Replace

Notes:

The keyboard shortcut for searching the word is Ctrl +F.

Word 2007 has a very powerful, Find and Replace feature which greatly simplifies editing of text. The Editing command is in Home tab for Finding and Replacing text. You can use this command to search for text, footnotes, graphics, etc. To replace these items, you can then use the Replace command.

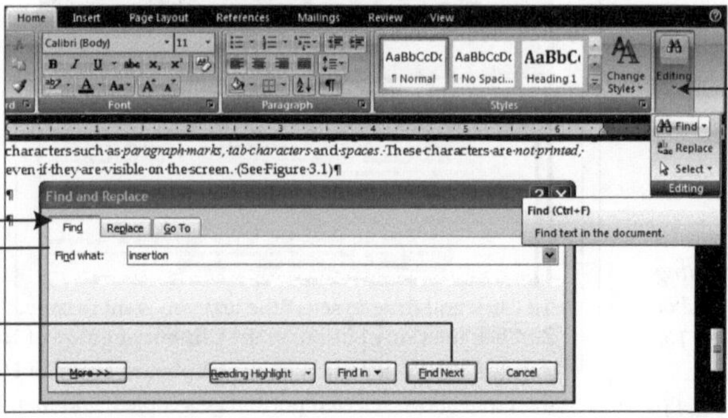

1. Click the **Home** tab and choose **Editing** command. Click a drop-down arrow and choose Find command
2. The **Find and Replace** dialog box appears with the **Find** tab selected.
3. In the **Find what:** text box, type the text you want to search for.
4. Click **Find Next** button. It searches the word given in the Find what: box.
5. If you want to highlight the selected word on the screen, click**Reading highlight** down arrow and click Highlight All. The selected word gets highlighted in the document.
6. To remove the highlighted word, select **Clear highlighting**. It removes the selected word.

Replacing Text

Notes:

If you want to confirm each change, click Find Next. When Word finds an occurrence of the text, click the Replace button to change the text.

You can replace searched text automatically using replacing text facility in Word 2007. For example replacing incorrect word *dcument* by *document.*

1. Click the **Home** tab and choose **Editing** command. Click a drop-down arrow and choose **Replace** command or press **Ctrl + H** keys together. The **Find and Replace** dialog box appears with the **Replace** tab selected.

Notes:

If you want to search for or replace text in only a portion of a document, then select the portion of the text and then follow the general instructions for finding or replacing text.

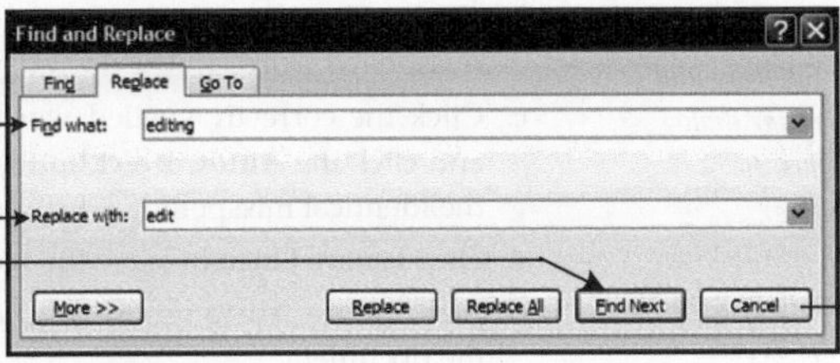

2. In the Find what: text box, type the misspelled word. (i.e dcument)
3. In the Replace with: text box, type correct spell word. (i.e document)
4. To check continousely, choose the **Find Next** button.
5. Click **Cancel** or press key to return to the document.

Notes:

The shortcut key to start a Spelling & Grammar is F7.

The wavy red line under misspelled words does not print.

When Word 2007 spelling checker detects double words, (say the the) then the Not in Dictionary: box changes to the Repeated Word: box, and the repeated word is highlighted in red. To delete the repeated word, click the Delete button.

Using Spelling Checker

Spelling checker is a flexible and powerful tool that will automatically check spellings in a paragraph or the entire document. When automatic spell checking is on, Word 2007 uses a red wavy line to underline words it thinks are not spelled correctly, so that you can spot them on the screen.

1. Select the word or select a document that you want to check for spelling. If you select nothing, Word 2007 checks the entire document.

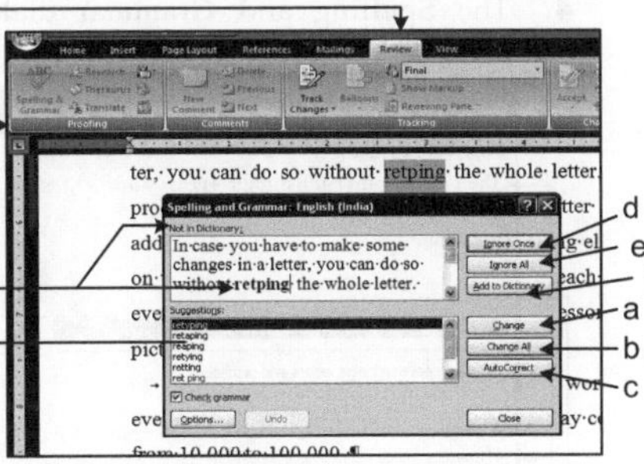

2. Click the **Review** tab.
3. In **Proofing** command group, click the **Spelling & Grammar** icon.
4. Word 2007 scrolls through your document and the misspelled word is highlighted in the text and displayed in the **Not in Dictionary:** box
5. Select the correct word from the **Suggestions:** list and then choose any one from the following list:

   a. Click the **Change** button to change the word.

Notes:

*The Spelling and Grammar dialog box has the **O**ptions... button. Clicking this button opens up the Word Options with Proofing page options dialog box appears. In this page, you can select different options to customize the spell checking operations.*

If you want Word to check your document's spelling but not the grammar, click to uncheck the Spelling & Grammar dialog box's option check grammar.

The Thesaurus dialog box also appears when you press Shift + F7keys together from keyboard.

b. Click **Change All** to change all occurrences of the misspelled words in the document.

c. Click the correctly spelled word in the **Suggestions:** list and click the **AutoCorrect** button to automatically correct the identical misspelling when you type it in future.

d. Click **Ignore Once** to leave the word as it is.

e. Click **Ignore All** to ignore all occurrences of the word in the document.

f. Click the Add to Dictionary button to add this word to the Word 2007 dictionary. The selected word will be added to the dictionary.

6. Word will now continue searching misspelled word. Click **Cancel** to stop the spell checking if so desired. Or

7. Click the **Close** button.

Using Grammar Check

The grammar checker evaluates a document for grammatical errors. Word 2007 uses collections of rules while reading a document.

1. Word 2007 may underline one or more words with a green wavy line to highlight some possible grammar errors.
2. Click the **Review** tab and choose Proofing command. Or
3. Click the **Spelling & Grammar** icon or press **F7** key.
4. The **Spelling and Grammar** dialog box appears on the screen.

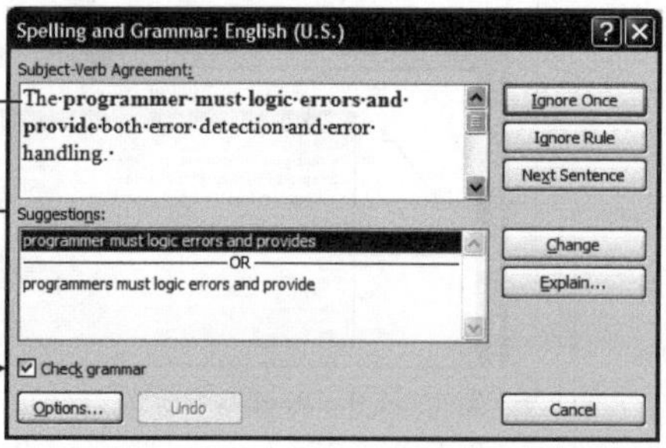

5. Click check grammar check box.
6. Word 2007 finds a sentence with a grammatical error i.e subject-verb agreement: options with a sentence appears in green line.
7. Word 2007 lists the suggestions in the Suggestions: text box if it finds error.

Notes:

You can turn off Word's automatic spelling checker by changing your Word Options dialog box. When correcting spelling and grammar in Word to uncheck, Check spelling as you type and Mark grammar errors options.

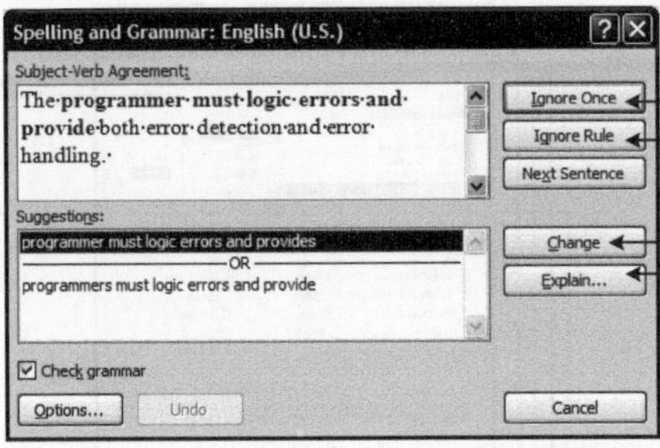

8. Correct the sentence by selecting a suggestion in the suggestions: box and then clicking the **Change** button. Or Correct the sentence by editing it in the upper text box and then click the **Change** button.
9. Click the **Explain** button for further details on the problem.
10. If Word finds a word that is not really misspelled, click the Ignore Once button. Word will ignore the word and continues checking the rest of the document.
11. If you want Word to ignore a grammatical problem it might find as it checks the rest of the document, click the **Ignore Rule** button.

Notes:

Fonts and Typefaces

A font or typeface is defined as a collection of characters and symbols with a common appearance or design. Courier is an example of a font. Times is a different font (or typeface) which is used in printing newspaper.

Text Formatting

Formatting is the process of specifying how a document should appear when printed. Formatting can be divided into three categories. These are Character formatting and Paragraph formatting

Character Formatting

Characters are the letters, numerals, punctuation marks and special symbols.

Using Font Dialog box

By formatting the font, you can change the typeface, appearance (such as bold or italic), size, color and other aspects of the type in documents.

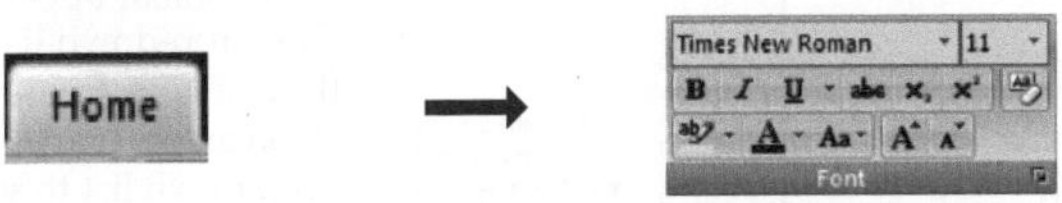

1. Select the text where you want to format.
2. Click the **Home** tab of **Font** group. Click **Font** launcher. The **Font** dialog box appears.

Notes:

Font Families

A collection of all of the variations of a font is called a font family. For example, the Arial font family. This family includes Arial, Arial Black and Arial Narrow characters.

Font Sizes

The size of the font is measured in points, and as the point size increases, the size of the letter also increases. One point equals 1/72th of an inch.

The keyboard shortcut to Bold the selected text is Ctrl + B.

The shortcut to word underline is ***Ctrl + Shift*** *+ W.*

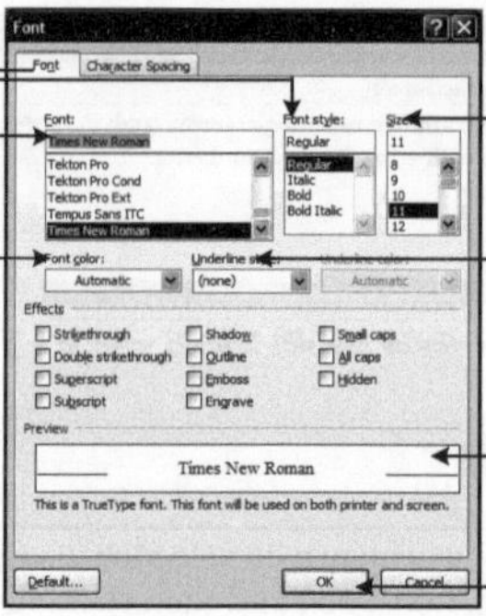

3. Click on the **Font** Tab of the **Font** dialog box. It offers the options for changing the font style and size.
4. Scroll through the fonts in the **Font:** list box and click the desired font.
5. Click a style in the **Font style:** list box, and choose desired style for the text.
6. Click a size in the **Size:** list box. Or type the desired point size in the **Size:** text box.
7. Click the **Font color:** drop-down arrow to choose the desired font color.
8. Click the **Underline style:** drop-down arrow to choose the desired underline color.
9. View a preview of the formatted font in the **Preview** box.
10. After choose the desired setting, click **OK** button.

Using the Ribbon

To modify character appearance, you can also use the commands in Ribbon or when you select the text, a mini toolbar appears.

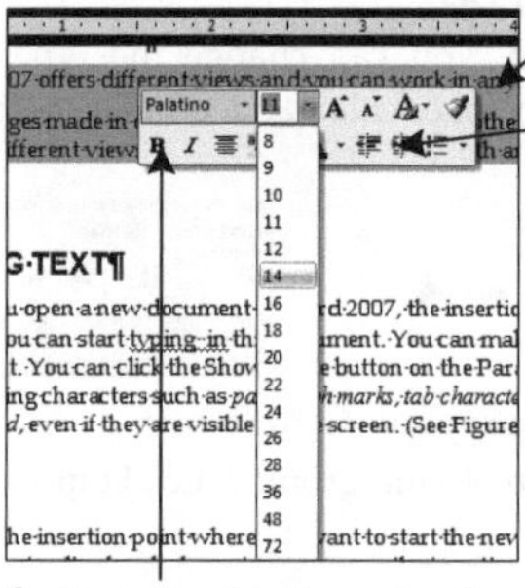

1. Select the text that you want to change the font.
2. After selecting text, a small mini toolbar appears.
3. The drop-down list shows all the available fonts. Use the scroll arrow on the right of the drop down list to scroll throught the list. When you move the cursor over the font you can see the changes in the appearance of text.
4. To make the character *Regular, Bold, Italic* click the corresponding button on the mini toolbar.

Notes:

The keyboard shortcut to open the Font dialog box is Ctrl +D.

Formatting Paragraphs

A paragraph can take the following characteristics. These are *alignment, Indents, Line spacing and Space before and after the paragraph.*

Align Text

The attribute *Alignment* of a paragraph refers to the position of the main document text on the page.

Notes:

When you want to create a new line without creating a new paragraph, press Shift + Enter keys at the point where you want to create the new line.

The keyboard shortcut for aligning text are:

Left: Ctrl + L

Center: Ctrl + E

Right: Ctrl + R

Justify: Ctrl +J

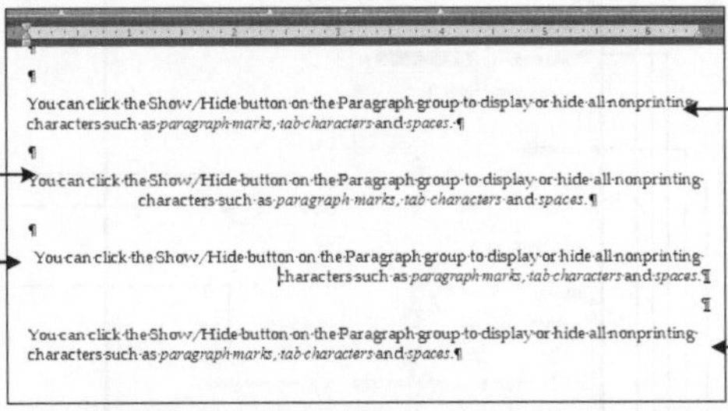

1. **Left align:** It aligns the text at the left margin and makes a zigzag right margin.
2. **Right align:** It aligns the text at the right margin and makes a zigzag left margin.
3. **Center align:** Center text between the left and right margins on the centre line. In this case both the margins are zigzag.
4. **Justify:** Aligns the text at both the margins by increasing the spacing between the words.

Indents

Indents are the white space added to the margins and thus decreasing the text area for paragraphs. So, when you have a "right margin and you want to add a right indent of 1.0", your text will be printed 2.0" from the right edge of the paper.

Once you change the indent, each new paragraph you start by pressing the **Enter** key will maintain the same indentation setting until you change it.

Line Spacing

Line spacing in a paragraph means the amount of space between the lines.

Space before and after Paragraphs

There is a spacing box in the Paragraph dialog box which lets you define the amount of white space that Word 2007 must place before and after paragraphs. Space settings can be entered in *points* (pts), *inches* (in), *centimetres* (cm), or *lines* (li). Thus, 12 points would be entered as **12 pt**, 2 lines as **2 li**, etc.

Using Paragraph Dialog box Launcher

1. Position the insertion point anywhere in the paragraph to be formatted or select multiple paragraphs.
2. Click the **Home** tab of **Paragraph** group. Click **Paragraph launcher** dialog box.

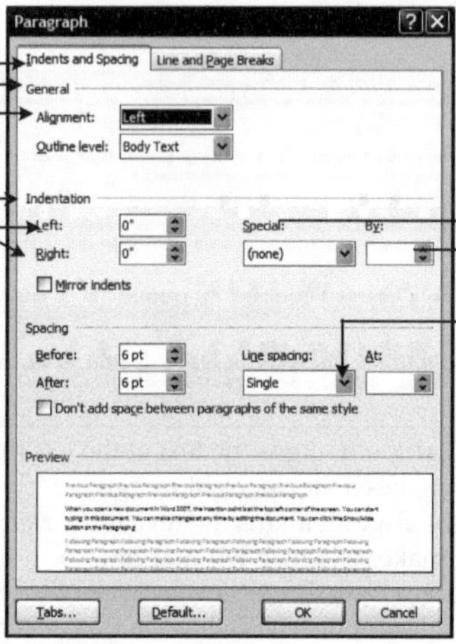

3. Click the **Indents and Spacing** tab
   In **General Options**:
4. In the **Alignment** drop-down arrow list, open it to show the list. From the list, click desired option as required.
   In **Paragraph Indentation Options**:
5. The **Left:** and **Right:** text box shows the left indentation. Enter the new value for indentation or use the up and down arrow keys to change the indentation.
6. To apply the first line indent or the hanging indent use the **Special:** list box. The options are:
   First line Indent: This indents only the first line of the paragraph.
   Hanging Indent: This indents all except first line of the paragraph.
7. In the **By:** text box, enter the indention or use the up and down arrow key to give the required indentation.
   In Spacing Options:
8. Line spacing drop-down has the options for controlling the line spacing.

Notes:

The keyboard shortcuts to change fonts are:

Bold:

Ctrl + B

Italic:

Ctrl + I

Underlined:

Ctrl + U

Increase font size: Ctrl + Shift + >

Ctrl + Shift + <

The keyboard shortcut key to indent paragraph

Ctrl + M

Ctrl + Shift + M

Ctrl + T

Ctrl + Shift + T

Ctrl + Q

The options are given below:

Single: Default value.

Double: Places a blank line between successive lines.

1.5 Lines: Leaves half the line space between the lines.

At Least: Indicate the minimum space between lines.

Exactly: Give the exact space between lines.

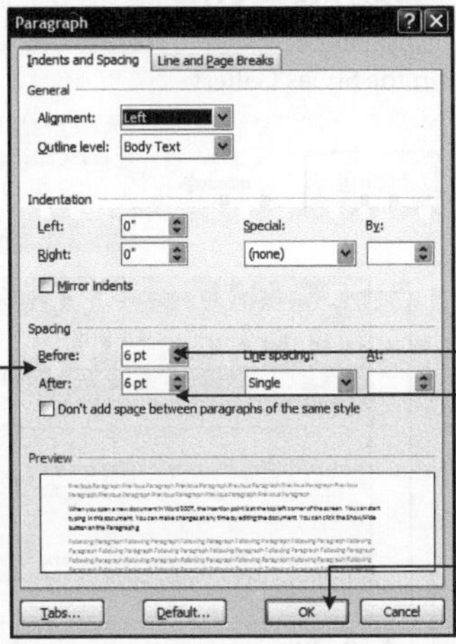

Space Before/After Paragraphs Options:

9. Type the space or select the space required in the **Before:** text box for adding space before the paragraph.
10. Type the space or select the space required in the **After:** text box for adding space before the paragraph.
11. Click **OK** press key to close the Paragraph dialog box.

Applying Border

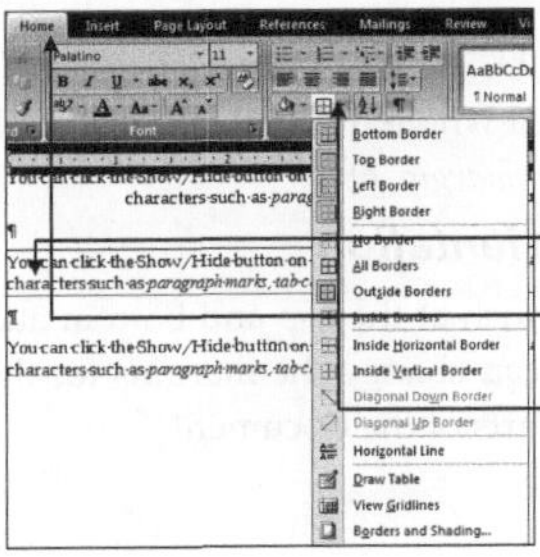

1. Position the insertion point anywhere in the paragraph.
2. Click the **Home** tab.
3. In the Paragraph group, click the borders drop-down and select the desired border you want to apply.

Notes:

The keyboard shortcut key to change the line spacing

Ctrl + 1 creates single spaced lines

Ctrl + 2 creates double spaced lines

Ctrl + 5 creates one and half spaced lines.

Ctrl + 0 adds or removes one line space preceding a paragraph.

Double-click the Format Painter button if you want to change the format of multiple selections in your document.

The vertical ruler is visible only in Print Layout view. The horizontal ruler is visible in Web and Layout views.

Applying Quick Formatting

In Word 2007, you can apply a specific style quickly and easily on the **Home** tab in the **Styles** group. For example, buttons for changing the font size, colour and other character attributes have been gathered in the **Font** group on the **Home** tab so that they are all easily accessible.

Applying a Style

Applying a style to a selection of text is easy as clicking a button in the Styles Gallery.

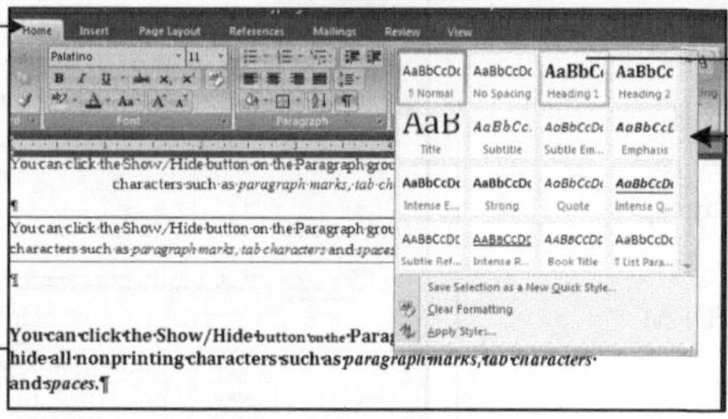

1. Position the insertion point where you want to apply a style.
2. For example, you can select text that you want to make into a **Heading 1**.
3. Click the **Home** tab of **Styles** group, as shown above icon.
4. Click the drop-down arrow. A list of styles gallery options appears.
5. Select the style called **Heading 1** in the Style Gallery.
6. The selected changed to **Heading 1** options.

Document Formatting

Formatting a document in Word 2007 is the process of changing the appearance of a document as a whole. It involves the length of the *printed page, left margin, right margin,* etc.

Document Margins and Orientation

Word 2007 default margins are 1 inch at the top and bottom and 1 inch on the left and right. You can change the margins for the entire document or for different parts of the document.

Notes:

In ***Full Screen Reading*** *and* ***Outline view****; you do not see the margins.*

You see the page as it will print. Always select the Print Layout view if you want to see *headers, footers, page numbers, footnotes,* etc.

You can also select one of the two types of page orientations namely, portrait (*vertical*) and landscape (*horizontal*). You can change the paper size and page orientation for a section or for the entire document.

Setting Document Margins

Page margins can quickly be changed using the ruler or they can be set to precise locations using page dialog box.

1. Select the sections for which you want to change margins. *Alternatively,* position the insertion point in the section whose margins you want to change.

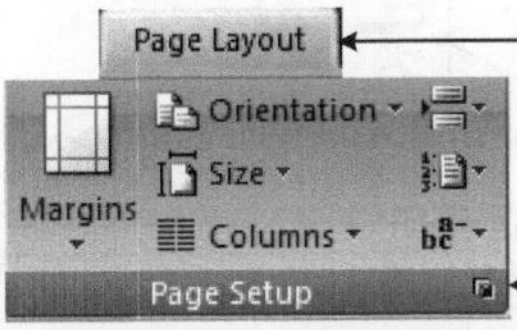

2. Click **Page Layout** tab.
3. Click the right corner arrow of **Page Setup.**
4. The **Page Setup** dialog box appears.
5. Click the **Margins** tab property sheet.
6. Select or type out the desired margin height from the **Top:** or **Bottom:** of the page.
7. Select or type out the desired margin width from the **Inside:** or **Outside:** of the page edge.
8. Select between **Portrait** (vertical) or **Landscape** (horizontal) page setting.
9. In the **Apply to:** choose the portion of the document from where you want to apply the new settings.
10. The **Preview** box displays the effect of the settings you select.
11. Click **OK.**

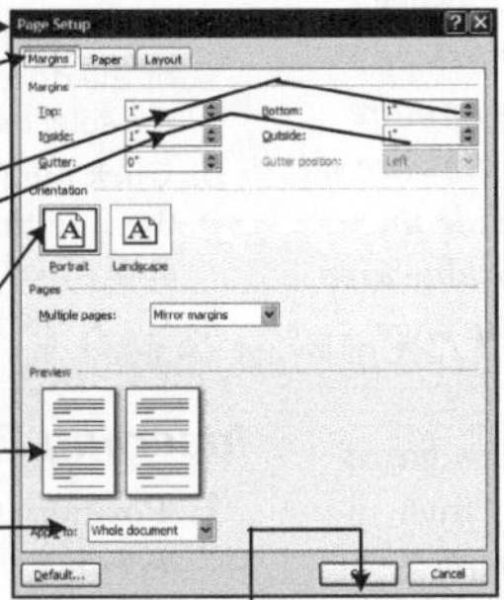

Indents are added to margin settings. That is, if you specify a 1.0" left margin and a 1/2" left indent, your text will print 1½ from the left margin. If you set a 1.0" right margin and indent the right edge of a paragraph 1.0", the text will stop 2.0" from the right edge of the page.

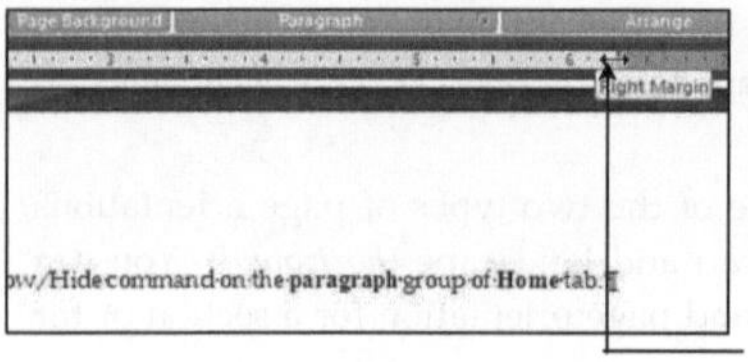

1. Switch to Print Layout view.

2. If the ruler is not displayed, click View tab. In the **Show/Hide** group, click the **Ruler** check box.

3. Position to the transition area on the ruler that is *where gray becomes white.*

4. The mouse pointer will become a two-headed arrow.

5. Drag the margin to the desired position with a mouse. The ruler's dimensions change as you drag.

Notes:

Most printers require a minimum width for margin settings, because they can't print all the way to the edge of the page. If you try to set margins that are too narrow, Word 2007 displays the message ***One or more margins are set outside the printable area of the page.***

Setting Paper Size

Page margins are usually set according to paper size you use.

1. Select the text, in the section that you want to change.

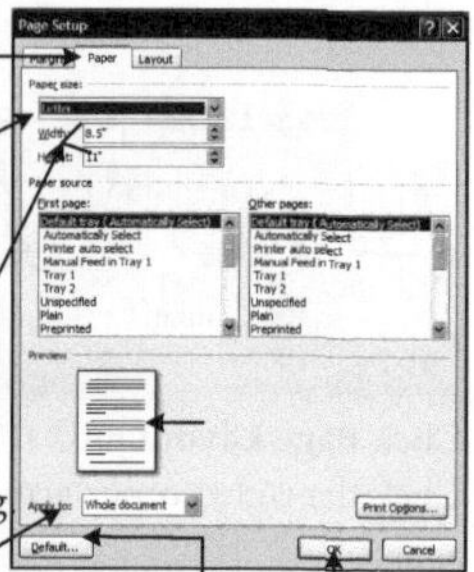

2. In the **Page Setup** dialog box, click **Paper** tab.
   In the **Paper size:** options
3. Click the drop-down list, it offers different standard paper size. Select the desired size you want. Commonly used paper size is A4 and legal size A3.
4. Type or select the **Width:** and **Height:** of the paper you are using
5. In the **Apply to:** select the portion of the document you want to print on the selected paper size.
6. Click the **Default...** buttons if you want to save these settings as default settings, so they can apply to all pages printed hereafter.
7. Click **OK** button.

Section breaks differ from paragraph marks (¶), in that a section break controls the information below it, while a paragraph mark controls the information that appears before it or precedes it.

Inserting Page Break

1. Position the insertion point where you want the break to occur.

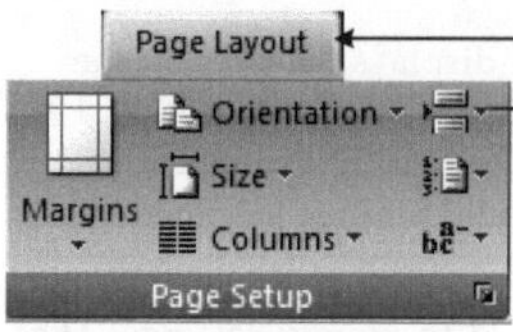

2. Click the **Page Layout** tab of **Page Setup** group.
3. In the top right corner, click **Insert Page and Section Breaks** drop-down arrow.

Notes:

The section break that controls the formatting of the last part of your document is not shown as part of the document. To change the document formatting, click in the last paragraph of the document.

***Deleting Page Breaks:** Select the page break. Now press the **Del** key. The Page Break is removed.*

To quickly edit a header and footer, view the document in Print Layout view, then double-click the header or footer.

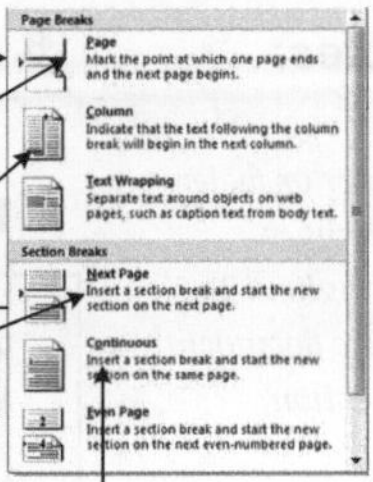

4. The list of options appear. Choose an desired options.
5. **Page** options mark the point which one page ends and the next page begins.
6. **Column** options indicates that the text following the column break will begin in the next column.
7. **Next page:** This selection would start the new section on a new page.
8. **Continuous page:** This selection would insert a section brek without starting it on a new page.

Inserting Header and Footer

You can insert a header or footer, and you can select the style you want from a gallery. Select the specified style to the document.

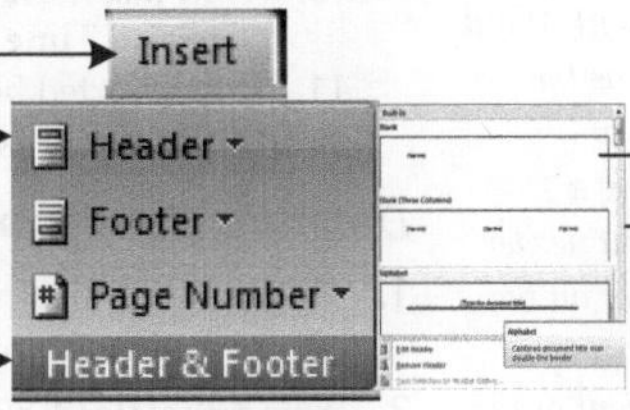

1. Click the **Insert** tab, in the **Header & Footer** group.
2. Click **Header** drop-down arrow.
3. A list of **Header** Gallery opens
4. Scroll through the gallery. You will notice the variety of headers that are available in the gallery. Select the desired style you want.

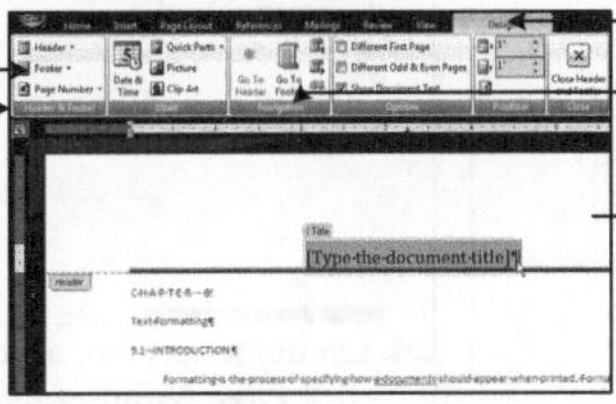

5. In the header, click the [Type the document title] placeholder, and then type the title
6. On the **Design** tab, in the **Navigation** group, click the **Go To Footer** button. Word displays the footer area at the bottom of the page. (OR)
7. In the **Header & Footer** group, click the **Footer** button. Click the down arrow, a list of footer Gallery opens.

Notes:

When you edit a header or footer, it changes throughout the entire document or section.

Headers and footers contain information at the top or bottom of the pages of a document. Word 2007 has the option of printing a different header or footer on the first page of a document or the section also.

While working in Header/Footer box, the main document appears grayed. To work in the main document double click the main document.

8. The page number and document name are included in the header gallery, if you want date and time to appear in the footer.

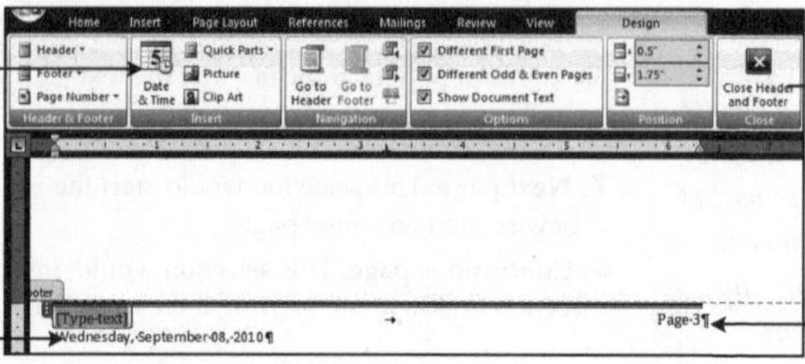

9. Word 2007 inserts the Footer pane in the bottom of the page with text and page number option in the Footer gallery list.
10. Word insertsDate and Time in the Footer by selecting **Date and Time** icon in the **Design** tab of **Insert** group.
11. After inserted header and footer in the document, click the **Close Header and Footer** in the **Close** group.

Deleting Header and Footer

1. Position the insertion point in the section with the header or footer you want to delete.
2. Select the **Header/Footer** you want to delete, and then press **Del** key.
3. If you have different headers or footers in other sections of the document, click the **Show Next** or **Show Previous** button on the **Navigation** group to find the next header or footer you want to delete.

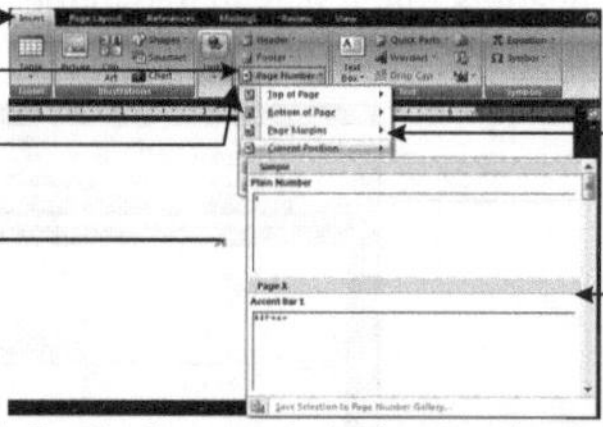

4. On the **Insert** tab, in the **Header & Footer** group, click **Page Number**.
5. The list of options appears, Click **Top of Page**, **Bottom of page**, or **Page Margins**, depending on where you to want page numbers to appear in the document.
6. Choose a page numbering design from the gallery. The gallery includes Page options such as **Bold numbers 1**, **Plain Number 1**, **thick line**, **Tildes**, etc. Select any options from the list.
7. You cansee the Bottom of Page appears in the document.

Notes:

You can format text in the header or footer by selecting the text and using the formatting options on the Mini toolbar.

If you created different first-page or odd and even headers or footers, or if you have sections that aren't linked, be sure to remove the page numbers from each different header or footer.

You can also remove page numbers by deleting a single page number from your document.

Format Page Number

Using the Page Number format feature to add page numbers to the top or bottom of the document.

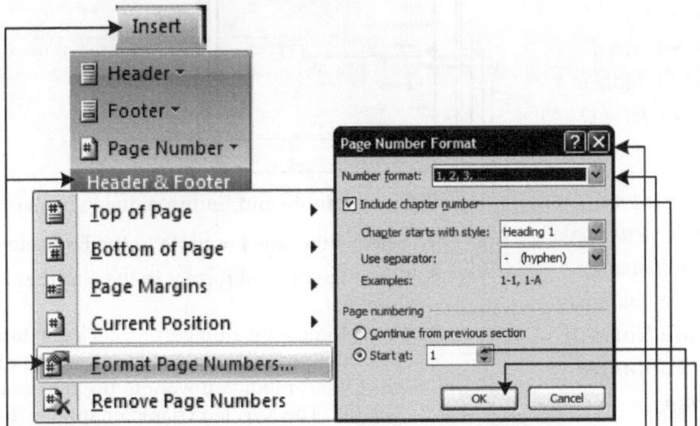

1. Double click the bottom of page, whose page number format you want to change.
2. In **Design** tab of **Header & Footer** group, select the **Page number** drop-down menu and choose **Format Page Numbers...** .
3. **Page Number Format** dialog box appears.
4. In the **Number format:** box select the format you want, from the drop-down list.
5. You can add the chapter number as part of the page number.
6. Click **Start at:** text box and type the beginning page number you want. (or click the arrow)
7. Click **OK** button.

Inserting Footnote and Endnote

Word 2007 footnote feature enables you to *enter, edit,* and *view* footnotes/endnotes in a variety of formats. The only difference between footnotes and endnotes is that, the *footnotes appear at the bottom of the page* and *endnotes appear at the end of the section or document.*

1. Position the insertion point after the text where you want to insert a reference mark. Word 2007 inserts the reference mark at the insertion point, unless you have selected text, in which case it positions the mark after the selection.

2. Click the **References** tab.
3. If you want to insert **Endnote**, click this icon.

   Or
4. If you want to insert **Footnote**, click this icon.

   Or
5. Click the arrow at the right corner of **Footnotes** group.

Notes:

The keyboard shortcut to insert Footnote is Alt + Ctrl + F and Endnote is Alt + Ctrl + D

*If you are in Draft view, leave the note pane visible and press **Show Notes** in the **Footnotes** group.*

*If you are in **Page Layout** view, you can Navigate next or previous footnote in the document*

*When you want to **delete** a note, you work with the note **reference mark** in the document window, not the text in the note.*

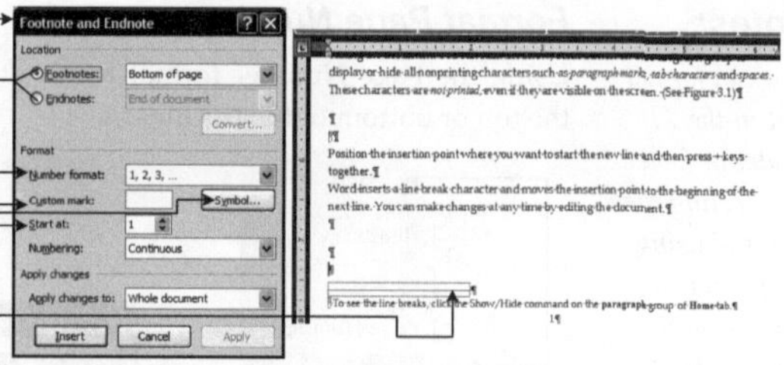

6. The **Footnote and Endnote** dialog box appears.
7. Select either the **Footnote** or the **Endnote** option.
8. Select the desired format in the **Number format:** drop-down list.
9. To customize the numbering, click **Custom mark:** now click the **Symbol...** button. The **Symbol** dialog box opens, select the symbol you want to use for numbering and then click Ok. The selected character appears in the **Custom mark:** text box.
10. In **Start at:** spinner box, select the format according to, in **Number format**. Select the desired changes in the **Apply Changes to:** drop-down box. Click Insert button to insert the footnote.
11. Word 2007 inserts the footnote, type the text in the footnote or endnote.

Inserting Symbols

In Word 2007, you insert symbol and mathematical equations in the documents such as characters like copyright © or registered (®) symbols, Currency symbols (such as £) etc.

1. Move the cursor where you want to insert a symbol in the document.

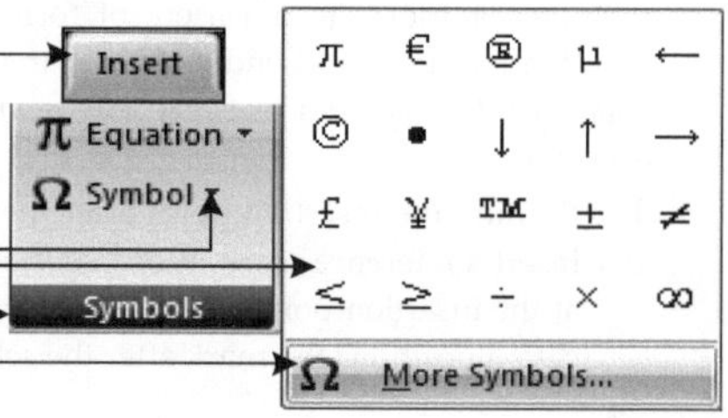

2. Click **Insert** tab of **Symbols** group, click the symbol drop-down arrow as shown above arrow.
3. A list of symbols appears, click the desired symbol you want. Word 2007 inserts your chosen symbol in the document.
4. If you want to see more options in the symbols, click the **More Symbols...** . A **Symbol** dialog box appears.

Notes:

Equation placeholders do not appear in the document on the screen or in print.

When you type an equation, Word 2007 automatically converts the equation into a professionally formatted equation.

*For symbols you use frequently, assign a shortcut key by clicking the **Shortcut key** button in the **Symbol** dialog box.*

*You can automatically insert some symbols with the **Autocorrect feature***

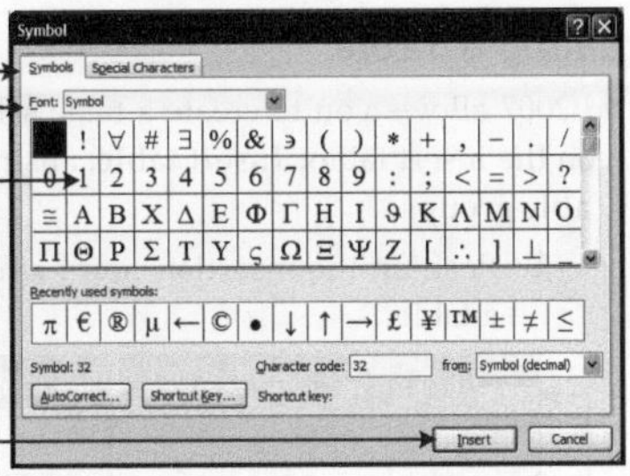

5. Click the Symbols tab.
6. Select the desired font in the **Font:** list, and you can see the selected symbol in the box.
7. If you click **Insert** button it will turn into **Close** button.

Inserting Equations

1. Move the cursor where you want to type equation in the document.

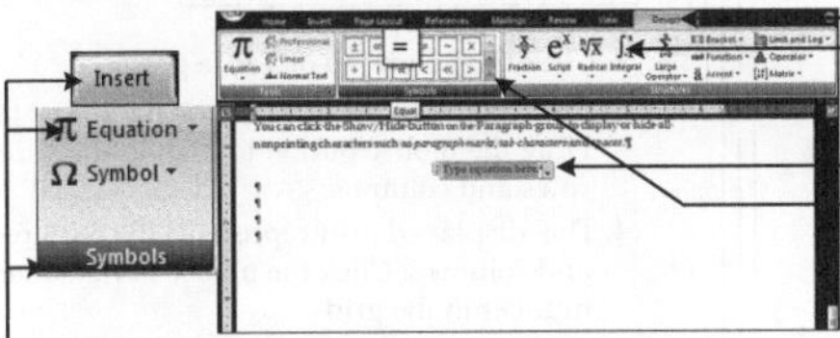

2. Click **Insert** tab of **Symbols** group. Click the **Equation** icon.
3. The Equation placeholder appears.
4. Select the equation in the **Design Contextual** tab, in the Structures group.
5. Choose from a list of frequently used or preformatted equations.

Or

6. In the **Symbols** group, click the drop-down arrow.

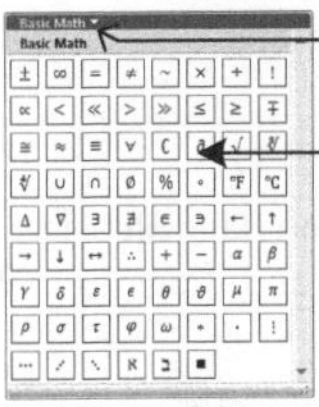

7. The Basic Mathematical sets are available in the drop-down list.
8. Select the desired symbol, in the basic gallery and click just once, it is automatically entered in the equation placeholder.

$$\frac{x}{y} = x^2 + y^2$$

9. After you complete the equation, you can see how it look in the document.

Notes:

*The insertion point will move left and down to the next row when you press **Tab** key in the last column and insert a new row in the table.*

*It will move right and up one row when you press **Shift + Tab** past the last column on the left.*

Selecting a Cell

The area between the first character in a cell and the left edge of the cell is called the cell selection bar. Clicking on this bar selects the contents of the entire cell.

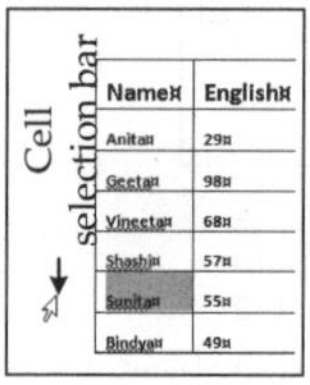

Creating a Table

Word 2007 allows you to create a table selecting the Insert Table grid on the insert tab or **Insert table...** using the **Table** options in the **Table** groups.

1. Position the insertion point where you want to insert a table.

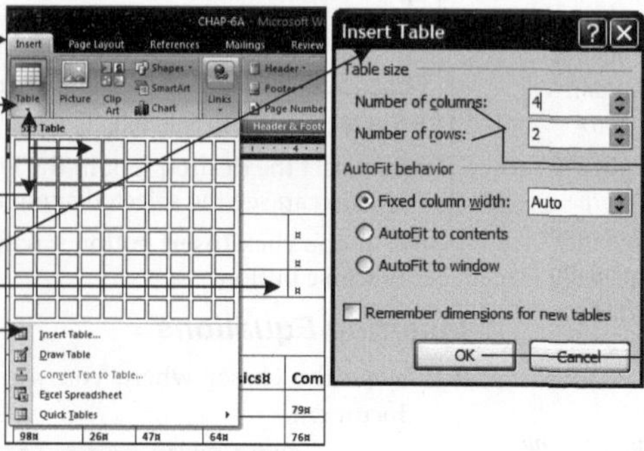

2. Click the **Insert** tab of **Table** group.
3. Click down arrow and choose the **Insert** table grid appears. Drag the mouse button to highlight the desired number of rows and columns.
4. The displayed grid represents the required number of rows and columns. Click the mouse button after getting the right number in the grid.
5. Word inserts an empty table when you release the mouse button.
6. Or you can click also, **Insert Table...** options.
7. The **Insert Table** dialog box appears.
8. Enter or type the desired **Number of columns:** and **rows:** spinner list box.
9. Click OK button.

Selecting Columns

To select a column, move the mouse pointer to the area at the top of a column called the *column selection bar*. At the column selection bar the pointer changes to a large, down-pointing arrow.

Selecting Rows

By clicking any cell's selection bar will select the entire row. By holding the left most button and dragging it the rest of the rows also.

Selecting Adjacent Groups of Cells

To select groups of adjacent cells, either drag through the cells or click in one cell and press **Shift** + click in the others.

Notes:

If you draw a table row or column line that you want to erase, click the ribbon's Eraser button and drag your mouse over the line you want to erase.

Alternatively, right click and select Insert, click the small triangle, a sub menu options appears. Select the Insert Rows Above or Below option.

Delete Rows

*Click the Layout Contextual tab. In Rows & **Columns** group, click **Delete** drop-down arrow. A list of options appears select **Delete Rows** option.*

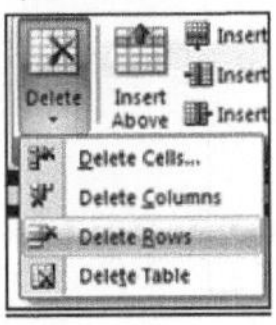

Selecting the Whole Table

To select a complete table, press down the **Alt** key and double click anywhere in the table.

Inserting Rows

To add a new row at the end of an existing table, position the insertion point anywhere in the last cell and press the **Tab** key. Word 2007 inserts a new row using the styles of the cells that are immediately above it.

1. Position the insertion point below the row where you want the new row to be inserted.

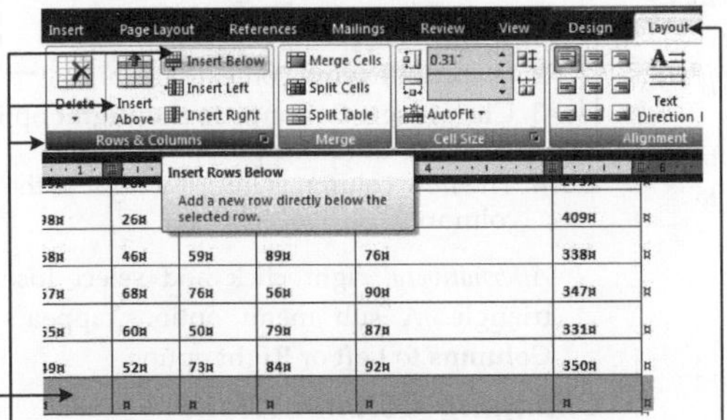

2. Click the **Layout contextual** tab.
3. Click **Insert Above** or **Below** in the **Rows & Columns** group.
4. The new row is inserted below the selected row.

Changing Row Height

Word 2007 sets the height of each row automatically in order to accommodate the cell containing the tallest entry.

1. Click anywhere in the row where you want to change its height.

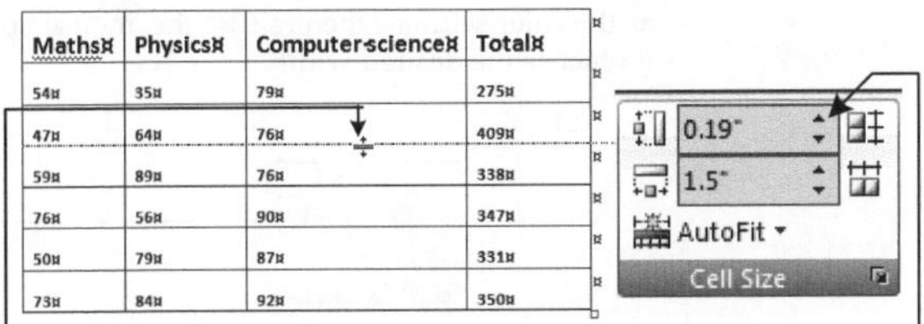

2. Move the pointer to the horizontal line. The pointer changes to up-and-down arrow. Use it to drag the row to the desired height.
3. Release the mouse button. Or
4. Click **Table Row Height** scroll box, to change the height of row in the cell size group.

Notes:

To insert a column at the right edge of a table.

1. Select an end-of-row marker.

*2. **Right** click and select Insert. A small triangle with sub menu options appears. Select the desired options you want to insert.*

Inserting Columns

1. Select the column to which you wish the new column to appear.

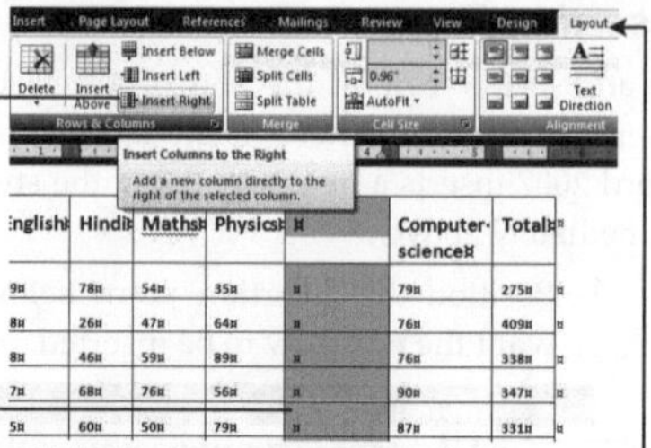

2. Click the **Layout** contextual tab.
3. Click **Insert Columns to the Rigtht** options in the **Rows & Columns** group.
4. The new column is inserted right to the selected column.

Alternatively, right click and select Insert. Click the small triangle. A sub menu options appears. Select the **Insert Columns** to **Left** or **Right** option.

Deleting Columns

1. Select the column(s) to be deleted.

*2. Click the **Layout** tab. Click **Table** down arrow and choose **Delete Columns.***

Changing Column Width

1. Point to a column boundary.

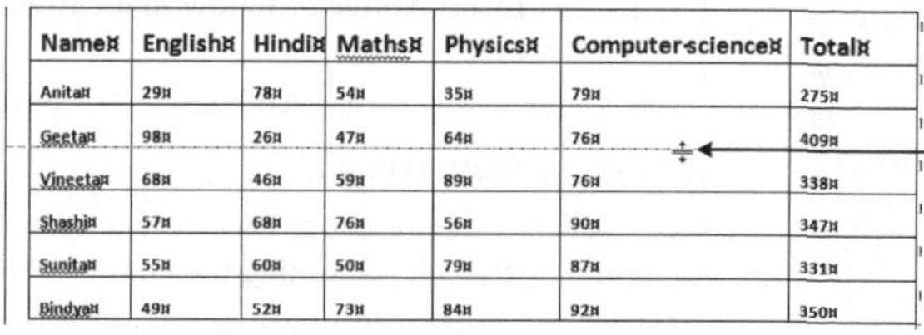

Name	English	Hindi	Maths	Physics	Computer science	Total
Anita	29	78	54	35	79	275
Geeta	98	26	47	64	76	409
Vineeta	68	46	59	89	76	338
Shashi	57	68	76	56	90	347
Sunita	55	60	50	79	87	331
Bindya	49	52	73	84	92	350

2. The pointer will change shape to a double arrow. Drag the column width marker. Watch the dotted line as well as the ruler settings, then release the mouse button when it reaches the desired width.

Or

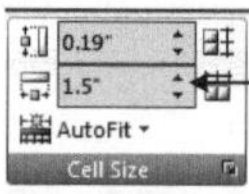

3. Click **Table Column Width** scroll box, to change the Table Column Width in the **Cell Size** group.

If you hold down the **Shift** key while dragging, the column to the right does not change size while the table's overall width increases.

Notes:

The split Cells feature allows you to split selected cells into multiple cells. Data already entered in cells to be split can be merged, if desired. This rearranges the data to fill the new cells.

Merging cells changes all selected cells into one. If there is information in the cells, it is also merged.

*If you hold down **Ctrl** key while dragging mouse, all columns to the right changes size but the table's overall width will not change. Thus, the width of the columns on the right will only change.*

Merging and Splitting Cells

Use the Merge Cells feature to join multiple cells. Similarly, use the split feature to separate cells.

1. Select the cells to be merged.

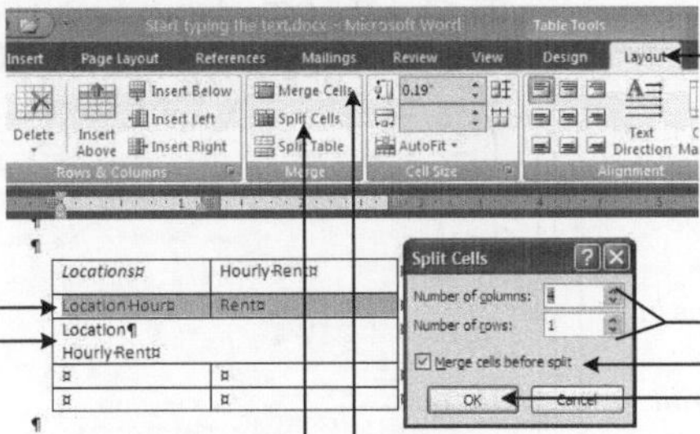

2. Click the **Layout** contextual tab, click **Merge** cells in **Merge** cells group.
3. The contents of the selection cells will merge.

   To split cells do the following:
4. Position the insertion point in a merged cell.
5. Click the **Layout** contextual tab and choose **Split Cells** in the **Merge** group.
6. Specify the **Number of columns:** or **rows:** you want to split in the **Split** dialog box.
7. The contents of the selection cell will split
8. Click OK

Aligning Text in a Table Cell

You can align text in a table cell in nine different ways: Top Left (the default alignment), Top center, Top Right, Center Left, Center Right, Bottom Left, Bottom Center, and Bottom Right as shown below icon.

1. Click the cell that contains text that you want to align.

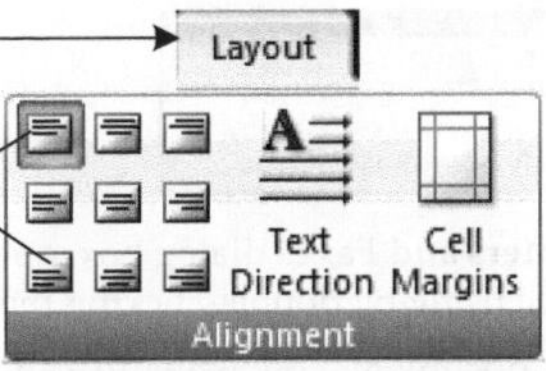

2. Click **Layout** contextual tab. In **Alignment** group choose the Text direction options you want in the cells.

For example, you want the text to be Top Right, choose Align text to the top right corner of the cell in the Alignment group options.

Notes:

The Shortcut key to print a command is ***Ctrl + Shift + F12*** *or*

Ctrl + P.

You can print different page range combinations in a document. From the Print dialog box, click to select a page range:

All *to print all the pages of the document*

Current page *to print the page on which the insertion point is resting.*

Selection *to print currently selected text and graphics.*

Pages *to print desired page numbers (use a hyphen to specify a page range: 6-11; or use a comma to separate individual pages: 6, 11)*

Print a Document

The simplest way to print is to open a document and click **Office button** and choose **Print.**

1. Open the document you want to print.
2. Click the **Office** button and choose **Print.**

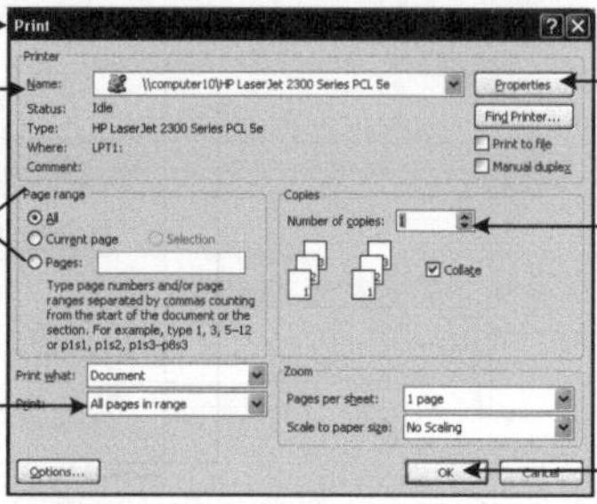

3. The **Print** dialog box appears.
4. Click the **Name:** drop-down list and choose the desired printer.
5. Click the **Properties** button to change printer propterties, such as pirnt quality (options will vary depending on your printer)
6. Check a desired **Page range** options to print.
7. Click **Number of copies** and type the desired number of copies to print.
8. Click the **Print** drop-down button to print odd or even pages only
9. Click OK button.

Cancel Printing

1. Click the Start button and then click **Printers and Faxes.**

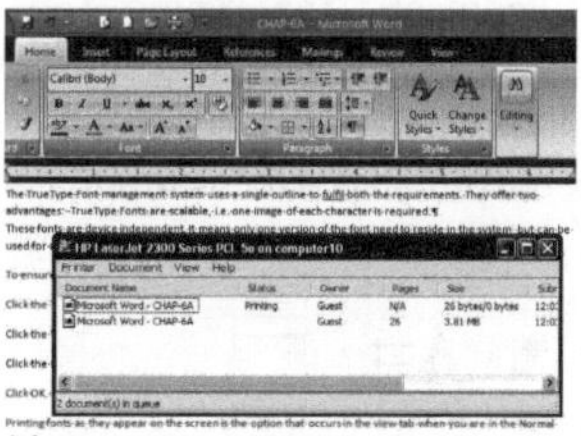

2. In the **Printers and Faxes** dialog box, open the printer that you are using by double-clicking the printer's icon.
3. Select the document you want to cancel printing, and then choose **Document Name,** right click and choose Cancel Printing.

MS Excel 2007

Getting Started

Excel is a popular spreadsheet program, where you can design worksheets using this software package. Excel 2007 uses a workbook-style presentation which is made up of several worksheets, like pages in a notebook. You can open Excel 2007 using Start button.

Notes:

Excel 2007 is a popular spreadsheet program, where you not only design worksheets but can plot graphs using this program.

Excel 2007 is a software package which accepts data in a tabular form, shows data in a tabular form and serves many functions to perform calculations.

Excel 2007 has a grid of columns and rows into which you can enter numeral, text, etc. Each box in the grid is called a cell.

Starting Excel using Start Button

1. Click the **Start** Button on the Taskbar.
2. Highlight **All Programs**, Click **Microsoft Office**.
3. Click **Microsoft Office Excel 2007**.

About Excel 2007 Interface

Excel 2007 includes the Microsoft Office Fluent interface, which consists of a customizable visual system of tools and commands. It shows the elements of the Excel 2007 application window and an open Excel 2007 workbook in detail.

Excel 2007 works in Windows XP, Windows Vista or Windows 7 installed as operating system on PC.

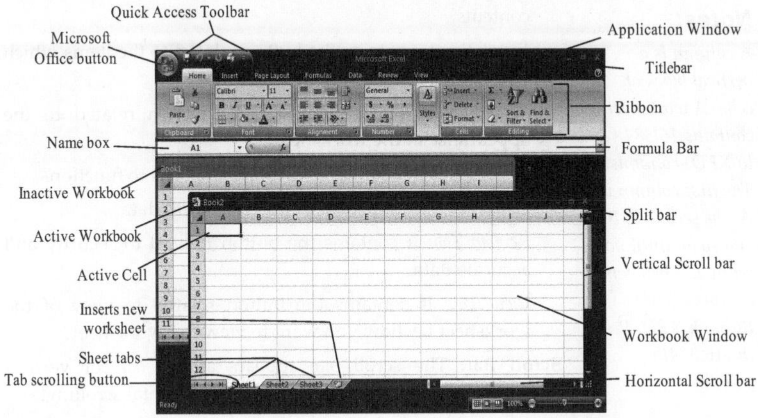

Title Bar: At the top of an Excel 2007 window, there is the title bar. The left edge of this bar has the Application window control icon next to which the name of the open document is displayed. On the right edge of the title bar, the *minimize, restore/maximize* and *close* buttons are placed.

Application Window: The window within which Excel 2007 runs.

Quick Access Toolbar: The buttons on the quick access toolbar represent a *command* or a *procedure*.

Workbook Window: A window within the Excel 2007 application window in which a worksheet, chart, or dialog box is shown.

MS Office Button: This button is located in the upper-left corner of the Excel 2007 window. It opens the menu containing commands like New, Open, Save, Save As, Share, Print, etc.

Active Workbook: The Excel 2007 workbook window that accepts entries and commands.

Inactive Workbook: A window that contains Excel 2007 information. It is not affected by commands. Such a window has a gray title bar and is behind the active workbook window.

Ribbon: Ribbon is displayed just below the title bar. In Ribbon, *Commands* are organized in logical *groups*, which are collected together under *tabs*. You can hide the Ribbon by double-clicking the active tab. Different types of Tabs described here under are available in the Ribbon of Excel 2007.

Home Tab: It contains the button related to the worksheet

Notes:

A worksheet is a sheet made up of rows and columns. It refers to the actual document you create by using the spreadsheet program. The worksheet is always stored in a workbook.

Row is a horizontal block of cells. The first row is numbered 1, the second 2, and so on. There can be a maximum of 1,048,576 rows in a worksheet.

Notes:

A column is a vertical block of cells. A worksheet contains 16,384 (A to XFD) columns. The first column is A, the second is B and so on until you reach Z. Then come columns AA through XFD. It is the 16,384th column.

Cell is the intersection of a row and a column.

Formulas are equations that perform calculations on values in a worksheet. A formula always begins with = (equal) sign.

Shortcut menus are meant to display frequently used commands relating to the selected item or object.

contents.

Insert Tab: It contains the button related to the items which you can insert in your worksheet.

Page Layout Tab: It includes the button related to the appearance of the worksheet.

Formulas Tab: It contains the button related to functions.

Data Tab: It contains the button related to data.

Review Tab: It contains the button related to security and accurate data.

View Tab: It contains the button related to view of the worksheet i.e. how you want to view the worksheet?

Scroll Bar: The scroll bar appears at the *left* for vertical scrolling and at the *bottom right* for horizontal scrolling.

To scroll one cell at a time, click the scroll button with arrows at the corners of the scroll bars.

To scroll more, drag the scroll button in the scroll bar.

Split Bar: The split bar is located at the top of the *vertical* scroll bar and to the right of the *horizontal* scroll bar. Double click the split button on the vertical scroll bar. It splits the sheet horizontally.

Tab Scrolling Buttons: These are the arrow buttons to the left of the sheet tabs for scrolling the worksheet.

To scroll between sheet tabs, click an arrow for the direction you want to scroll.

To scroll one sheet tab at a time in left or right direction, click the middle tab scrolling buttons.

To scroll through a group of sheet tabs in left or right direction, click the tab scroll buttons at the left and right corner.

To display a list of the sheets in the workbook right click a tab scrolling button to display the menu.

Sheet Tabs: A tab is near to the bottom of a work book window that displays the name of a sheet. Click the sheet tab to move to the next sheet. To display the shortcut menu right click the sheet tab. To scroll through the sheet tabs, use the tab scrolling button.

Name Box: The *name box* is at the left end of the formula bar. It identifies the selected *cell, chart item* or *drawing object.*

Formula Bar: The *formula bar* displays the constant value or formula used in the active cell. The formula bar is also used for editing the cell contents.

Status Bar: Status bar appears at the bottom of the Excel 2007 window. It displays information regarding a selected command or an operation in progress. Note that the right side of the status bar shows zoom slider, different views tool such as Normal, Page

Notes:

You can create a blank workbook or create new workbook based on an existing workbook, the default workbook template, or any other template.

Creating New Workbook

A workbook is a collection of many worksheets. By default, a workbook opens with three worksheets and it can contain a maximum of 255 worksheets.

1. Click on the **MS Office button.**
2. Then choose **New...** .

To create new workbook, you can also press Ctrl + N keys together.

3. In New dialog box, click **Blank Workbook.**
4. Then click **Create** button.

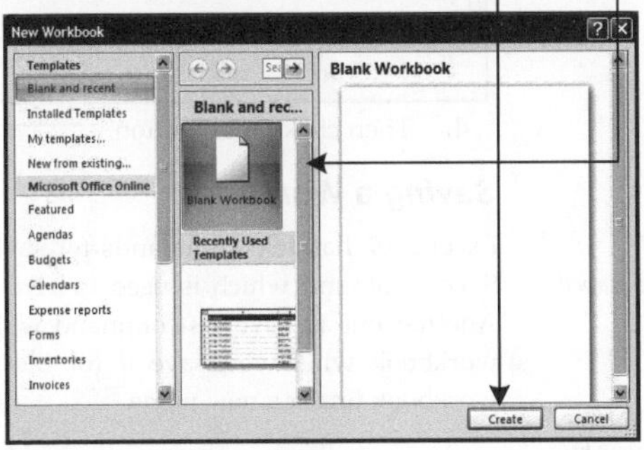

Notes:

To open recent used files choose the recent files from the right side of the MS Office menu.

Opening a Workbook

Excel 2007 makes use of several workbooks and their worksheets. To work on any worksheet first of all, you have to open a workbook.

Notes:

To open workbook, you can also press Ctrl + O keys together.

To open more than one workbook simultaneously, click the name of one file name and then hold down Ctrl key and click another file name and then press Enter key.

1. Click on the **MS Office button**.
2. Then choose **Open...** .

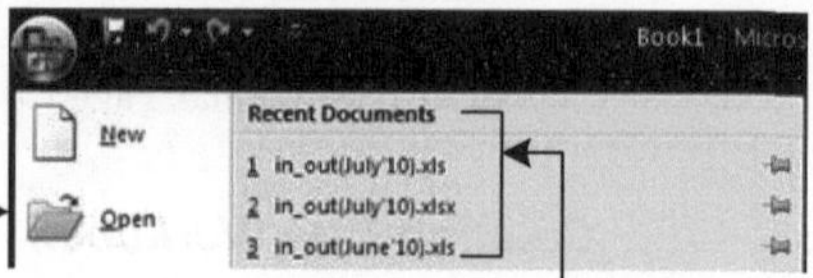

List of Recent document list

3. In Open Dialog box, choose the drive, folder name that contains the workbooks. After finding the required workbook, select it.

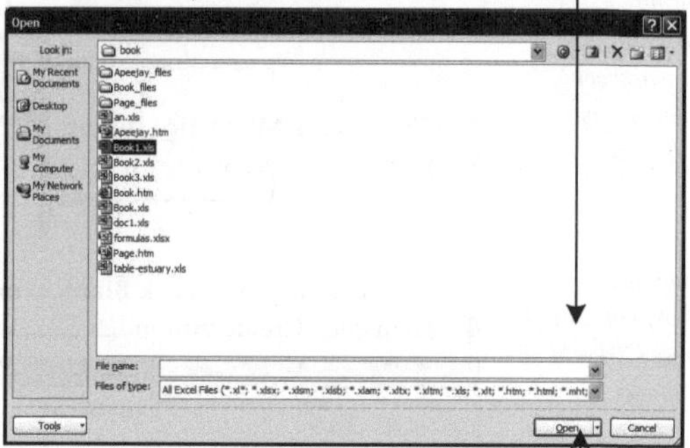

4. Then click **Open** button.

Notes:

Excel 2007 worksheet is saved with .xlsx.

You can also save your workbook by pressing  *(Save) button from the Quick Launch Toolbar.*

Saving a Workbook

Excel 2007 has two commands for saving workbooks. One is Save command which is used to save an existing workbook. Another one is Save As command which is used to save the workbook when you save it for the first time or save the workbook under a new name.

1. Click on the **MS Office button**.
2. Then choose **Save As...** .

3. In Save As Dialog box, specify the location where you want to save the file in **Save in** box.

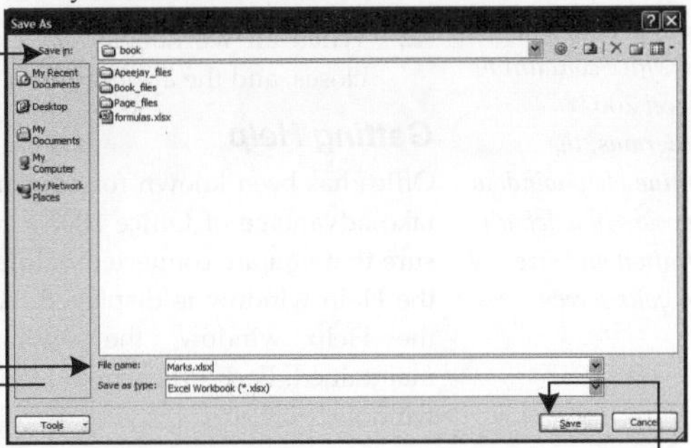

4. In the **File name:** box give the name of the file.
5. In the **Save as type:** box give the type of file.
6. Click **Save** button.

Notes:

You can also quit from Excel by pressing Close button (X) or by pressing Alt + F4 keys together.

The Search button shown in Help window is a drop down control that lets you specify what and where to search.

Closing a Workbook

When you finish using worksheet or chart, you close its window. If you have made any changes since the last time you saved the workbook, Excel 2010 displays an alert dialog box, asking whether you want to save your work before closing.

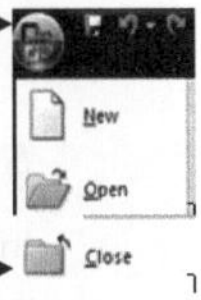

1. Click on the **MS Office button**.
2. Then choose **Close**.
3. The window closes provided no change has been made to the workbook since it was saved last.
4. If you have made changes to the workbook since the last save, the Alert dialog box appears. In the dialog box, choose No if you do not want to save a changed version of the file, or choose Yes if you do want to save changes. Type a new file name and choose Save.

Quitting Excel 2007

Notes:

When first time you use the Help feature in Office containing Excel 2007 programs, the online Help window appears in a default location and sizes on your screen.

1. Click on the **MS Office** button and then choose **Exit Excel**.
2. When all workbooks are closed, Excel 2007 window closes, and the application is terminated.

Getting Help

Office has been known for offering very helpful advice. To take advantage of Office 2007's full help feature set, make sure that you are connected online. You can change the way the Help window is displayed. After that, when you open the Help window, the settings that you made are maintained. Each program in MS Office has a separate Help window.

A default workbook opens with 3 worksheets. However, you can change the number of sheets depending upon your needs. The maximum sheets that you can open are 255.

1. Click on the **Help button** (circle with question mark inside) or Alternatively, press **F1** key.
2. Type the particular word which you want to search in the search box and press **Enter** key.

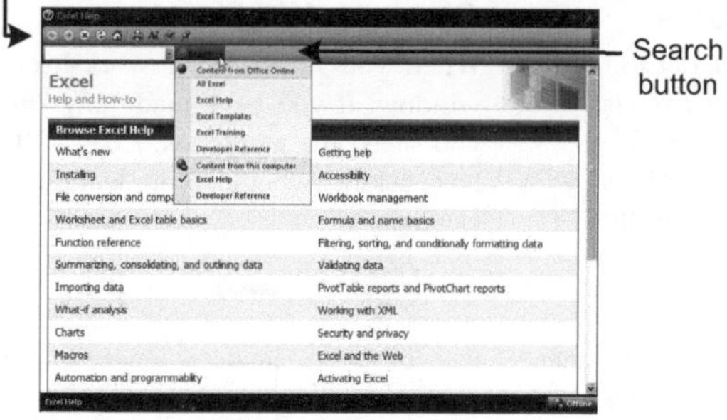

Switching between Workbook Windows

In Excel 2007, you can also get multiple workbooks open, each in its own document window. To work on a workbook you need to activate it.

1. Click on the **View Tab**.

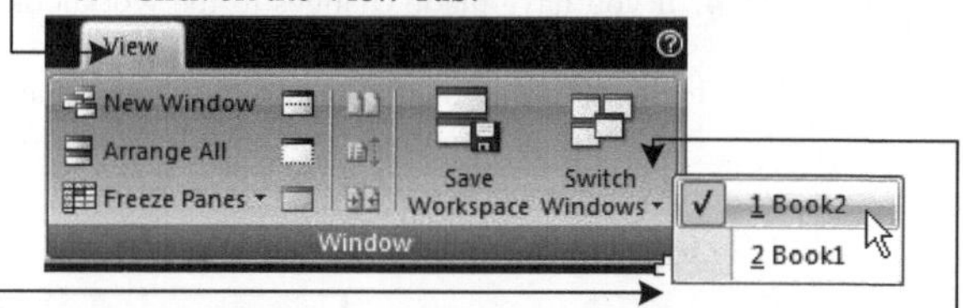

2. In the **Window** group, click arrow next to the **Switch Window**.
3. Then select the workbook window from the list of open windows.

Inserting and Deleting Sheets

Notes:

To insert or delete worksheet, position the mouse pointer on the tab of any sheet and then choose the desired option.

You can insert a new sheet in the workbook at any location you desire.

If you revise workbooks, you will want to *insert/delete* sheets from the workbook. Excel 2007 gives you the flexibility to easily insert and remove sheets.

To Insert a sheet in a workbook:

1. Activate the workbook into which you want to insert the sheet.
2. Select the existing sheet before which you want to insert the new sheet by clicking its sheet tab or by pressing **Ctrl + PgUp** or **Ctrl + PgDn** as the case may be.
3. Select **Insert Sheet** option from **Insert** drop down list of the **Cells** group of the **Home Tab** Or, Press **Alt + Shift + F11** keys together to insert a new worksheet.

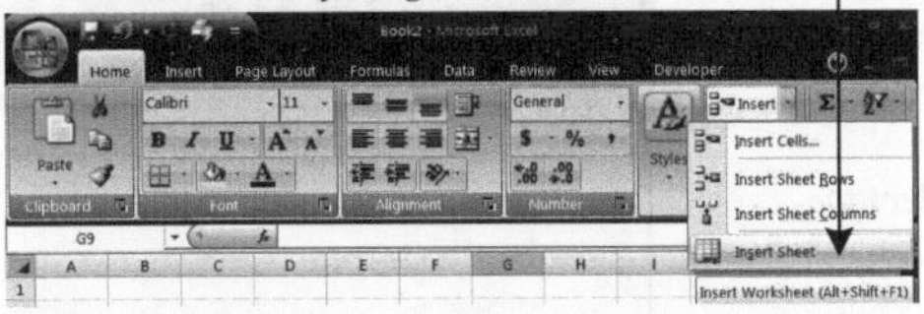

Notes:

You cannot undo or get back a worksheet after deletion. Therefore, you should be very careful before you delete a worksheet.

Double clicking the sheet tab will allow you to change the sheet name.

An active sheet is the sheet in which you can operate.

To Delete a sheet in a workbook:

1. Select the sheet you want to delete.
2. Click on the **Home tab**, in the **Cells** group. Select **Delete Sheet** from the **Delete drop down list.**

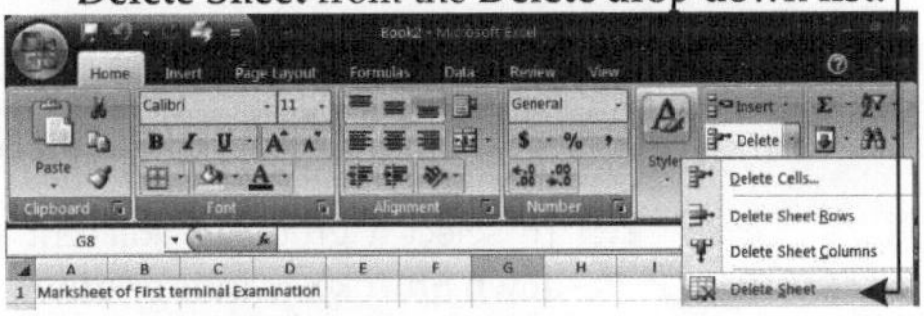

Renaming a Sheet

The names assigned to worksheets in a workbook by default are Sheet 1, Sheet 2, etc. However, you can also name the sheets as per your needs.

1. Open the sheet which you want to rename.

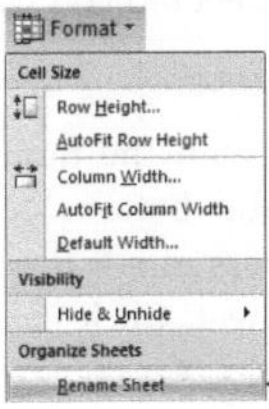

2. In **Home Tab**, under the **Cells** group, from the **Format** drop down list, select **Rename Sheet**.

Notes:

To rename sheet, click the right mouse button on the sheet tab whose name you want to rename, then choose ***Rename.***

When you select a group of sheets, the word ***|Group|*** *is displayed in the title bar which indicates that a group of sheets is selected.*

To ***deselect*** *the group, click any sheet tab that is not selected.*

3. Type the new sheet name, using up to 31 characters including spaces.
4. Press **Enter** key. The new sheet name appears on the sheet tab.

Grouping Sheets

You can perform operations on several sheets at one time by creating a *group selection*. This group selection is useful to edit or format a group of sheets *identically* or to reorganize a group of sheets. You can group the worksheets and then add text or format them all at once.

1. Select the first sheet tab.

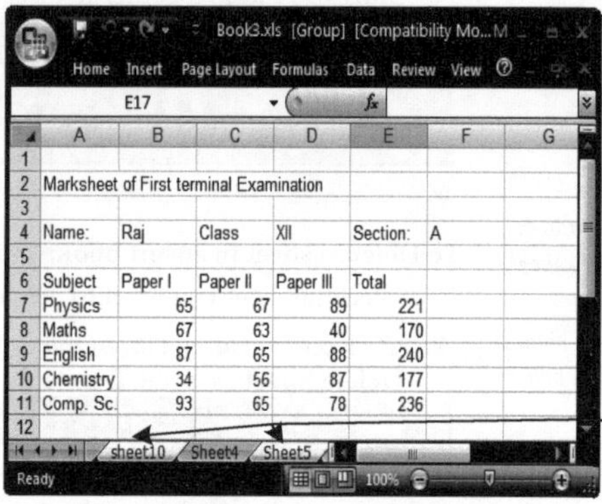

Group sheets

2. To select a group of adjacent sheets, press and hold down **Shift** key, while selecting the last sheet tab in the group. All sheets in between, including the first and last sheet you clicked are selected.

OR

To select a group of non-adjacent sheets, hold down Ctrl key and click the next sheet tab you want to select. Do this for each sheet tab you want to select.

Notes:

The vertical and the horizontal scroll boxes give you the position in the worksheet.

Scrolling with Mouse

To scroll the window with the mouse, use the scroll bars located at the right and bottom of each worksheet. The arrows in the scroll bars show the direction the window moves over the worksheet. Click the arrow to scroll in that direction.

Scrolling with Keyboard

When you scroll using a keyboard, the cell selected by you changes as you scroll. Following table shows some keys to scroll.

Key	Movement
↑	Scrolls up one row.
↓	Scrolls down one row.
←	Scrolls left one column.
→	Scrolls right one column.
PgUp	Scrolls up one screen.
PgDn	Scrolls down one screen.
Alt + PgUp	Scrolls right one window.
Alt + PgDn	Scrolls left one window.
Home	Moves to the beginning of the row.
Ctrl + Home	Moves to the beginning of the worksheet.

Selecting a Single Cell using Keyboard

Before you can *enter, edit* or *modify* the contents of a cell, you must select or activate the cell or cells you want to change. Following table shows some keys to select single cell.

Key	Movement
↑	Moves the active cell up one cell.
↓	Moves the active cell down one cell.
→	Moves the active cell right one cell.
←	Moves the active cell left one cell.
Tab	Enters data and moves the active cell right.
Shift + Tab	Enters data and moves the active cell left.
Enter	Enters data and moves the active cell down.
Shift + Enter	Enters data and moves the active cell up in the selected range.
Ctrl + Arrow	Moves the active cell in the direction indicated by arrow until the edge of a block of data is reached
Home	Moves the active cell to column A of the current row
Ctrl + Home	Moves the active cell to the first cell in the worksheet (cell A1)
Ctrl + End	Moves the active cell to the last cell in the used portion of the worksheet
PgUp	Moves the active cell up one full window
PgDn	Moves the active cell down one full window
Alt + PgUp	Moves the active cell one screen left
Alt + PgDn	Moves the active cell one screen right

Notes:

To select a single cell using mouse, move the mouse pointer over the cell and click the cell.

The single cell that receives the data or formula you enter is the ***active cell****. A selection of multiple cells is referred to as a* ***range****.*

If you want to see the active cell, but it is not visible in the window, press ***Ctrl + Backspace*** *keys together.*

To select a large range of cells using ***GoTo*** *command, type a range address in the Reference: box, such as* ***A5:F12****, and then click* ***OK.***

Selecting a Range of cells

Select a range of cells when you want to apply a command to all the selected cells or want to enter data into the cells in the range.

1. Click the cell at one corner of the range.

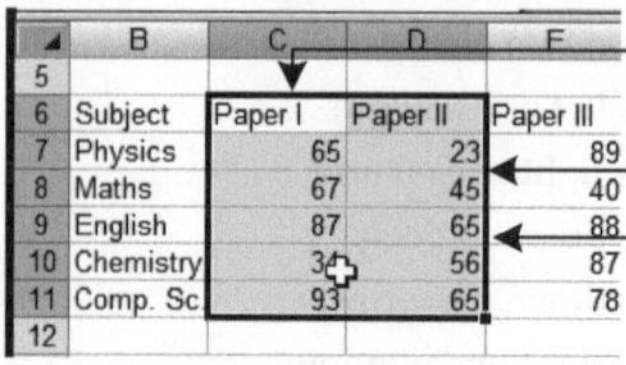

2. Drag to the opposite corner of the range and release the mouse button.
3. A rectangular range of cells is selected.

Selecting Large Range of Cells Using Go To Command

The Go To... command moves you to any cell or address in the sheet you request. If you choose a named cell or a range of cells, with Go To, the entire range is selected.

1. Select one corner of the range.
2. Click on the **Home tab.**

3. In the **Editing** group, click arrow next to **Find & Select.**
4. Then click **Go To...** or press **F5** key or press **Ctrl + G**. The Go To dialog box appears.

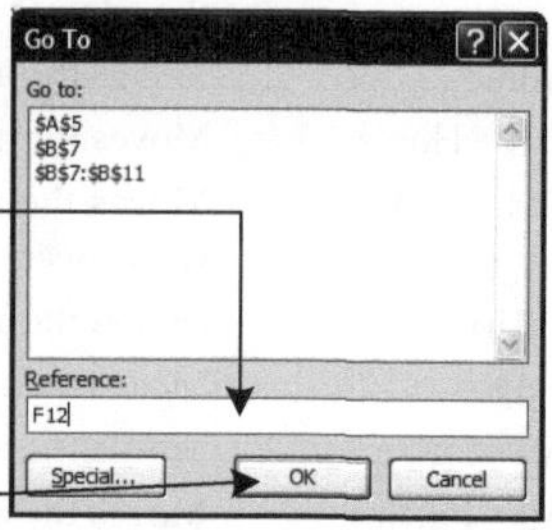

5. Type the cell reference of the opposite corner in the **Reference:** text box.
6. Hold down **Shift** key when you click the **OK** button, or press **Enter** key.

Selecting more than one Ranges of Cells

Excel 2007 has the capability to select multiple nonadjacent ranges at a time. This feature helps you to format multiple ranges with a single command. You may even print different parts of the worksheet with a single print command. Similarly, you can erase multiple data-entry cells with one keystroke.

1. Select the first range of cell.
2. Press and hold down **Ctrl** key as you select each additional range of cells.
3. Release **Ctrl** key.

Following figure shows an example of selecting multiple ranges of cells.

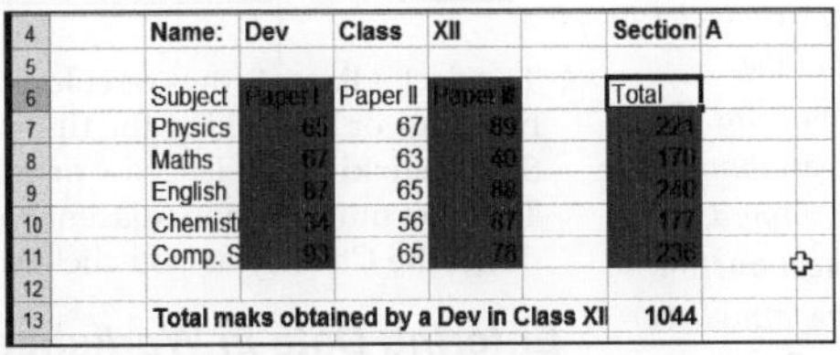

Notes:

You can use AutoCalculate feature to find total or sum count, average, or to find the maximum or minimum number in the selected range of cells without creating a formula or using a calculator.

Excel 2007 has a very useful command that enables you to select cells by contents or the relationship to formulas.

AutoCalculate

When you select a range of cells, Excel 2007 displays the sum of the selected ranges in the status bar.

1. Right-click the Status bar.
2. From the pop-up list that appears, select the function you want to use for AutoCalculate.
3. Then, select the range you want. Excel 2007 displays the appropriate results in the Status bar.

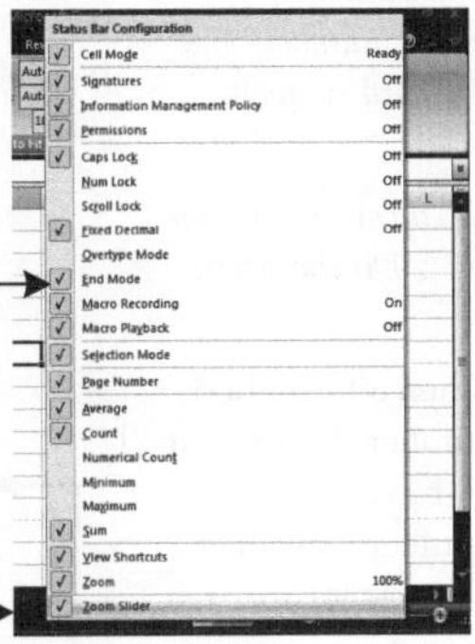

Selecting Entire Row/Column with Mouse

Some operations are quicker if you select an entire row or column at one time. For example, formatting is simple and more efficient if you select and format the entire row or column instead of formatting each cell in the row or a column

Notes:

The active cell appears with a dark border and its row and column headings appear to be raised to easily identify the cell address.

If you make a mistake before finalizing data entry, press ***Backspace*** *key to delete the character to the left of the insertion point. To erase everything that you have typed, click the* ***cancel button*** *from the formula bar or press* ***Esc*** *key.*

Text in a cell can include any combination of letters, numbers and keyboard symbols

A cell can contain up to 32,000 characters.

When a formatted number does not fit within a cell, number signs like hash (####) are shown.

To select single row or column, click the row or column's heading. The complete row or column is selected.

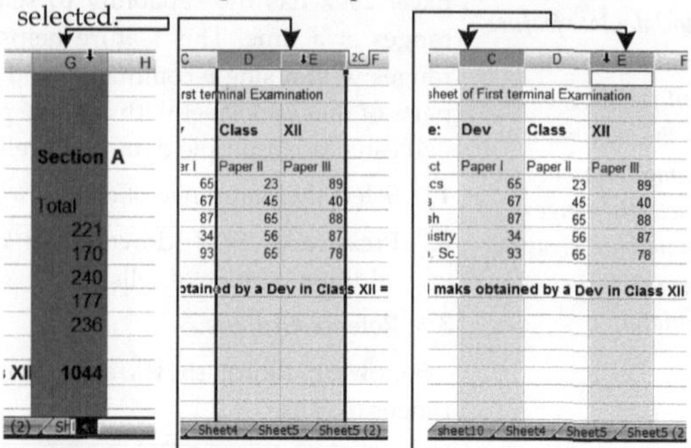

To select adjacent rows or columns, drag across the headings or by clicking the first row and pressing the **Shift +clicking** the last row or column.
To select multiple nonadjacent rows and columns, hold down the **Ctrl** key as you click each heading

Entering Data in Worksheet

The power of Excel lies in storing, manipulating, and displaying data items. Before you can manipulate and display data, you must enter it correctly.

When you see the message *Ready* in the status bar then you can enter data items in a worksheet. You can enter different type of data in a cell of the Excel worksheet.

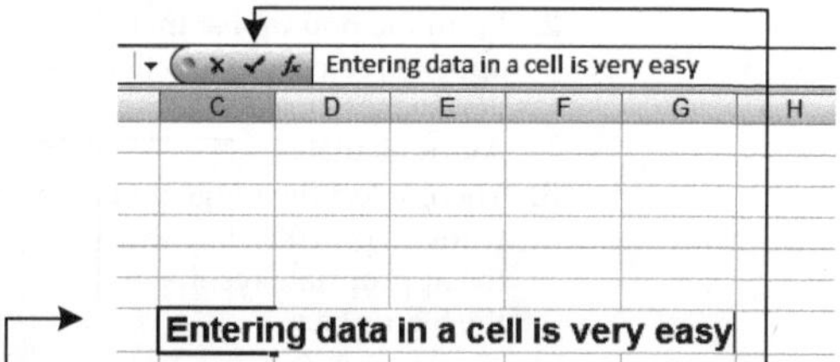

1. Click on the desired cell where you want to enter data.
2. Type your data in the active cell.
3. Click on **Enter** button from the Formula bar or press **Enter** key or **Tab** key.

✍ ***To enter and edit data directly in the cell, you need to turn on the in-cell editing option, if not done already.***

Notes:

You can different types of series in two ways:
1. Using the mouse to drag the fill handle.
2. Using a command that gives you the capability to create many types of series.

Dragging the fill handle to the right and down fills the series in increasing order; dragging the fill handle up or left fills the series in decreasing order.

The fill handle is the small square located at the lower right corner of a selection.

The area enclosed with the gray border fills with a series of numbers determined by the first two cells you selected.

Autofill Feature

Excel 2007 makes it very easy to enter a series of dates, number or text. For example, you can insert column heading like *Jan, Feb, Mar,* etc. or enter number at equal intervals such as 2, 4, 6, 8, etc. very easily.

Creating Linear Series:

1. Enter the first two elements of data in the series in adjacent cells, namely 1 and 3 in cells B6 and C6. Excel uses these two data items to determine the amount of increment in each step and the starting number for the series.

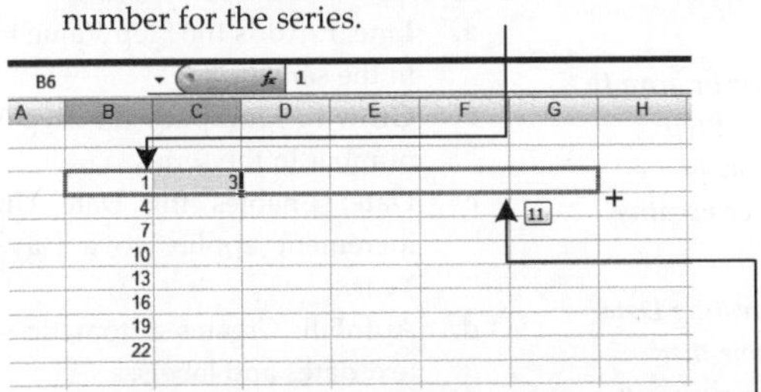

2. Select these two cells and then drag the fill handle down or right to fill in increasing and drag the fill handle up or left to fill in decreasing order.
3. Release the mouse button.

Create a Number Series using Fill Series Dialog Box:

1. In the first cell, enter the *first number.*
2. Select the range of cells you want filled.
3. Click on the **Home tab.**

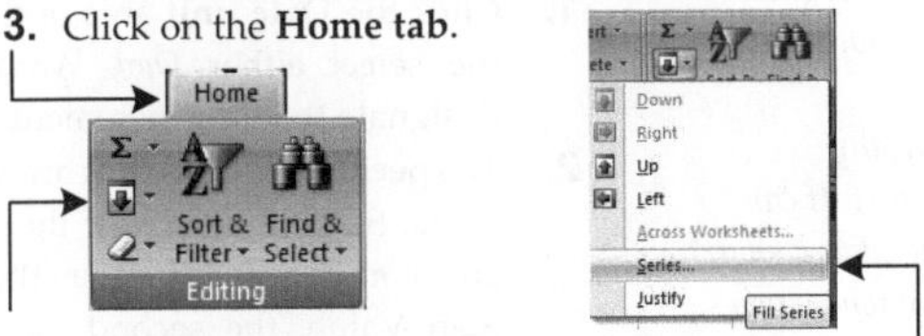

4. In the **Editing** group, click arrow next to **Fill.**
5. Then choose **Series...** to display the Series dialog box.

The AutoFill feature in Excel recognizes key words, such as days of the week, month names, and Quarterly abbreviations. Excel extends a series to repeat correctly, namely, Qtr1 follows Qtr4 and then the series continues.

Notes:

*When the series reaches either the end of the selected range or the **Stop Value**, Excel stops filling the cell. If you use a negative **Step Value**, the **Stop value** must be less than the starting value.*

*In **Linear or growth** series, the **Step Value** may be positive or negative.*

While creating Data series, note that Weekday gives you dates without Saturdays and Sundays.

***AutoCorrect** feature working both as a correction tool because it recognize common typing errors. It automatically corrects text. It can also be used as a short hand tool where you enter the abbreviations for long words so that on entering the abbreviation, it is replaced with the actual word.*

6. Click the Rows or Columns option that matches the type of range you want filled.
7. Select the Trend check box if you want selected values to be replaced by values for a linear or exponential best-fit.

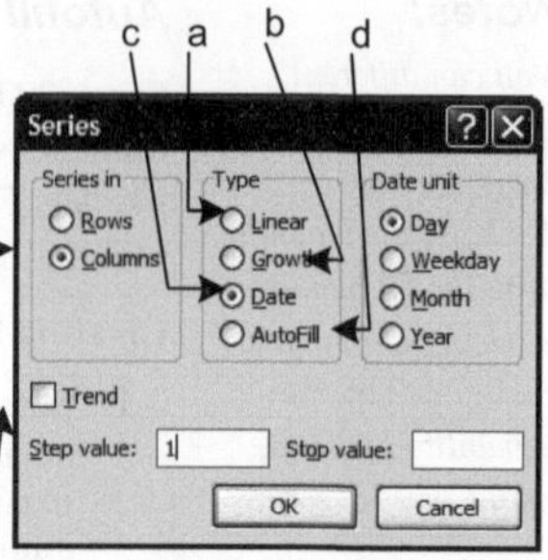

a. Linear: Adds the Step Value to the preceding number in the series.
b. Growth: Multiplies the Step Value by the preceding number in the series.
c. Date: Enables the Date Unit group so that the increment applies to a Day, **W**eekday, **M**onth, or Year.
d. AutoFill: Creates automatic series that may include text dates and labels.

To create a Linear or Growth series:

1. In Series dialog box, in the Step value: box enter the step value. This number is the constant amount by which the series changes from cell to cell.
2. In the **Stop value:** box enter a value at which you want to stop the fill.
3. Click OK.

To create a Date Series:

1. Click the **Date unit** area of the **Series** dialog box and the select either *Day, Weekday, Month,* or *Year* to designate the date increment.
2. To specify the increment amount, enter the Step value in the Step value box. If the starting value is **12/1/09**, and you choose Month as the Date Unit and 2 as the Step Value, the second date in the series becomes **2/1/10**.

AutoCorrect Feature

Excel 2007 has the AutoCorrect feature that recognizes common typing errors and automatically corrects them as you type. AutoCorrect will also correct two initial capitals. You can also use AutoCorrect to expand abbreviations. When you type *incl,* AutoCorrect will expand it to the full word *include.*

Notes:

You can add your own AutoCorrect entries and also delete any features already available which you do not want to use.

You can also add AutoCorrect entries during a spell check. For this, you have to choose the AutoCorrect button when Excel stops on the mistake.

*To delete an AutoCorrect entry, select the entry you want to Delete from AutoCorrect dialog box and then click **Delete** and then click **OK** button.*

*With the AutoComplete feature of Excel 2007 for repeated words you only have to type just few letters and the complete word is displayed. To accept the word press **Enter** key.*

To add AutoCorrect Entry Manually:

1. Click the **MS Office Button** and then click **Excel Options**. Excel Options dialog box appears. In this dialog box, Click on **Proofing** button on the left side. Under **AutoCorrect options** group, click on the **AutoCorrect Options...**

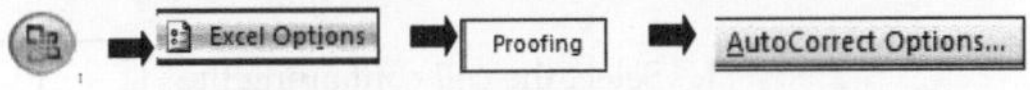

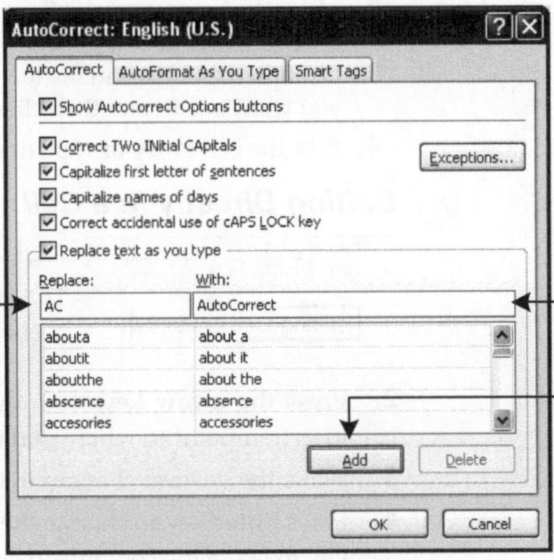

2. In the **Replace:** text box, type the error or abbreviation as you would usually type it.
3. In the **With:** text box, type the correct spelling of the word or phrase or expansion of an abbreviation i.e. short form of the word.
4. Click **Add** to add the new entry to the list of AutoCorrect entries.
5. Follow steps 2-4 for each entry you want to add.
6. After completing the entries click OK.

AutoComplete

Excel includes a feature called AutoComplete to make it easy to enter repeated text items in a column.

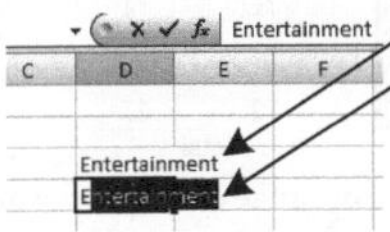

1. First time, type the complete name.
2. Next time you have to type only first letter.
3. Then press **Enter** key.

Excel 2007 matches and completes the entry automatically.

Notes:

A flashing insertion point indicates where typing and editing will take place.

Editing Data

While editing a cell entry, you can edit the text either in the formula bar or in the cell itself.

Editing Cell Entry in the Formula Bar

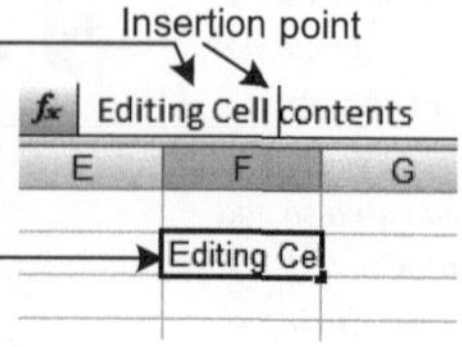

1. Select the cell containing the data you want to edit.
2. Move the insertion point into the text in the formula bar.
3. Position the pointer in the text you want to edit and then click.
4. Edit the cell entry or type new text.

Editing Directly in a Cell

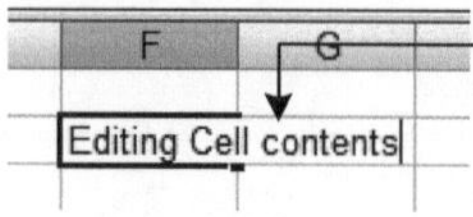

1. Double-click the selected cell or press **F2** key.
2. Press the **arrow** keys to move the *I-beam* that marks the insertion point to where you want to edit.
3. Make the desired changes to the cell entry.
4. Press **Enter** key to change the text. Alternatively, press **Esc** key to leave the contents unchanged.

Notes:

As you move the range of cell, you can see the range reference where the selection will be pasted.

Using the drag-and-drop method, you can make only a single copy. You cannot copy to multiple locations.

Moving and Copying Cell Contents

Cutting and pasting is a valuable function for reorganizing a worksheet. You may *cut* a range of cells to *paste* them elsewhere. This operation can move cell contents, format, and any note attached to the moved cells. You can also copy a range of cells and paste it into another location.

Moving Cell Contents by Dragging and Dropping

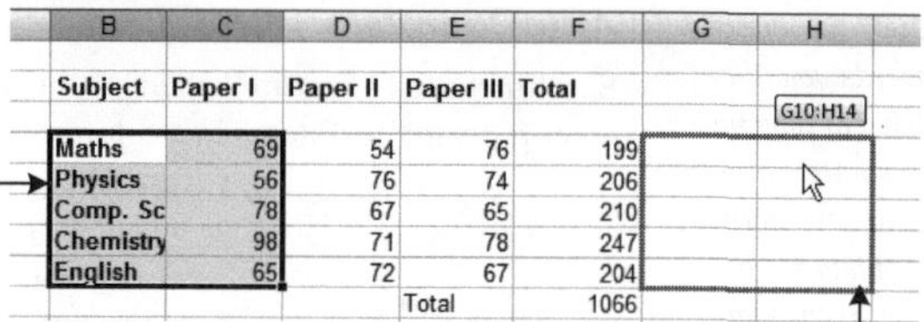

1. Select the cell or range of cells you want to move.
2. Move the mouse pointer over the selection's border. The pointer changes to an arrow.

3. Drag the pointer and the gray outline of the selection to the new location.
4. Release the mouse button when the gray outline is where you want to place the selected range.

Copying Cell Contents by Dragging and Dropping

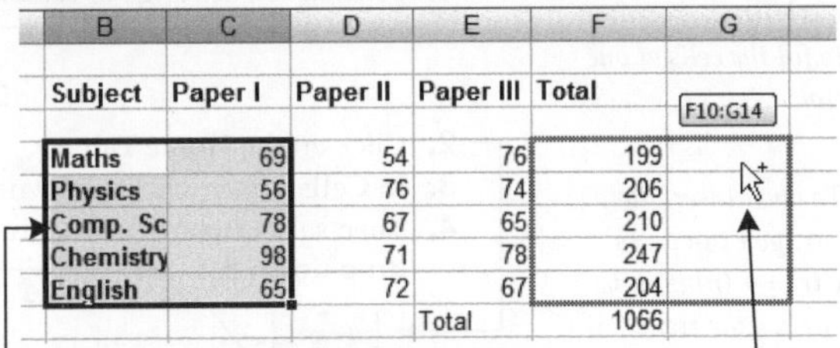

1. Select the range of cells you want to copy.
2. Hold down the **Ctrl** key and move the pointer over an edge of the selection. The pointer becomes an arrow with a **+ (plus)** sign.

3. Continue holding down **Ctrl** key as you drag the edge of the selection to where you want to copy.

Moving Cell Contents with Menu Command

1. Select the cell or range of cells you want to move.

2. Click on the **Home Tab.**
3. Then click **Cut** button under the **Clipboard** group, or press **Ctrl** + **X** keys together.
4. Select the cell at the upper-left corner, where you want to paste the selected cells.
5. Click **Paste** button under the **Clipboard** group.

Copying Cell Contents with Menu Command

1. Select the cell or range of cells you want to move.

2. Click on the **Home Tab.**
3. Then click **Copy** button under the **Clipboard** group, or press **Ctrl** + **C** keys together.
4. Select the cell at the upper-left corner, where you want the duplicate to appear.
5. Click **Paste** button under the **Clipboard** group.

Notes:

*If you release the **Ctrl** key before you release the mouse button, the copy operation becomes a move operation. The plus (+) sign next to the arrow disappears.*

*To move or copy data to another application such as **Word,** you cannot use drag and drop technique. For this, you can use menu commands or shortcut keys*

*While moving or copying cell contents with menu command press **Ctrl + V** keys together to paste and retain the copy in clipboard memory or press **Enter** key to paste only one time.*

*You can also drag a selected range to another worksheet in the workbook. To do so, hold down the **Alt** key and then drag the selection to the sheet tab. The sheet pops up and you can then drag the selection to the location you want on the sheet.*

Notes:

*To fill multiple rows or columns at one time, select all the original cells and then use the **Ctrl+drag** procedure to fill the cells at one time.*

*To open Insert dialog box, you can press **Ctrl + + (plus)** keys or click the right mouse button and select Insert... .*

Inserting Cells, Rows or Columns

Sometimes you may need to insert cells, rows, or columns to make room for new formulas or data. You can insert cells, rows, or columns as easily as you can delete them.

Inserting Cells:

1. Select a cell or range of cells where you need new cells inserted.

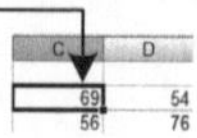

2. Click on the **Home** Tab.
3. In **Cells** group, click arrow next **Insert.**
4. Then select **Insert Cells...** from the **Insert** drop-down list.

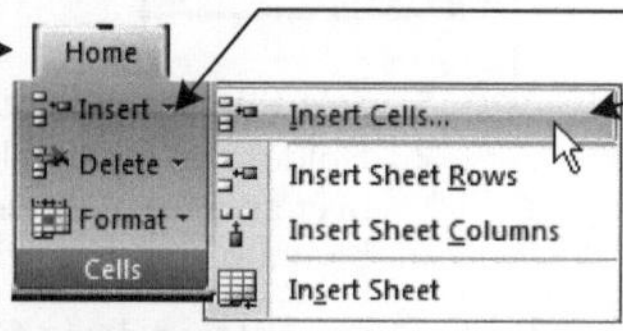

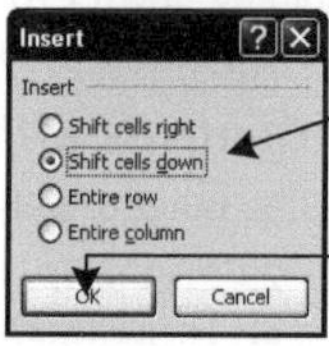

5. To insert cells, select the direction you want selected cells to be inserted.
6. Click Ok.

Inserting *Rows* or *Column:*

1. Select cell in the *rows* or *columns* where you want to insert *new* rows or columns.
2. Select **Insert Sheet Rows** from **Insert** drop down list of the **Cells** group of the **Home** Tab to insert rows.
3. Select **Insert Sheet Columns** from **Insert** drop down list of the **Cells** group of the **Home** Tab to insert columns.

Notes:

To clear the contents of a cell or range of cells, using shortcut menu, select the cell(s), click the right mouse button and choose Clear Contents.

Clearing Cell Contents

You can clear or erase everything in a cell or erase the format only, or erase the formulas only, or erase the comments only.

To clear the contents of a cell, select the cells and then press **Del** key. Only the contents are deleted. Formats and notes will remain intact.

If you accidentally clear a cell's contents, immediately press Ctrl + Z keys together. This will undo your most recent edit action.

Notes:

As you drag the column to adjust the width, the Width box appears, displaying the numeric value for the column width.

1. Select the cell or range of cells you want to clear.

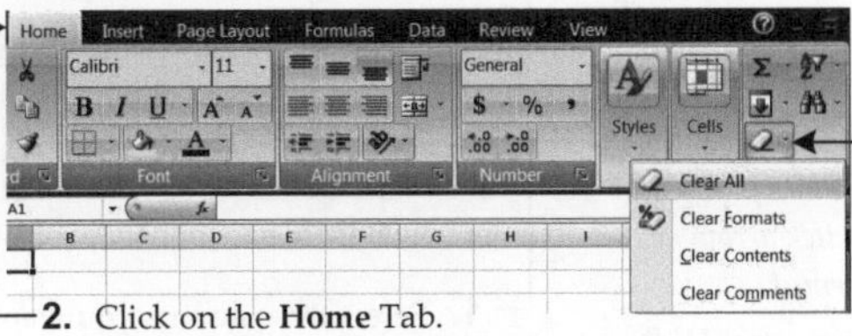

2. Click on the **Home** Tab.
3. Then click arrow next to **Clear** button under the **Editing** group and then select the option that you want.
4. Select the command according to your need.
   a. **All:** Clears cell contents and notes; returns the format to General format.
   b. **Formats:** Returns the format to General format.
   c. **Contents:** Clears contents but does not change formats or notes.
   d. **Comments:** Clears comments but does not change contents or formats.
5. Excel 2007 will clear the contents.

Notes:

If a column is not wide enough to display a number, date, or time, Excel 2007 displays it using # characters in the cell.

Adjusting Columns Width

You can adjust the width of one or more columns to get better look in a worksheet.

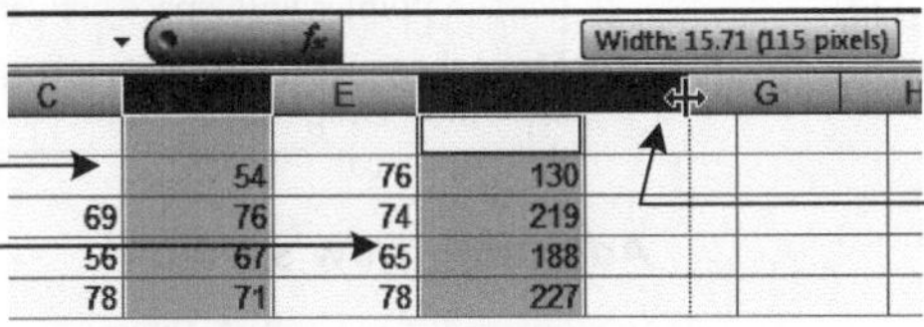

1. Select the columns to change the width.
2. Move the pointer onto the column separator to the right of the column heading. Pointer changes to a two-headed, horizontal arrow.
3. Drag the column left or right until the column is of the required width.
4. Release the mouse button.

✍ ***If you work on a large worksheet, you may not require to print or view the whole worksheet at one time. For this reason, you can hide columns temporarily so that they do not print or appear on the screen.***

Hide Columns in a Worksheet

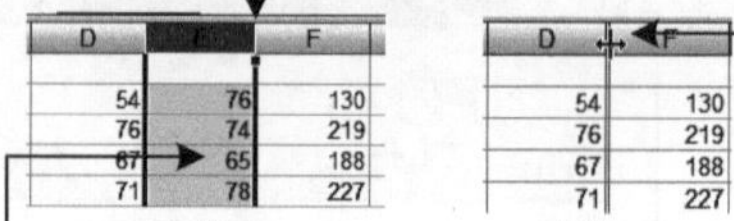

Before After

1. Select the columns you want to hide.
2. Move the mouse pointer over the column separator line i.e. on the right of the column you want to hide.
3. The mouse pointer changes to a two-headed pointer. Drag the column separator left until crosses the separator on its left.

Unhide Columns in a Worksheet

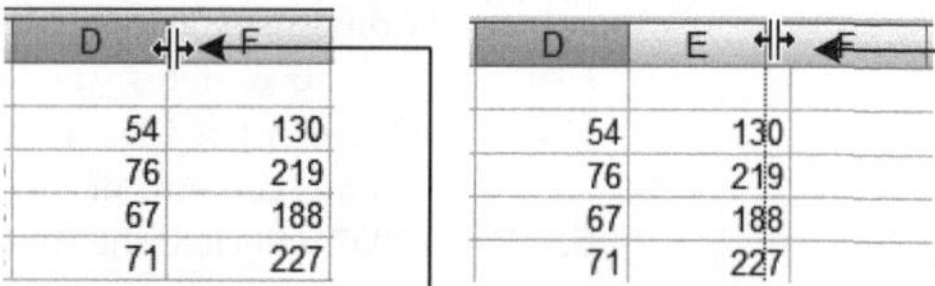

Before After

1. Move the pointer over the column separator on the right of a hidden column. The mouse pointer changes to a two-headed pointer with space between the two heads.
2. Move the pointer so that its left tip touches the column separator. Drag the column separator to the right, and then release it.

Adjusting Row's Height

You can adjust row height in a worksheet to create enough space for *titles, subtotals, grand totals,* etc.

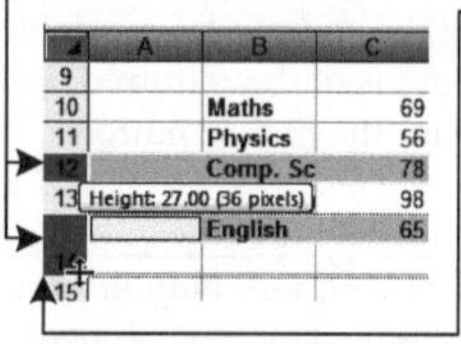

1. Select the rows for which you want to adjust the height.
2. Move the mouse pointer to the line directly under the header of the row you want to change. The mouse pointer changes to a two headed vertical arrow.
3. Drag the two-headed arrow pointer up or down until the row is of the required height.
4. Then release the mouse button.

Notes:

To hide column using Ribbon,
1. Select the columns.
2. Under ***Home*** *Tab, click* ***Cells*** *group and then click arrow next to* ***Format****.*
3. Here, select ***Hide & Unhide*** *and then select* ***Hide Columns****.*

To unhide column using Ribbon,
1. Select the columns between which hidden columns appear.
2. Under ***Home*** *Tab, click* ***Cells*** *group and then click arrow next to* ***Format****.*
3. Here, select ***Hide & Unhide*** *and then select* ***Unhide Columns****.*

Hide Rows in a Worksheet

1. Select a row or rows which you want to hide, in a worksheet.

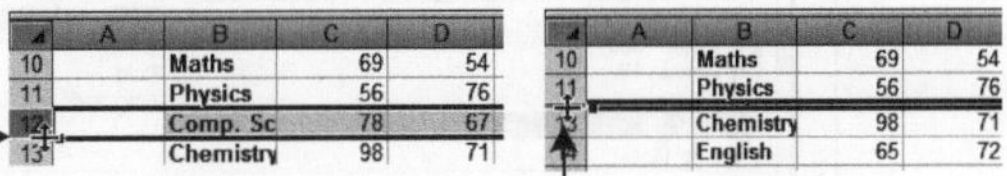

Before **After**

2. Move the mouse pointer over the row to separate till it changes to double arrow.
3. Now drag till the row is hidden or all the selected rows are hidden.

Notes:

To hide column using Ribbon,
1. Select the rows.
*2. Under **Home** Tab, click **Cells** group and then click arrow next to **Format**. Here, select **Hide & Unhide** and then select **Hide Rows**.*

There are two methods to format cells in a worksheet.
1. By using Dialog Box Launcher
2. By using Ribbon command.

Unhide Rows in a Worksheet

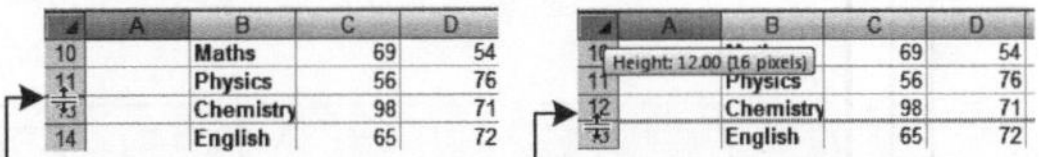

1. Move the pointer over the row number that is under the hidden rows.
2. Move the pointer up slowly until it changes to a double-headed pointer with space in between the two headings.
3. Drag the line down to display the hidden rows.

Formatting Cells and their Entries

You can use different character fonts and styles in an Excel 2007 worksheet. You can also change font colours, which appear on screen. If you have a colour printer, you can print worksheet with these colours.

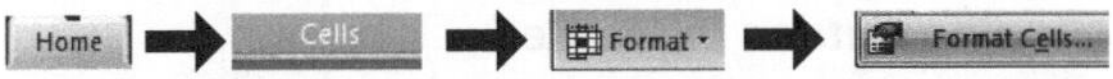

Format Entries within a Cell or a Range of Cells

1. Select the cell, range, or multiple ranges.
2. Under **Home** Tab, click **Cells** group.
3. Then click arrow next to **Format.** Here, select **Format Cells... .**
4. **Format Cells dialog box** appears. In this dialog box, click on the **Font** tab

Notes:

*You can open **Format Cells** dialog box by pressing keys **Ctrl + 1** or by clicking on the **Dialog Box Launcher** i.e. the small icon*  *that appears on the bottom right corner of the* ***Font*** *group i.e.*

*of the **Home** tab.*

Fonts of various typefaces are used in printed materials. Font height is measured in points, and there are 72 points in an inch. Fonts also appear in different styles: plain, bold, italic, underline and strike- through. Excel 2007 can use up to 256 different fonts in a worksheet.

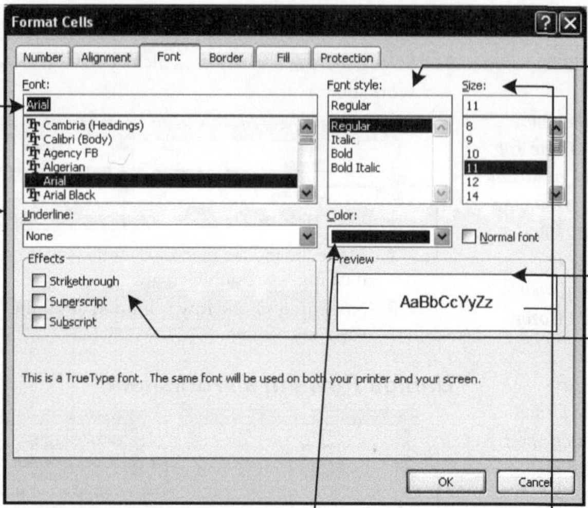

5. Select the font from the **Font:** list.
6. Select the font style from the **Font Style:** list.
7. Select the font size from the **Size:** list.
8. Select underline style from **Underline drop-down** list.
9. Select a colour from the **Color dropdown** list.
10. From the **Effects** group, select any combination of *Strikethrough, Superscript* or *Subscript* check boxes.
11. The **Preview box** shows the result of the chosen formatting options.
12. Click OK.

Aligning Entries in the Cell

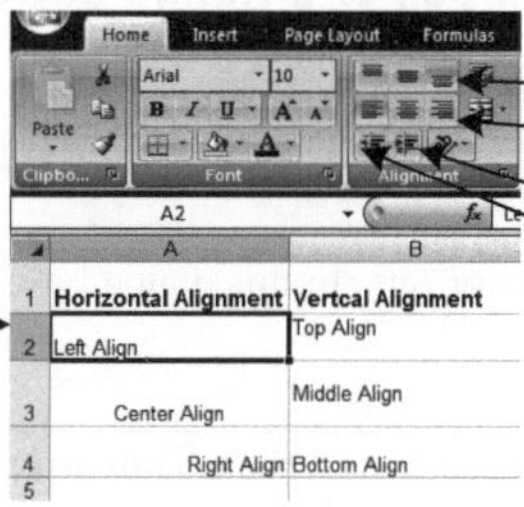

1. Select the cell or range of cells.

To horizontal alignment, click the **Left**, **Center**, or **Right** Align button from the **Alignment** group under the **Home** Tab.

To vertical alignment, click **Top align**, **Middle Align,** or **Bottom align** button.

To indent the cell contents, click the **Increase Indent** button.

To decrease indent, click **Decrease Indent** button.

Aligning a title across a selection of cells enables you to center a heading over a table or report.

Merging Cells

1. Type and format the title in the left cell of the range in which you want to center the title

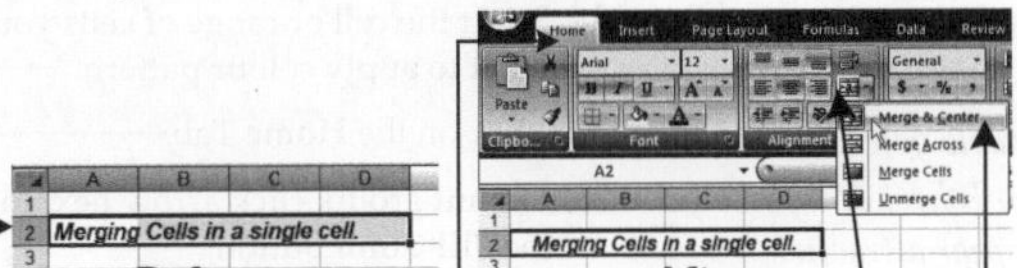

Before **After**

2. Select the range.
3. Click on the **Home** Tab.
4. In the **Alignment** group, click arrow next to **Merge & Center.**
5. Then Select **Merge & Center.**

Wrapping Text so as to Fit within a Cell

1. Select the cell or range of cells containing the text you want to wrap.

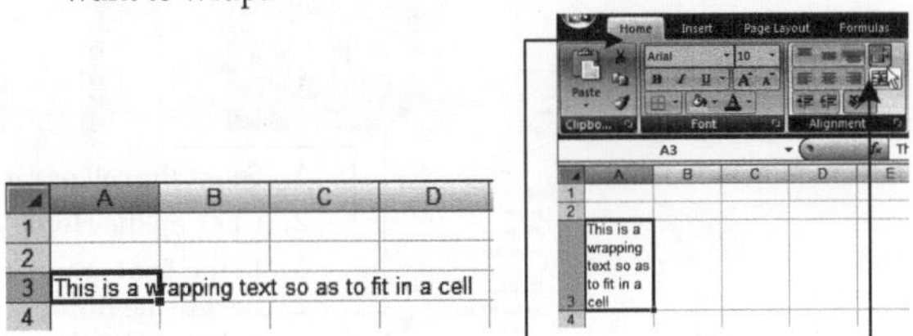

Before **After**

2. Click on the **Home** Tab.
3. In the **Alignment** group, click on the **Wrap Text** button.

Rotating Numbers and Text

1. Select the cells containing the title or label to be rotated.

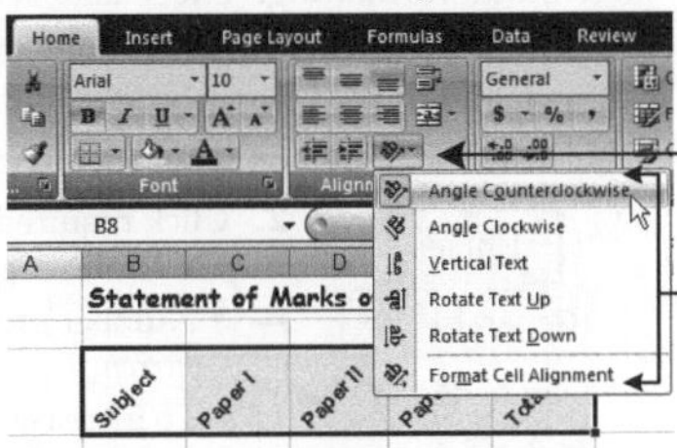

2. Click on the **Home** Tab.
3. In the **Alignment** group, click arrow next to **Orientation** button.
4. Then click on the desired option.

Notes:

*The **Merge and Center** button does two things in one step. First, it merges the selected cells and then it centers the text in the left-most cell within the merged cell.*

Excel 2007 gives you the option to wrap the text and to adjust it like a paragraph fitting within a cell. The cell's height increases to accommodate many such lines.

*To wrap text in a cell, press **Alt + Enter** keys together to enter a line break, as you type in the text. Wrap text option is automatically applied to the cell.*

Text is seen in horizontal and read from left to right. But, Excel 2007 gives you the option to align text so that the letters can be stacked. It means, you can read text from top to bottom.

Notes:

Shading, borders and colours in a worksheet would enable you to make worksheet or reports appear attractive.

Adding a Pattern or Colour

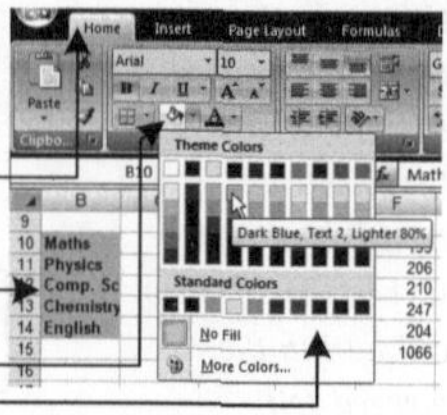

1. Select the cell or range of cells you want to apply colour pattern.
2. Click on the **Home** Tab.
3. In **Font** group, click arrow next to the **Fill Color** button.
4. Click the colour you want to use.

Adding Borders and Lines to Cells in a Worksheet

You can place border around cell(s) or lines and double lines. This is to add emphasis as well as to define data-entry areas. This also helps to mark total and subtotal, to appear distinct.

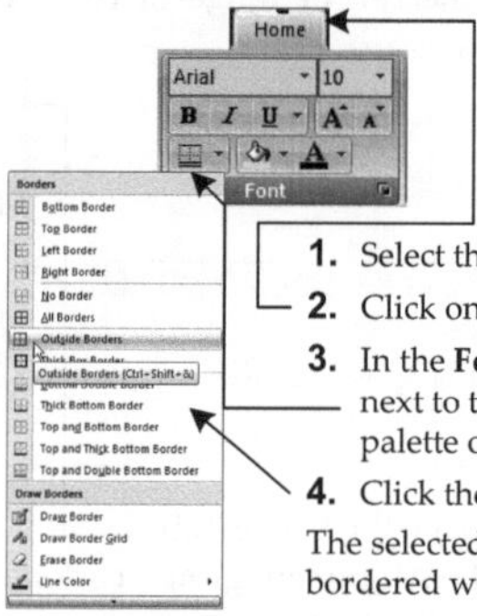

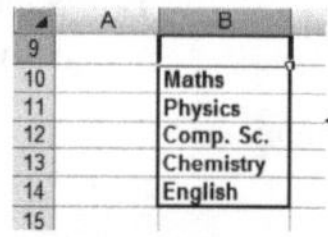

1. Select the cell or range of cells.
2. Click on the **Home** Tab.
3. In the **Font** group, click the down arrow next to the **Borders** button to display a palette of border selections.
4. Click the desired border.

The selected cell or range of cells is now bordered with the selected border.

Numeric Formatting

Numbers, dates and *time* are stored in cells as pure numbers without formatting. Excel 2007 examines the format of the number you enter, to determine whether the application can format a cell for you according to the type of data entered.

1. Select the cell or range of cells you want to format.

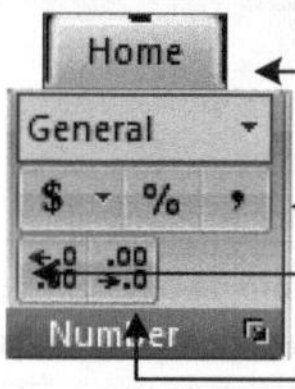

2. Click required formatting button from the **Number** group of the **Home Tab**.
   - Number group offers buttons for *currency, percentage,* or *comma* format.
   - To increase the decimal places, click the Increase Decimal button.
   - To decrease the decimal places, click the Decrease Decimal button.

Applying Numeric Formatting using Dialog Box Launcher

1. Select the cell or range of cells you want to format.
2. Click on the **Home** tab.
3. In the **Number** group, click the **Dialog Box Launcher** i.e. the small icon ( ) that appears on the bottom right corner of the Number group.
4. **Format Cells** dialog box with **Number** Tab appears.

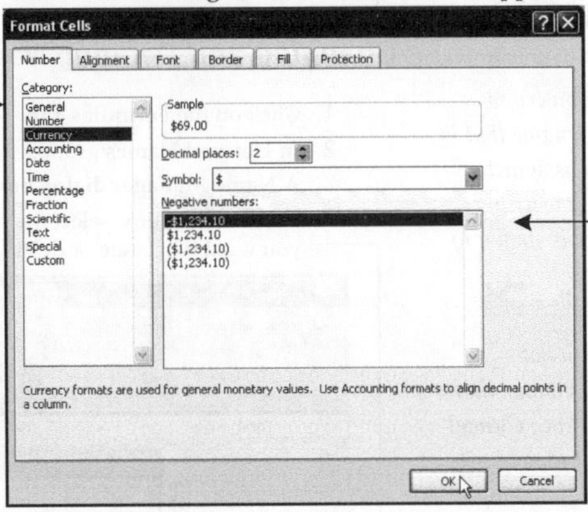

5. In the **Category:** list, select the type of number format you want to use. Depending on what category you select, you will notice different options.
6. Click OK.

Notes:

If the active cell contains a number, the Sample area shows you the appearance of the numeric format.

Shortcut keys for format cells are:

General:

Shift + Ctrl + ~

Number:

Shift + Ctrl + !

Currency:

Shift + Ctrl + $

Percent:

Shift + Ctrl + %

Scientific:

Shift + Ctrl + ^

Enter Date/Time using Shortcut keys

1. Select the cell.
2. Press one of the following keys:

Ctrl + ;	**Inserts current date.**
Ctrl + Shift + :	**Inserts current time.**
Shift + Ctrl + @	**Formats in h:mm AM/PM**
Shift + Ctrl + #	**Formats in d-mmm-yy.**

Applying Names to Workbook / Worksheet

Names can be given at *workbook level* (i.e. *global names*). They can also be applied at the *worksheet level* (i.e local names).

Names that you define globally (i.e. at the workbook level) apply to all the sheets in that workbook. But, the area of the local name is limited only to the sheet.

Notes:

Sheet-level names i.e. local names take precedence over book-level i.e. global names.

Notes:

If you enter a name that is already used, the cell or range of cells with that name is selected, rather than the current selection being given that name.

When you try to assign a name that is already assigned earlier, a warning message is shown to you.

*After you have deleted a name, note that clicking **Cancel** does not undelete it. Any cell referring to a deleted name will display the #NAME? Error, since the name will no longer be valid.*

Excel 2007 gives you the option to display formulas on a worksheet or the results of the formulas.

*The shortcut key for switching between viewing formulas and the results of formulas is **Ctrl + '** keys pressed together.*

Define a Name Using the Name Box

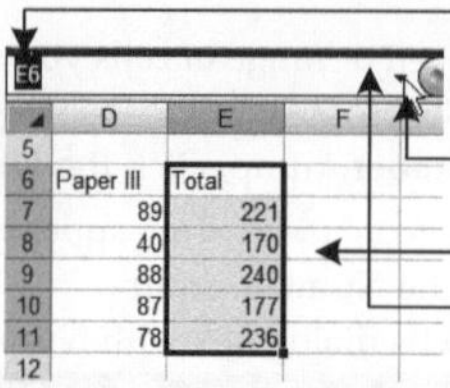

1. Select the cell or range of cells.
2. Click the arrow to the right of the **Name box.** The active cell reference appears in the name box.
3. Type the name in **Name box.**
4. Press **Enter** key.

Changing and Deleting Names

1. Click on the **Formulas** Tab.
2. In **Defined Names** group, click **Name Manager.** A **Name Manager dialog box** appears.
3. In this dialog box, select the name from the list box you want to change or delete.

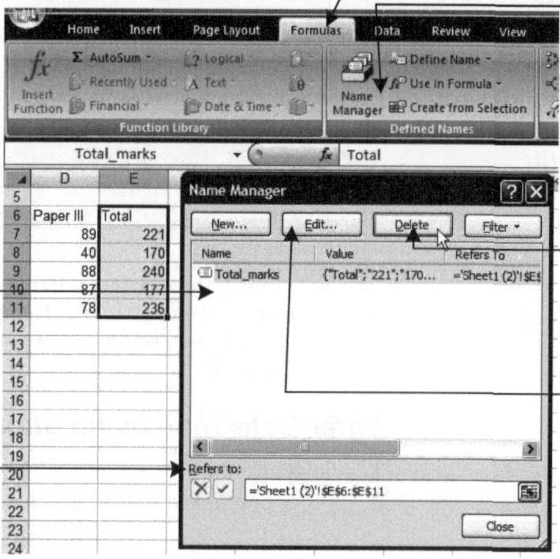

4. To change the name, click on **Edit...** Button. To change the cells reference, select the **Refers to:** box.
5. Edit the name or cell reference in the appropriate text box.
6. To delete a name, select the name you want to delete and click **Delete** Button.
7. Click Close button.

Using Formulas

Formulas in Excel 2007 always begin with an equal sign (=) and can include following types of data items:

Notes:

*Always start the formulas with an equal sign (=). If you forget the equal sign, Excel 2007 does not interpret the entry as a formula. Suppose, you enter B12*D15 (no equal sign), then B12*D15 is actually entered into the cell as text.*

Always separate terms in a formula with operators or parentheses.

When you point to a cell to include it in a formula, you actually move the pointer to the cell you want it in the formula.

The easiest method to enter cell references in a formula is by pointing to the cell you want to include in a formula.

a. *numeric* and text values (constants)

b. arithmetic operator, comparison operators, text operators, functions, parentheses

c. cell references and names

Entering Formulas

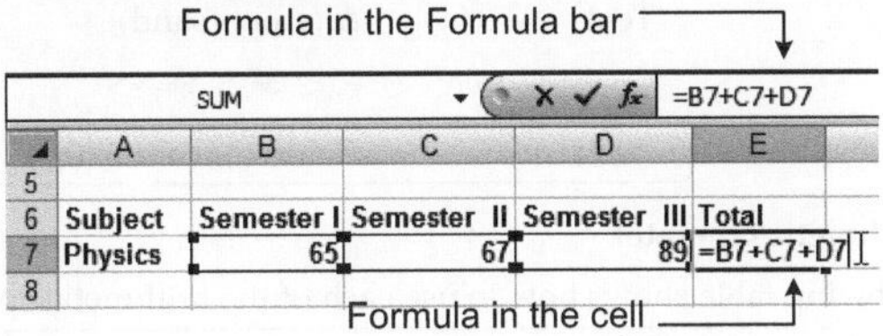

1. Select the cell in which you want to enter the formula.
2. Then type an equal sign (=).
3. Type a *value, cell reference, function*, or *name*.
4. If the formula is complete, press Enter key or click the Enter box (✓) in the formula bar. If the formula is incomplete, go to step 5.
5. Type an operator such as + or - signs.
6. Return to step 3.

Entering Cell Reference

Cell references allow you to use values from different parts of a worksheet and execute. This enables you to do the desired calculation. You can use any cell or group of cells in a formula.

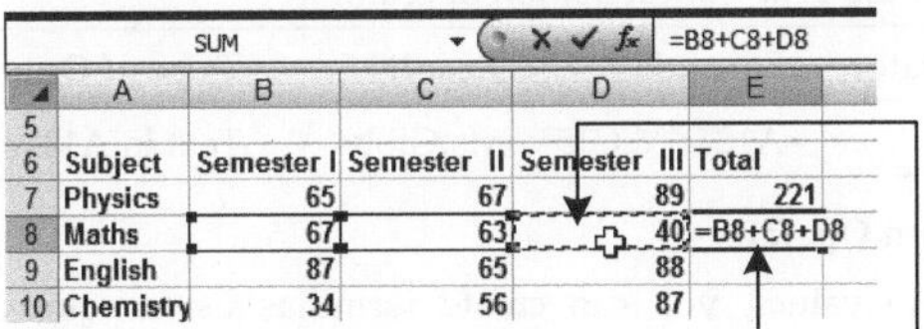

1. Select the cell for the formula.
2. Type an equal sign (=).
3. Point to the cell you want it in the formula and click, or press the arrow keys to move the dashed marquee to the cell you want in the formula.
   The address of the cell you point to appears at the cursor location in the formula bar.

The cell reference in a formula changes after you copy the formula to a new location or after you fill a range with a formula.

Using Operators in Formulas

Operators are used in formulas to execute operations on the values taken by formulas.

Operators	Signs
Arithmetic	+, , *, /, %, ^
Text	& (ampersand)
Comparative	=, <, <=, >, >=, <>
Reference	Colon (:), comma(,), space ()

Arithmetic Operator

Following table shows how to use each of the arithmetic operators.

Operator	Formula	Result	Type of Operation
+	=5+2	7	Addition of 5 with 2
–	=5–2	3	Subtraction of 2 from 5
–	–5	–5	Negation (negative of the number)
*	=5*2	10	Multiplication of 5 with 2
/	5/2	2.5	Division of 5 by 2
%	5%	.05	Percentage
^	=5^2	25	Exponentiation (to the power of)

Text Concatenation Operator

The ampersand (&) operator, joins text within quotation marks or text contained in referenced cells. Joining text is known as *concatenation.* Following table shows how to use each of the Text Concatenation operators.

Operator	Formula	Result	Type of Operation
&	=A12&""&C15	Ms.Gibbs	Text in A12 and C15 is joined

Comparison Operators

To compare values, you can create formulas using comparison operators. These operators return a TRUE or FALSE result, depending on how the formula evaluates the condition. Examples of comparison operators in formulas are shown in the following table:

Formula	Type of Operation
=A12<15	TRUE if the contents of cell A12 is less than 15; FALSE if the contents of cell A12 is 15 or more.
=B36>=15	TRUE if the contents of cell B36 is 15 or more; FALSE if the contents of cell B36 is less than 15.

Reference Operator

Reference operators make no changes to constants or cell contents (See Following Table)

Operator	Formula	Result	Type of Operation
:	SUM (A7:A11)	Range	Evaluates as a single reference.
,	SUM (A7:A11, B11)	Union	Evaluates two references as a single reference
Space	SUM (A9:A11 A7:A11)	Intersect	Evaluates the cells common to both references (if no cells are common to both, then #NULL results.
Space	=Yr10 Sales	Intersect	Cell contents at the intersect of the column named Yr07 and the row named Sales

Range Operator

Use the range operator (:) to reduce your work in formulas. If you want a formula to refer to all cells in column B, type B:B. Similarly, the range that includes all cells in rows 5 through 12 is entered as 5:12.

Evaluation (Precedence) of Formulas

Excel 2007 follows a set of rules when applying operators in a formula. Working from the first calculation to the last, Excel 2007 evaluates operators in the order shown in the following table.

Operator	Definition
:	Range
Space	Intersect
,	Union
–	Negation
%	Percentage
^	Exponentiation
* and /	Multiplication and division
+ and –	Addition and subtraction
&	Text joining
=, <, and <= >, >=,	Comparisons

If you want to change the order in which calculations are performed then enclose in parentheses the terms you want Excel 2007 to calculate first.

For example, you will notice the difference between the results of the following formulas:

Formula	Result
=6+21/3	13
=(6+21)/3	9

✍ ***Reference operators enable you to combine absolute and relative references and named ranges. Reference operators are valuable for joining cells (union) or referring to a common area shared between different ranges.***

Entering Functions In a Worksheet

You can operate a function by using following methods:

1. **Enter Function directly:** You can type the function name and the required arguments in the formula bar. To use this method you need to remember the name of the function and the arguments to be passed.
2. **Insert the function:** This is an easier method because Excel 2007 inserts the function and asks you to fill in the parameters only.

Entering a Function Directly

1. Activate the cell.
2. Type the function and the argument in the formula bar.

Using the Insert Function

Use the Insert Function to make your job much easier. The Insert Function guides you through the process and explains each function as well as each argument within a function

1. Select the cell where you want to enter the function.

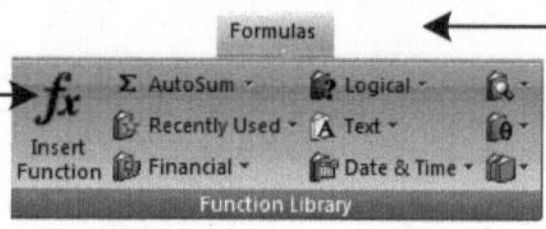

2. Click on the **Formulas** Tab.
3. Then click on the **Insert Function**.

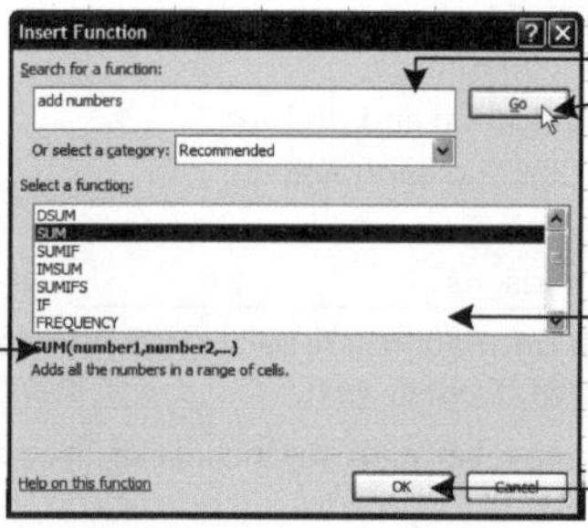

4. Insert Function dialog box appears. In this dialog box, in **Search for a function:** box, type a brief description of what you want a function to do.
5. Then click **Go**.
6. In **select a category:** drop-down list, select a function category according to your need.
7. Click on the Specific function that you want from the **Select a function:** list box.
8. To read the description in the lower part of the dialog box to verify that this is the function you want.
9. Then click **OK** or **Double click the function** whichever you want to use. It will display a dialog box **Function Arguments.**

Notes:

Functions are the predefined formulas or programs that perform calculations in Excel on specific values, called arguments. Each function takes specific types of arguments, such as numbers, references, text, or logical values.

*You can also display the **Insert Function dialog box** by clicking on the **Insert Function** button on the center of the formula bar i.e. or by pressing **Shift + F3** keys together*

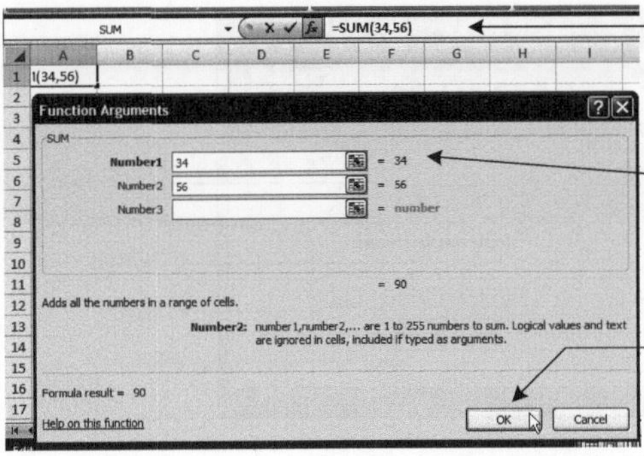

10. Selected function displays in the **Formula bar** as well as in cell.
11. In **Function Arguments dialog box,** enter the arguments in each **argument text box**. You can type the cell references or numbers
12. Click **OK** to complete the function. You can also choose **Cancel** if you decide not to insert the function.

Editing Function

After you enter function into a formula in the formula bar, if need be, you can edit it in two ways. You can use Insert Function to step through the functions in a formula, or you can manually edit the formula and functions.

Edit a function using Insert Function

1. Select the cell containing a function.
2. Under the **Formulas** tab, click on the **Insert Function**. The Function Arguments dialog box appears and shows the function in the formula.
3. Change any arguments necessary in the function.
4. When you finish making changes, click **OK**.

Edit a Function Manually

1. Select the cell containing a function.
2. Press **F2** key to activate the Formula bar or click in the Formula bar.
3. Select the argument in the formula you want to change.
4. Enter the new argument by typing, dragging, pasting a name, or inserting a function.
5. Press **Enter** key.

Working with Charts

You can create different types of charts using Excel 2007 that will help you to analyze data in a worksheet and give you a visual presentation of results. There are two types of charts namely, *embedded charts* and charts that appear in a *chart sheet.*

An *embedded chart* appears in a worksheet next to tables or text.

A chart can be created by itself in its own chart sheet within a workbook

Notes:

*In the Insert Function, use the **Most Recently Used** category to quickly get to functions you use very often.*

*You can move across arguments by pressing **Ctrl** + → or **Ctrl** + ← keys together. To select as you move, hold down **Shift** key.*

Select a term or argument in the formula bar by double-clicking it.

Embedded charts are required when you want a chart side-by-side with the data for the chart, as in the case of a report document.

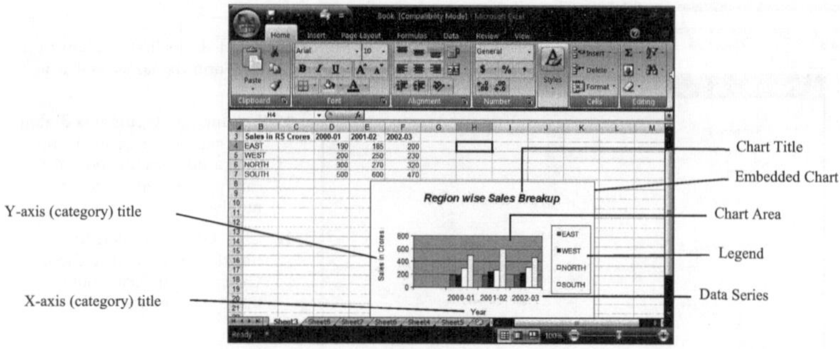

Notes:

If you need to print a chart on its own, creating the chart on a chart sheet is the best approach.

*To quickly create a chart, select data and press **F11** key then Excel 2007 insert a chart in a **chart sheet**, using the default chart type. But, when you press **Alt + F1** keys together, the chart is displayed as an **embedded chart**.*

Chart Terminologies

An Excel 2007 chart may contain objects that you may like to modify individually. These objects are described as under:

Axis (*x-axis* and *y-axis*): The horizontal or x-axis along the bottom of charts is also referred to as *category* axis. The vertical or y-axis against which data points are measured is also referred to as *value* axis. This axis contains the scale against which data is plotted.

Data point: A single piece of data.

Data series: A collection of data points.

Legend: The name of each data series is used as a legend title.

Marker: An object that represents a data point in a chart such as bar, pie and symbols. Markers that belong to the same data series appear in the same shape, symbol and colour.

Plot area: The Rectangular area bounded by the two axes.

Text: Text associated with data points or free-floating text that can be moved easily. The box containing the text can be resized.

Creating a Chart

1. Select the data items you want to appear as chart.
2. Click on the **Insert** tab.
3. Then in **Charts** group, click arrow next to that chart which you want to insert.
4. Then select the chart from the chart subtype.
5. Chart will appear.

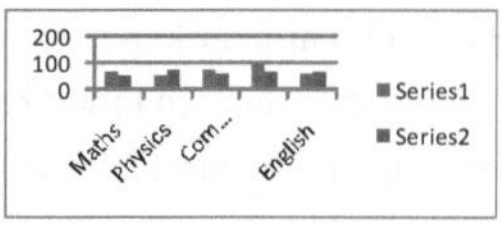

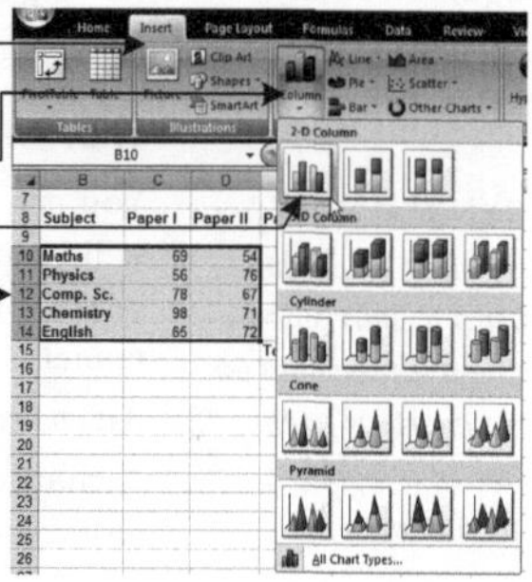

Notes:

When you create a chart, chart tools become available and the ***Design, Layout*** *and* ***Format*** *tabs are displayed. You can use command on these tabs to modify the chart so that data is presented the way you want.*

Positioning a chart along with data items helps you to analyse data easily. By making changes in the data items, you can immediately preview the effects in the chart.

Previewing Charts

After creating a chart and before printing, it is a good practice to see the full page view (preview) of the chart.

Preview a chart if chart is in a Chart sheet

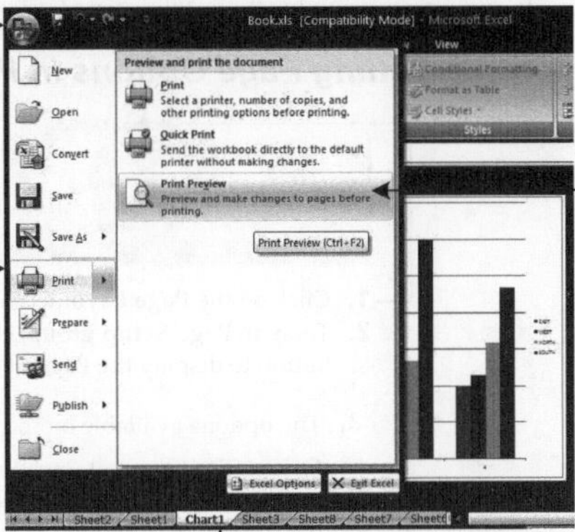

1. Activate the chart sheet.
2. Click on the **MS Office button**. Menu appears.
3. Here, point the cursor in **Print** option (no need to click).
4. Now click on **Print Preview** from the option of the print.
5. A window containing the preview of the chart sheet appears.

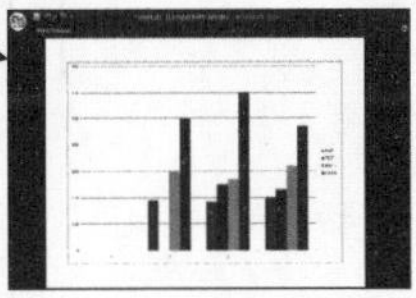

Preview a chart if chart is Embedded on a worksheet

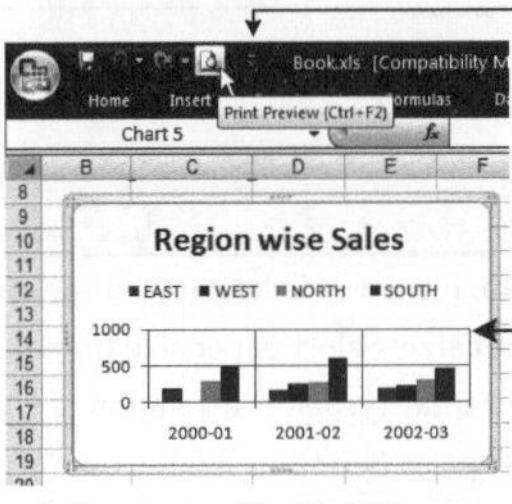

1. Activate the sheet containg the chart.
2. Click on the Print Preview button i.e. [icon] from the Quick Launch Toolbar.
3. A window containing the preview of the chart along with data appears.

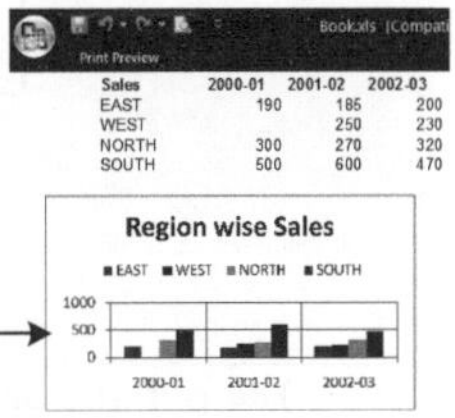

Notes:

When you choose ***Fit To:*** *option, Excel 2007 ignores any page breaks you have set, and fits the entire worksheet or print area to the specified number of pages.*

Setting Up Worksheet for Printing

Before you print worksheet, it is better that you change the page setup as per the printer and paper which is used for printing a worksheet. Page Setup dialog box in Excel 2007 involves four tabs namely, *Page, Margins, Header/Footer* and *Sheet.*

Setting Page Options in Page Setup Dialog Box

1. Click on the **Page Layout** Tab,.
2. Then in **Page Setup group**, click on the **Dialog box launcher** button to display the **Page Setup dialog box with Page tab**.
3. The options available on the Page tab are given below:

   Orientation: Portrait (meaning page length is more than the page width). Landscape (meaning page width is more than the page length).

   Scaling Adjust to: Allows you to enlarge or reduce the printed worksheet. You can reduce it to 10% to fit more of the worksheet on a page. You can also enlarge it to 400% to enhance details.

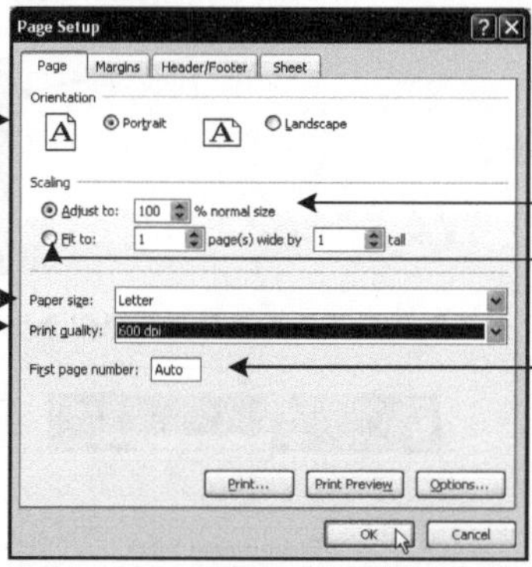

Fit to: Fits a worksheet onto a specific number of pages.

Paper size: Select paper size from drop-down list.

Print quality: Select resolution (dpi) from list.

First page Number: Begins numbering at specified page number.

You can also set the orientation from Ribbon by clicking the orientation option from the Page Setup group of Page Layout Tab.

Setting the Margins in a Worksheet

Notes:

To set the margins and select the position of headers, footers and print area, you have to click on the ***Margins tab*** *in the* ***Page Setup dialog box.***

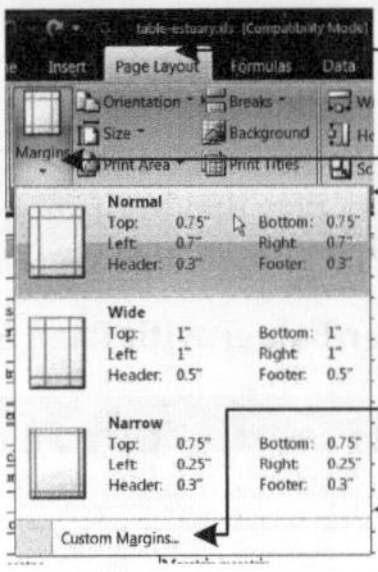

1. Click on the **Page Layout** Tab, then click on the **Page Setup group**.
2. Then click arrow next to the **Margins**.
3. It will display the predefined margins. Select from here or

   if you want to set the margins manually then select the option Custom Margins... .

4. It will display the **Page Setup dialog box with Margin Tab**.

   Following Options are available in Margin Tab:

   Top: Give the distance between the top edge of the page.

   Left: Give the distance between the left edge of the page and the data printed on a page.

   Right: Give the distance between the right edge of the page and the data printed on a page.

   Bottom: Give the distance between the bottom edge of the page and the data printed on a page.

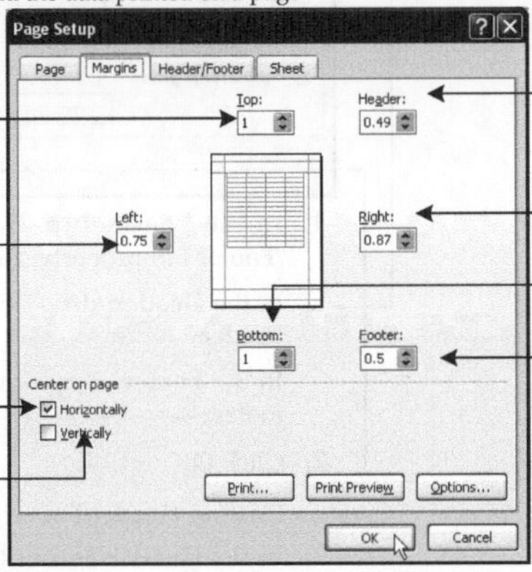

   Header: Give the distance between the top of the page and the header.

   Footer: Give the distance between the footer and the bottom of the page.

   Center on Page: Use this option to center the print area vertically or horizontally between margins.

   Horizontally: Give this option to horizontally center the page.

   Vertically: Give this option to vertically center the page.

You can preview the worksheet as an area on the dialog box showing how the margins are set.

Notes:

Headers and footers are not actually a part of the worksheet. They are part of the printed page. Therefore, they are allotted separate space on the printed page.

Setting Headers and Footers

You can use headers for company's name and report titles, etc. The footers are commonly used for page numbering and printing date/time.

If need be, you can use the built-in header/footer option in Excel 2007 or you can specify custom headers/footers.

Use Built-in Header/Footer with Page Setup Dialog Box

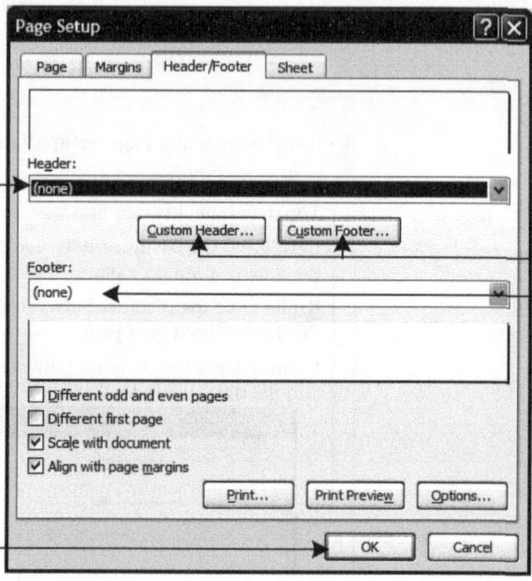

1. In the Page setup dialog box, click **Header /Footer tab** property sheet .

   In the **Header:** drop down list select the built-in header.

   In the **Footer:** drop down list select the built-in footer.

2. Click **OK**

Create a Custom Header/Footer with Page Setup Dialog Box

1. In the **Header/Footer tab** of Page Setup dialog box, click the **Custom Header...** button or **Custom Footer...** button.
2. According to the button you click, Header or Footer dialog box appears. Select the options according to your need.

Setting Sheet Options

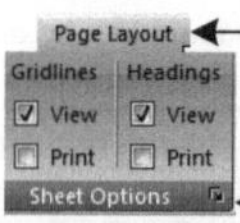

1. Click on the **Page Layout** tab.
2. Then in the **Sheet Options group**, click **Dialog Box Launcher button.**

It will display the Sheet Tab of the Page Setup dialog box. The Sheet tab options with function are given below:

Print area: Select area of worksheet you want to print.

Print titles-Appears rows or columns on each page when printing a multiple-page document.

Rows to repeat on top: You can specify the number of rows you want to repeat on each page.

Columns to repeat at left: You can specify the columns you want to repeat on each page.

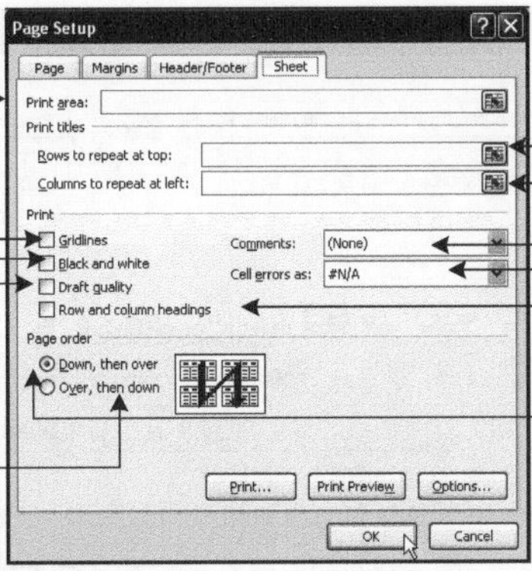

Print Options- Select print options:

Gridlines: Turns gridlines on/off (on the printed pages).

Black and white: Prints all pages in black and white.

Draft quality: Gridlines, graphics will not be printed.

Row and column headings: Includes row and column headings on every printed page.

Comments: This allows printing cell comments.

Cell errors as: This allows options for cells errors i.e. Displayed, Blank, (hyphen), or #N/A.

Page order Options-Select page order for multiple-page worksheet.

Down, then over: This option would print the page from top to bottom and then left to right.

Over, then down: This option would print the page from left to right and then from top to bottom.

Printing Worksheet

You can set *margins* and *fonts* and include *headers/footers* as well as *titles* while printing a worksheet. You can even print multiple copies of the entire worksheet or a part of it.

1. Click on the **MS Office button**. Menu appears.
2. Here, click on the **Print** option. A Print Dialog box appears.

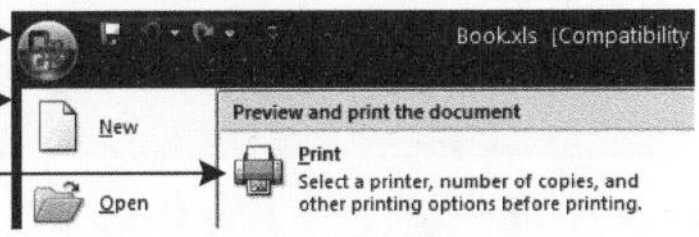

Print titles are not the same as page headers. However, they can be used for similar purposes. Also, a page can be set up both print titles or page headers or both.

Print dialog box options are as follows:

Printer Option box:

Name: This shows selected printer, printer status, type, and the port. Select the desired printer from the Printer drop-down list.

Print to file: Allows you to create a disk file for the selected printer.

Print range option:

All: Prints all pages in a worksheet or a workbook.

Page(s) From:/To: Select this option to print pages you wish to print.

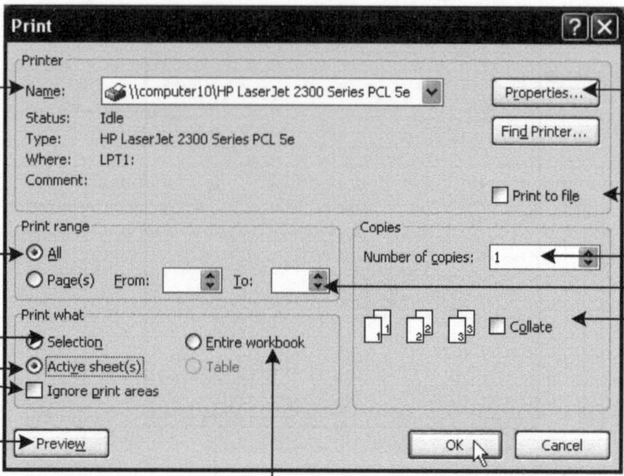

Print what option:

Selection: Prints selected cells.

Active sheet(s): Prints only selected worksheet.

Entire Workbook: Prints currently open workbook

Ignore print areas: Select this check box if you want to ignore the print area you have selected.

Copies options:

Number of copies: Prints assigned number of copies of selected pages in a worksheet.

Collate: Check box allows you to collate multiple copies.

Other options:

Preview button: Click this to switch from the Print dialog box to the print preview mode.

Properties button: Click this to show a dialog box which controls the printing options.

MS Access 2007

Getting Started

Access 2007 is a software package for database management. Access is an easy to use with full featured database development application. It can be used to develop a simple mailing list as well as a complex accounting package.

Notes:

Access databases consist not only of the basic data items, but also of related items you use to work with them. Every database may contain six different types of objects. These objects are Tables, Queries, Forms, Reports, Macros and Modules.

In Access database, you store information in objects called ***Tables****. Tables are rectangular arrangements of rows and columns, where each column represents a field and each row represents a record.*

Starting Access using Start Button

1. Click the **Start** Button on the Taskbar.
2. Highlight **All Programs**, Click **Microsoft Office**.
3. Click **Microsoft Office Access 2007**.
4. A starting page of Access is displayed.

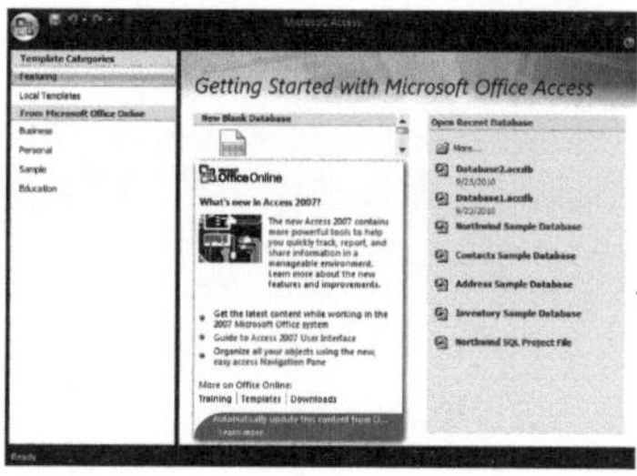

About Access 2007 Interface

Access 2007 includes new user interface which is the result of extensive research and usability testing, and it is designed to make it easier to find the commands.

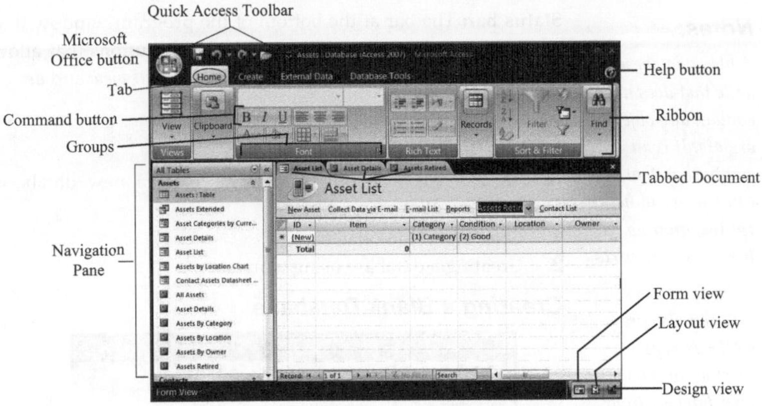

Notes:

The new user interface makes it easy to work in Access 2007. Major new interface elements in Access 2007 are Ribbon, Command tab, Contextual command tab, Gallery, Quick Access Toolbar and Navigation Pane.

***Layout view** lets you make common design changes while you view a live form or report.*

New Interface elements of Access 2007 are given below:

MS Office Button: This button is located in the upper-left corner of the Excel 2007 window. It opens the menu containing commands like New, Open, Save, SaveAs, Print, Manage, etc.

Ribbon: The area at the top of the program window where you can choose commands. It contains a series of command tabs that contain commands. In Access 2007, the main command tabs are Home, Create, External Data, and Database Tools. Each tab contains groups of related commands and these groups surface some of the additional new user interface elements, such as the gallery, which is a new type of control that presents choices visually.

Quick Access Toolbar: A single standard toolbar that appears in the ribbon and offers single-click access to most needed commands.

Navigation Pane: The area on the left side of the window that displays your database objects. When you open a database or create a new one, the names of your database objects appear in the Navigation Pane. It replaces the Database window from earlier versions of Access.

Tabbed documents: Tabbed document is the new feature of Access 2007. With the help of this, you can display your database objects in tabbed documents instead of overlapping windows. Now tables, queries, forms, reports, pages, and macros are displayed as tabbed documents.

Status bar: The bar at the bottom of the program window that displays status information and includes buttons that allow you to change your view i.e. *form view, layout view* and *design view.*

Creating New Database

Access 2007 gives you two ways to create a new database. These are as follows:

1. Creating a blank database
2. Creating a database using template

Creating a Blank Database

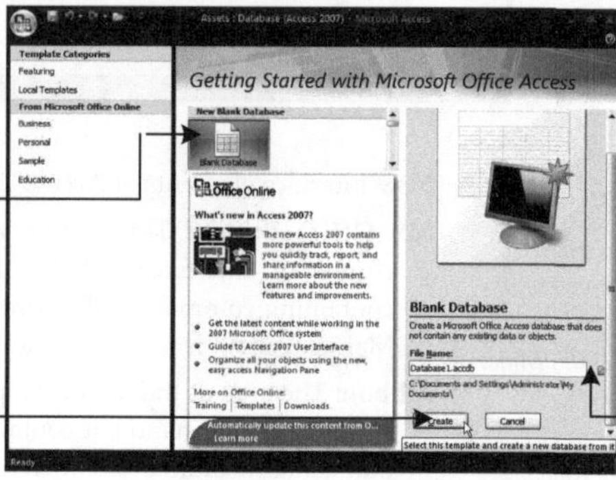

1. In the **Getting Started with MS Office Access page,** under **New Blank Database**, click **Blank Database.**
2. In the **Blank Database right pane**, type a file name (say *Database1.accdb*) in the **File Name:** box.
   If you want to change the location of the file, click on the **Browse button** .
3. Click **Create.**
4. Access creates and opens the database with an empty table named **Table1** in **Datasheet view.**
5. The cursor is placed in the first empty cell in the **Add New Field** column to add data.

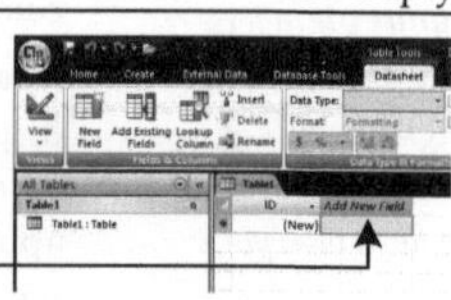

Creating a Database using Template

Access provides you with a variety of templates that you can use to speed up the database creation process.

Notes:

A blank database is a file that does not contain any objects or data. It is an empty shell that you can use to add new ***tables, queries, forms,*** *and* ***reports.***

You can also press ***Ctrl + N*** *keys together to start a new database from anywhere in Access. After you give the database a name, Access closes the database that you were working on and opens a blank database window.*

A template is a ready-to-use database containing all the tables, queries, forms, and reports needed to perform a specific task.

Access 2007 includes a suite of prebuilt tracking applications in the form of templates that you can use to get started quickly and refine them to track information in your way.

Notes:

In order to make data entry easier, you can create objects called Forms. Forms provide you with a "template" that you fill in whenever you enter the information for record.

To make your data more easily readable and understandable, you create a report. Reports let you define how you want the data printed on paper or shown on the screen

Access has a feature that you can use to perform several actions with a single command. Such a feature, called Macros operate by running a series of actions that can do various jobs again and again by just typing single word command only.

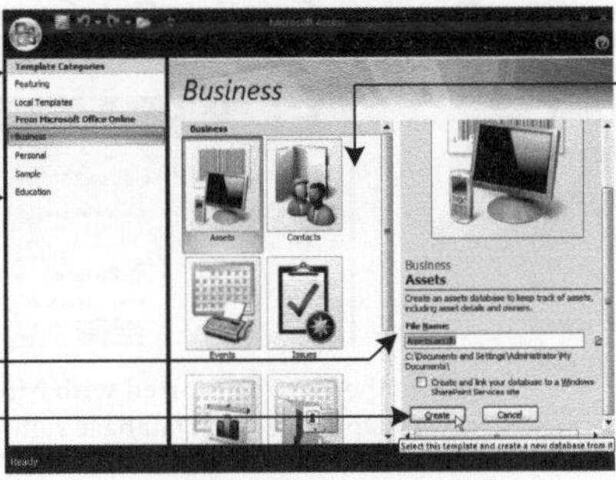

1. In the **Getting Started with MS Office Access page,** under **Template Categories,** click on the category that suits to your need.
2. Then, click on the *template* from the center of the window.
3. Now, in the right side of the window, Access suggests a file name in the **File Name** box. You can change the file name.
4. Click **Create** button.
5. Access creates the database and then opens it.

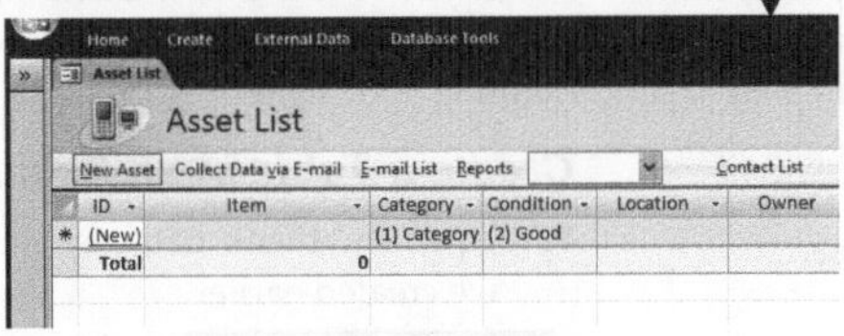

Open an Existing Database if You are Already in Access

1. Click on the **MS Office button.**
2. Then choose **Open... .**

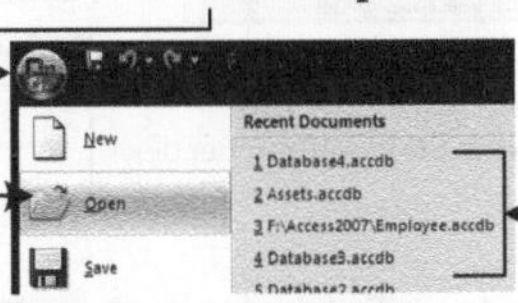

List of Recent document list

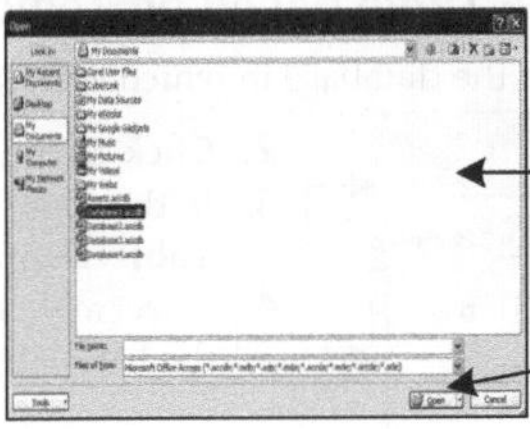

3. In Open Dialog box, choose the *drive, folder name* that contains the workbooks. After finding the required workbook, select it.
4. Then click **Open** button.

Notes:

Access 2007 offers easy access to both end-user help and developer help from the same Help viewer window. The new help experience has been redesigned in response to user feedback.

With the new rich text support in Access 2007, you are no longer limited to plain text. You can format text with options, such as bold, italic, different fonts and colours and store the text in your database.

Open an Existing Database if You just Launched Access

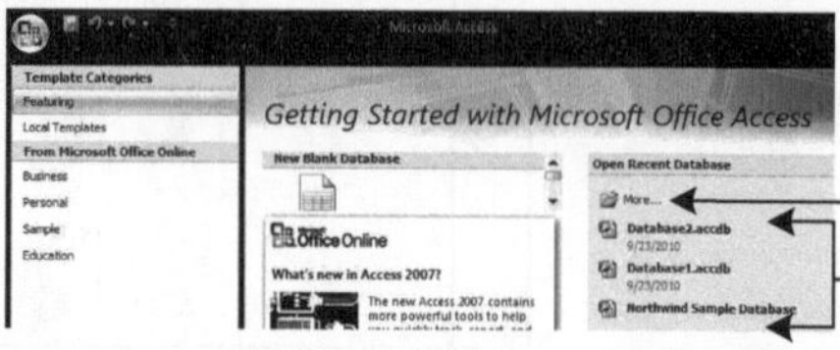

1. In the **Getting Started with MS Office Access page,** in **Open Recent Database** right pane, Access displays list of recent files.
2. Click on the file name. Excel will open the file.
3. If file you need is not listed in recent database, then click on the More... button.
4. Then Excel will display Open dialog box, select file from this dialog box.

Create a Table in Blank Database

When you create a new blank database, a new empty table is automatically inserted for you. You can then enter data to start defining your fields.

Create a Table in an Existing Database

1. Open the blank database named as **Database1.accdb** that we created earlier.

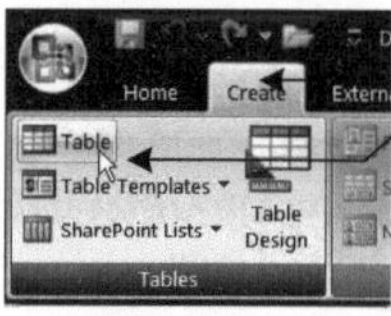

2. Click on the **Create** Tab.
3. In the **Tables** group, click **Table.**
4. A new table is inserted in the database.
5. Double click on the **Add New Field** Column to add a field (such as Name, Address, etc.)
6. Now, type data in the cell below the **Add New Field**column header.

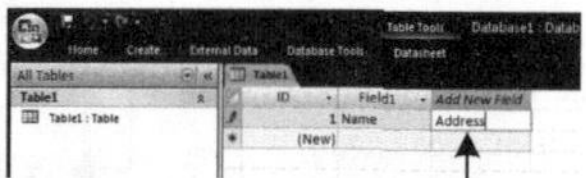

Create a Table based on Template

1. Open the database in which you want to create table.

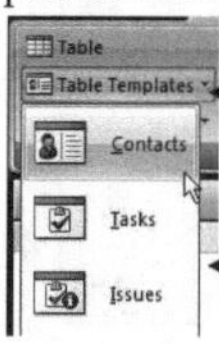

2. Click on the Create Tab.
3. In the Tables group, click **Table Templates.**
4. Select any one template from the list.

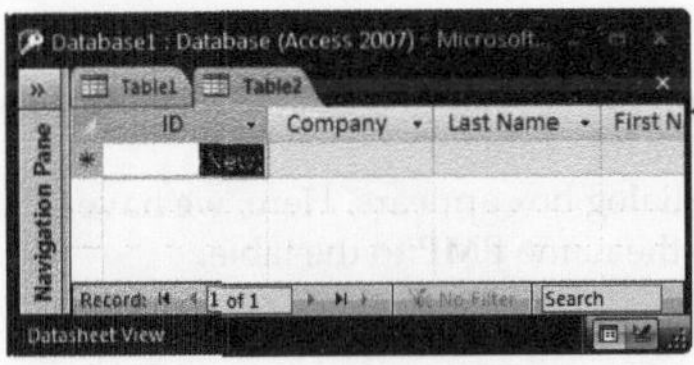

5. A new table is inserted based on the table template (i.e. Contacts) you selected.

Create a Table using Design View

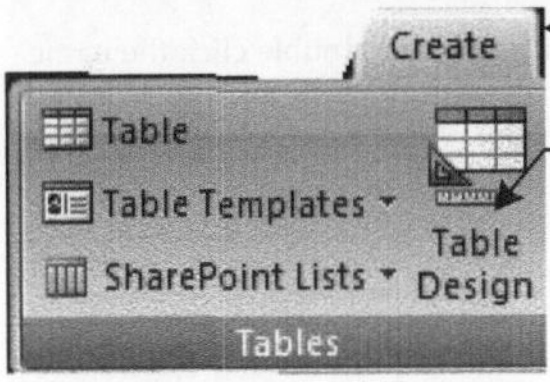

1. Click on the **Create** Tab.
2. In the **Tables** group, click **Table Design**.
3. You will find **Design** Tab and a grid that has three columns across the top.

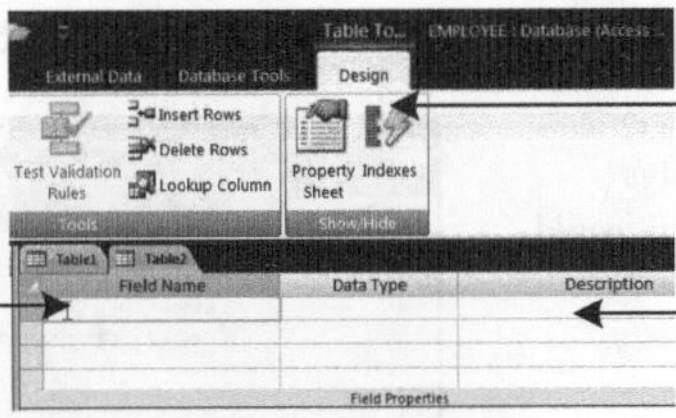

4. Under the **Field Name** column, type the name of the field which you want to insert into the Table.

Notes:

Each field in a table has a set of properties that you use to customize how a field's data is stored, handled, or displayed.

*To set the primary key for a table you have to use **Design** view.*

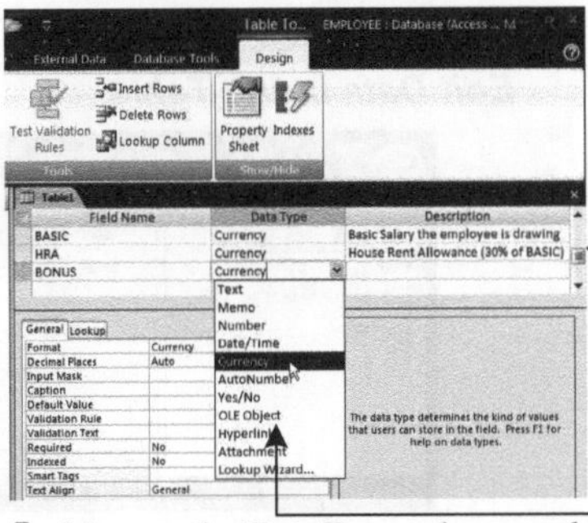

5. Move to the **Data Type** column and select a data type for the newly entered field.
6. Type a small description about the field in **Description** column. You may leave it blank also.

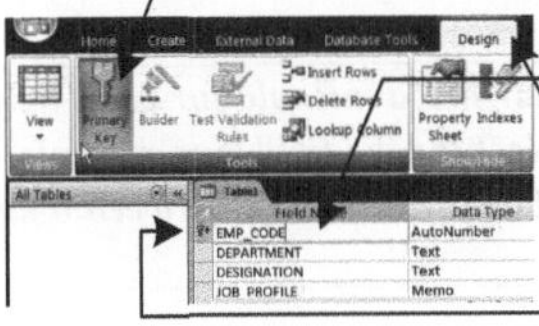

7. To set a field as the primary key, click the field.
8. Then click on the **Design** Tab.
9. In the **Tools** group, click **Primary Key**.

This field will now be assigned as the primary key.

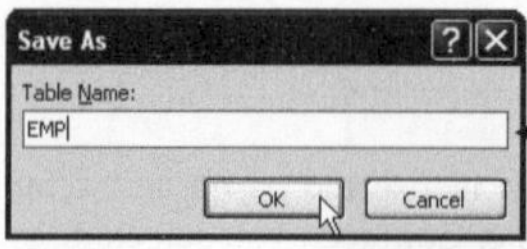

10. Click on the **MS Office** ( ) button and then choose **Save** ( ) option and type a name for this Table.
11. Save As dialog box appears, Here, we have assigned the name **EMP** to the table.

Notes:

When you enter data in the new column, Access 2007 uses the information you type to recognize the appropriate data type for the field.

When data entered in a record is complete, it would get saved automatically.

Opening Table

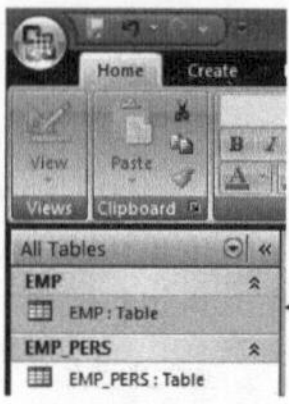

In the **Navigation Pane**, double click the name of the table you want to work on..

Add Data in the Table

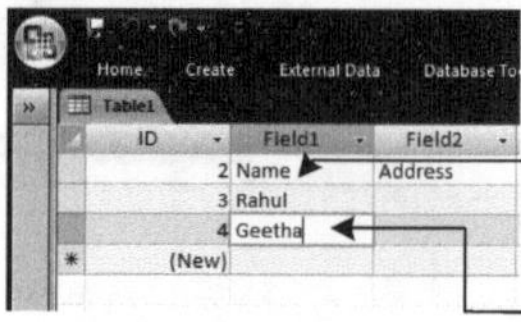

1. Open the table.
2. By default, MS-Access opens the table in **Datasheet view**.
3. Click on the first field and then enter data.
4. After entering data in the first field, press **tab** to move cursor to the second field. Type in the second field and so on.

Edit Data in the Table

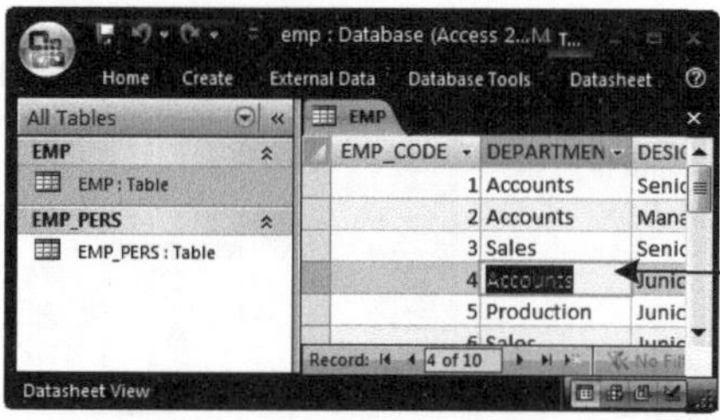

1. Open the Table to be edited.
2. *Double click* the field you want to edit.
3. Make changes in the field(s).
4. Click the **Close** button. Changes you applied will get automatically saved.

Data Type Properties are the properties that are available for each field. They are determined by the data type you select for the field. For example, if data type property is set to Text, then the Field Size can be between 0 and 255 (the default setting is 50).

Delete a Record in a Table

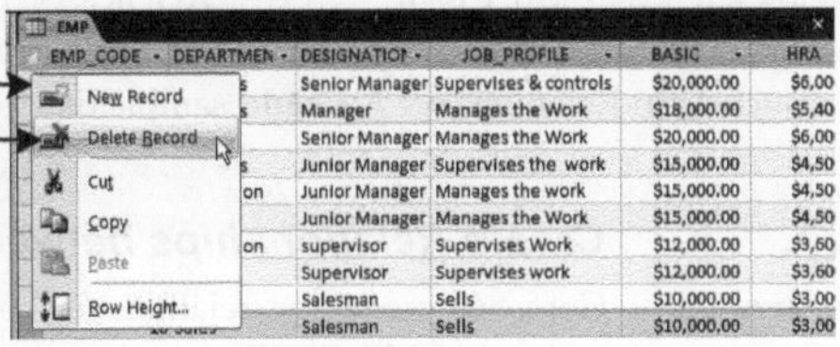

1. Open the Table.
2. Right click the record which is to be deleted.
3. Click **Delete Record** from the shortcut menu You will observe a dialog box. Click **Yes**.
4. The record is deleted.

Notes:

To change the position of a column in datasheet view, click on its header and drag it to the desired location.

Changing Field's Data Type

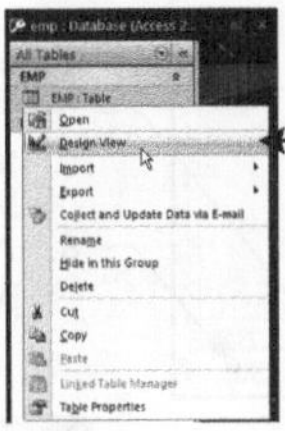

1. In the **Navigation Pane**, right click the table name and then choose **Design View**.

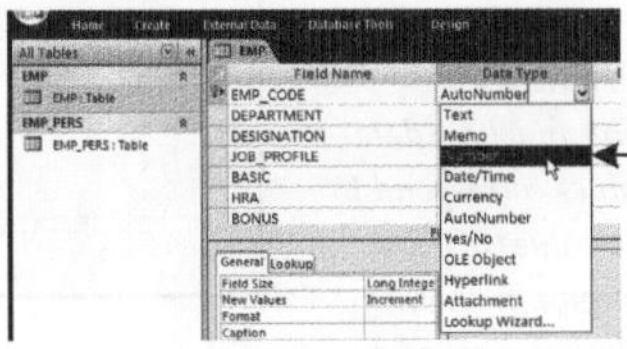

2. Move to the field and click the **Data Type** column, then choose the new data type you want.
3. Click **Close** button on the right side of the tab and choose **Yes** when prompted to save the changes.

Notes:

*When you create a table, you specify the different data types such as **Text, Number, Date/Time, Currency and logical (Yes/No)** for each field in the **Table Design View**.*

Sorting Data in the Datasheet

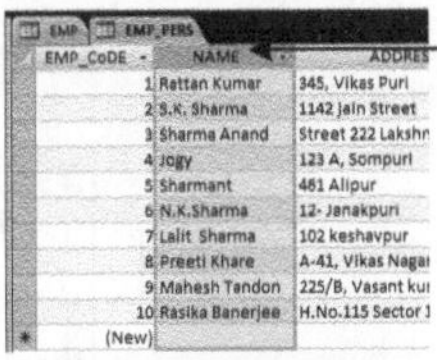

1. Click on the desired column. (Here, we select **NAME** column).
2. Then click on the **Home** Tab.
3. In the **Sort & Filter** group, click on the **Ascending** or **Descending** button

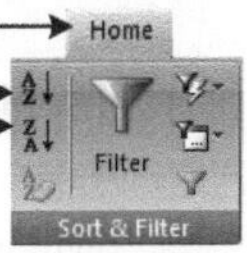

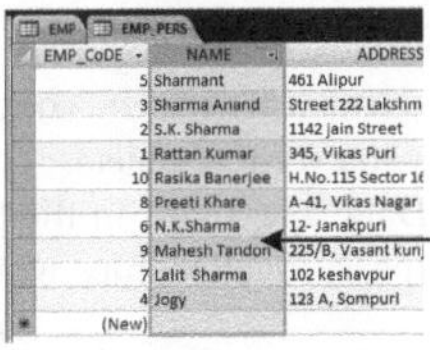

After clicking on the descending option, the result should look like one given here.

Notes:

*To return the data back to its original sort order, click under the **Home** Tab, in the **Sort & Filter** group and then click on the **Clear All Sorts**.*

You can sort on any type of data type except Memo, Hyperlink and OLE Objects.

Create another table EMP_PERS, using the methods described earlier. This table will contain fields such as EMP_CODE, NAME, ADDRESS, PHONE, EMAIL DOJ. We will be using these two tables named EMP and EMP_PERS in our further study of MS-Access such as in Relationship. Also add sample data to the MS-Access Table just created.

Create Relationships between Tables

Here, we create the relationship between two tables i.e. **EMP** table and **EMP_PERS**.

1. Open the database which contain **EMP** and **EMP_PERS** tables.
2. Click on the **Database Tools** tab.
3. In the **Show/Hide** group, click **Relationships**.

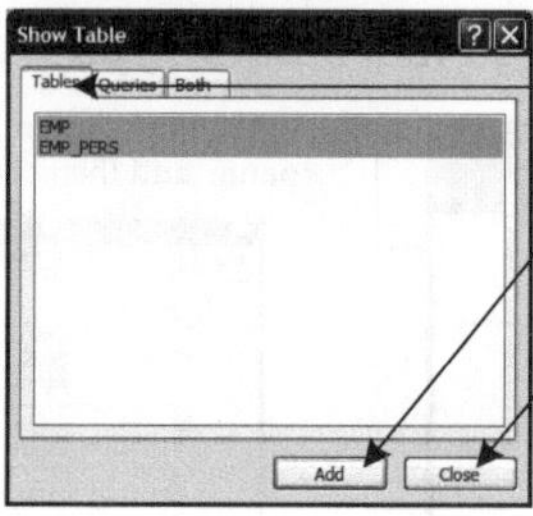

4. A Show Table dialog box appears. In this dialog box, click **Tables** Tab.
5. Then select one or more tables and Click **Add** button.
6. After that click **Close** button.

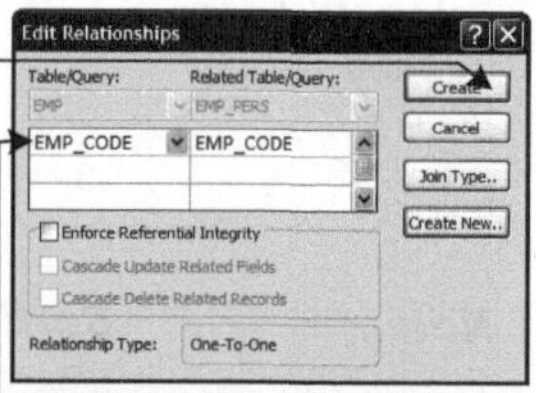

7. Now drag fields (primary key) from one table to the common field (foreign key) in the other table.
8. After that **Edit Relationships** dialog box appears. In this dialog box, verify the fields name shown that are common field for the relationship.
9. Then Click **Create New.**

Access makes a relationship between tables by lines.

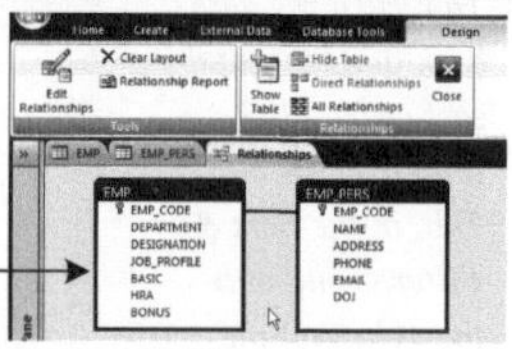

Notes:

Relationships *are those attributes defined from one table to another in the same database.*

Field or group of fields that is the unique identifier for a table is called the ***primary key****. But, In a relation, the column whose data values correspond to the values of a key column in another relation is called a* ***Foreign key****.*

There are three types of relation-ships that can be established among tables. These are:
1. One to one Relationship,
2. One to many Relationship,
3. Many to many Relationship

Delete Relationships

1. Open the database which contain the tables whose relationship you want to delete.
2. Under the **Database** Tools, in the **Show/Hide** group, click **Relationships**. A Relationships window appears.

If you create relationship first time then the Show Table dialog box automatically appears. If it does not appear, click under the Design tab, in the Relationships group, click Show Table.

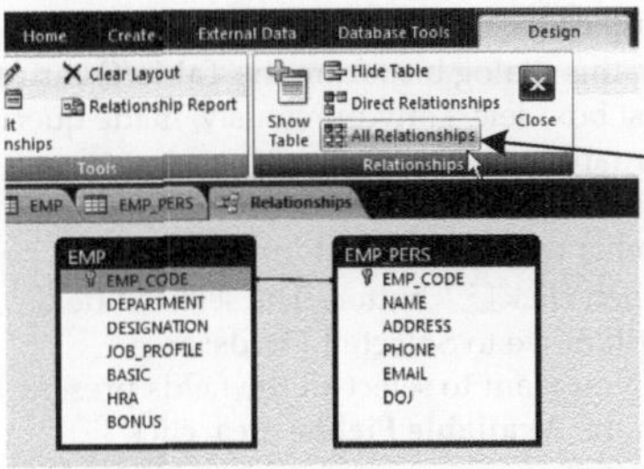

3. Click Under the **Design** Tab, in the **Relationships** group, then click **All Relationships**. All tables that have relationships are displayed, showing relationship lines.
4. Click the line of that relationship which you want to delete. *When you select the line, the relationship line appears thicker*.
5. After that Press **Del** key.
6. Access displays the confirmation dialog box showing the message **"Are you sure you want to permanently delete the selected relationship from your database?"**
7. Click **Yes**.

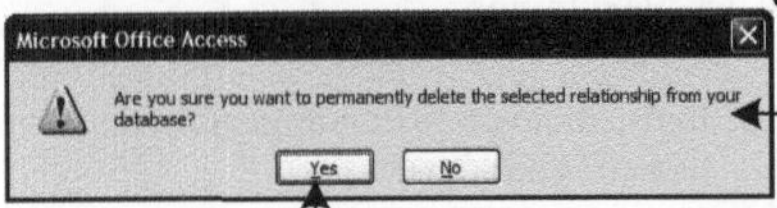

Notes:

*A **simple query** strips away fields so that you can see only the fields that you want to see.*

Handling Queries

Queries are questions you ask from database. Access 2007 has powerful search capabilities. For example, suppose from the **EMP_PERS** database you want to know how many Employees have surname *Sharma*? Such an enquiry can be easily put to Access and you will get the answer very fast. Access lets you create queries in two ways:

1. **Using the query wizard:** When you create a query using the query wizard, the wizard guides you through a series of dialog boxes where you make the selection for the query.
2. **Using the design view:** When you use the design view you have more control over the query and Access 2007 lets you create complete queries in the design view.

Create a Simple Query using the Query Wizard

1. Click under the **Create** tab.
2. In the **Others group**, click **Query Wizard**.

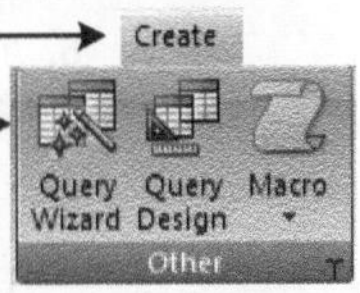

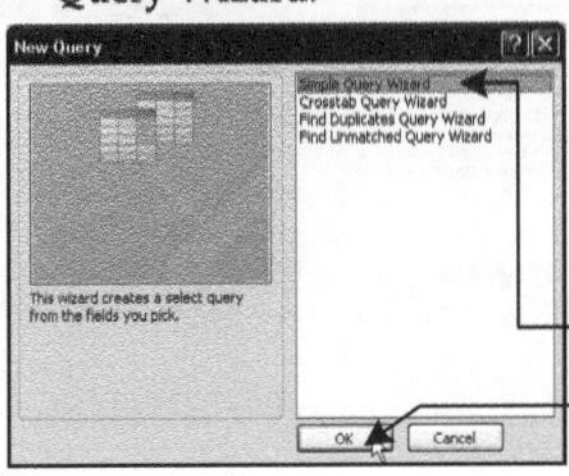

3. A New Query dialog box appears.
4. In this dialog box, click **Simple Query Wizard**.
5. Then click **OK**.

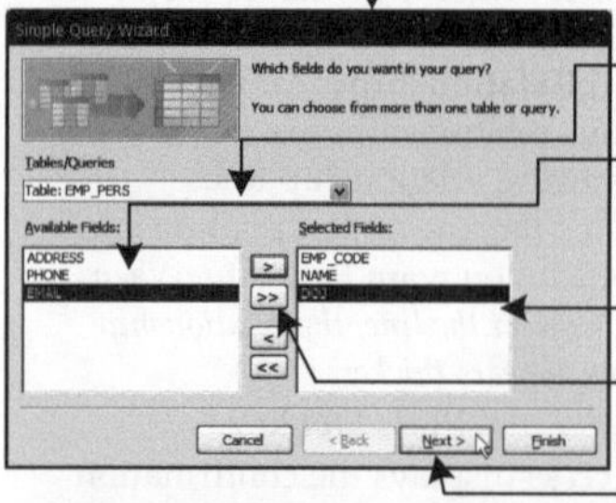

A Simple Query Wizard dialog box appears.

6. In this dialog box, from the **Table/Queries:** list box, select any previously, made query or table.
7. From the **Available Fields:** area select the fields which you want in your query.
8. Then click [>] button. The selected fields will move to **Selected Fields:** area.
   If you want to select all the fields present in the **Available Fields:** area, click [>>] button.
9. Click **Next** button.

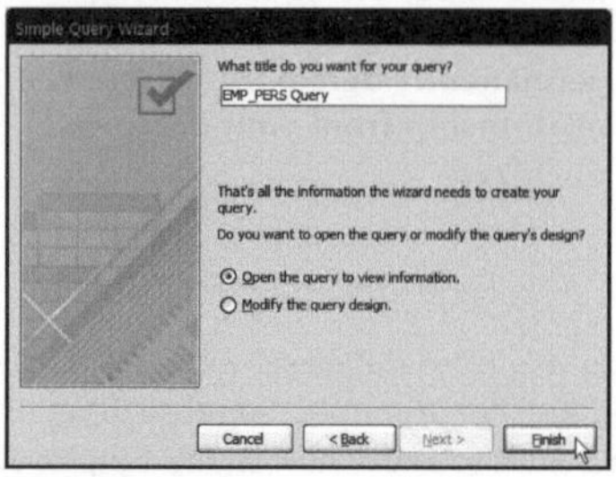

10. In the dialog box that appears type a title for your Query.
11. Then click **Finish** button.

Access 2007 displays the result of the query in a Datasheet View

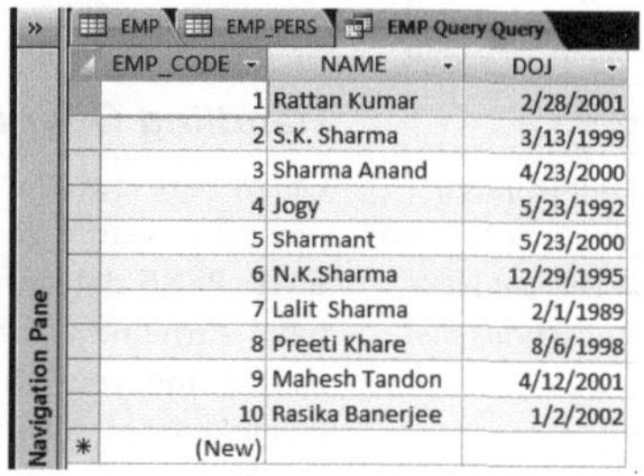

Notes:

*A **crosstab query** lets you combine two or more fields to calculate and display a calculation based on a third field.*

*To remove a field from the **Selected Fields:** area click the [<] button. To remove all the fields, click the [<<] button.*

Create Crosstab Query using the Query Wizard

1. Click under the **Create** tab.
2. In the **Others** group, click **Query Wizard**.
3. A New Query dialog box appears. In this dialog box, click **Crosstab Query Wizard.**
4. Then click **OK**.
5. In Crosstab Query Wizard dialog box, click on the table name.
6. Then click **Next** button.

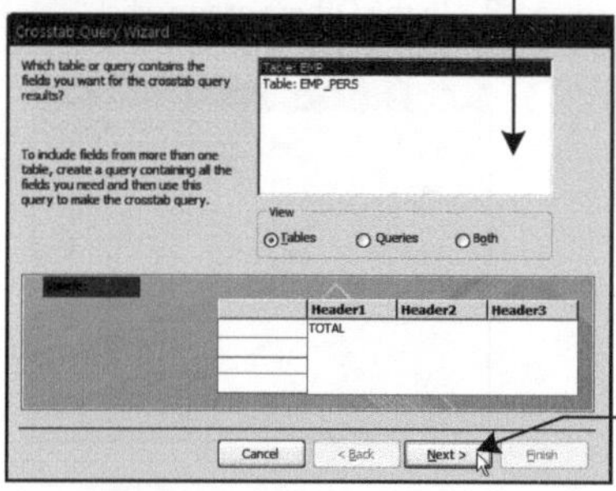

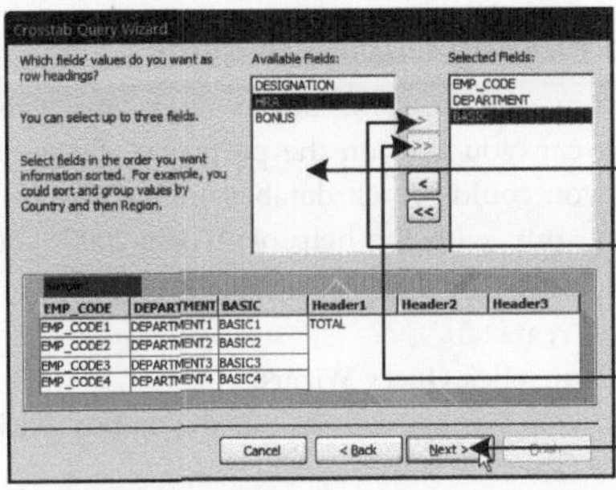

Another dialog box appears that asks for the fields.

7. In this dialog box, from the **Available Fields:** area select the fields which you want in your query.
8. Then click [>] button. The selected fields will move to **Selected Fields:** area.
   If you want to select all the fields present in the **Available Fields:** area, click [>>] button.
9. Click **Next** button.

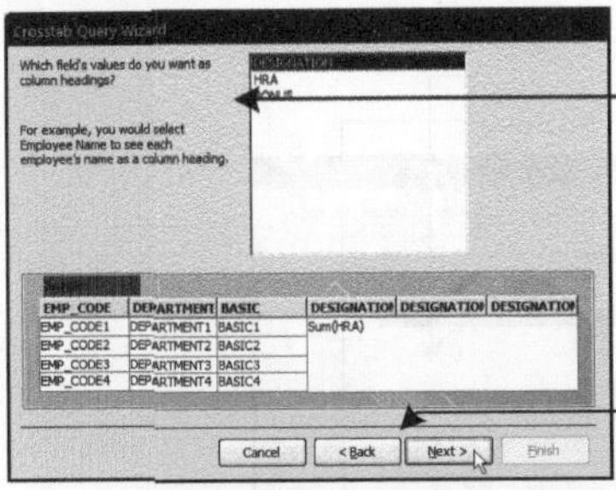

10. In the dialog box that appears, asking for a single field to use to crosstabulate data with the field you choose from last dialog box. In this dialog box, selected field should consist text information that lists different data. Click the field.
11. Then click **Next** button.

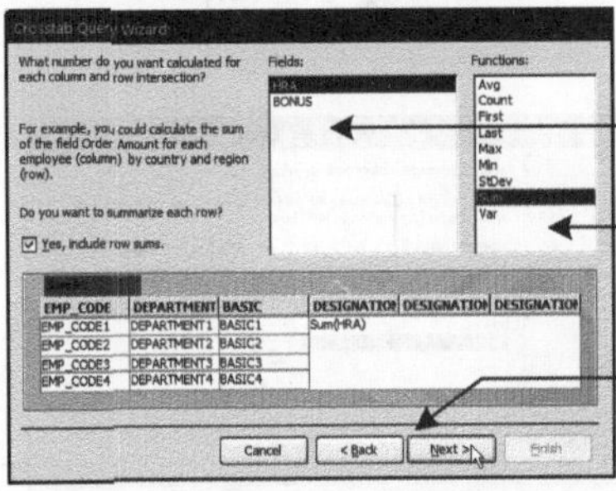

Another dialog box appears

12. Click a field that contains numerical data.
13. Then click mathematical function that you want to Access to calculate sum, average or count.
14. After that click on the **Next** button.

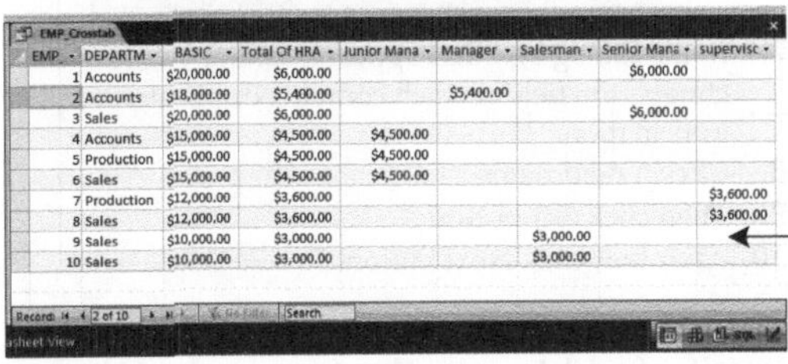

15. In the dialog box that appears, type a name for the Query.
16. Then click **Finish** button.
17. Access displays the result of the query in a **Datasheet View** as a separate tab.

Create Query to Finding Duplicate Items

Notes:

With the help of queries you can also find the duplicate data items in your database.

Suppose, In a company, on the same day several employees had joined. But how can you find on the particular day who had joined. For this you could search database manually. It is very time consuming. But, with the help of Access 2007, you can create a query that finds the duplicate data items.

1. Click under the **Create** tab.
2. In the **Others** group, click **Query Wizard**.
3. A New Query dialog box appears. In this dialog box, click **Find Duplicates Query Wizard.**
4. Then click **OK**.
5. In Find Duplicates Query Wizard dialog box, click on the table name.
6. Then click **Next** button.

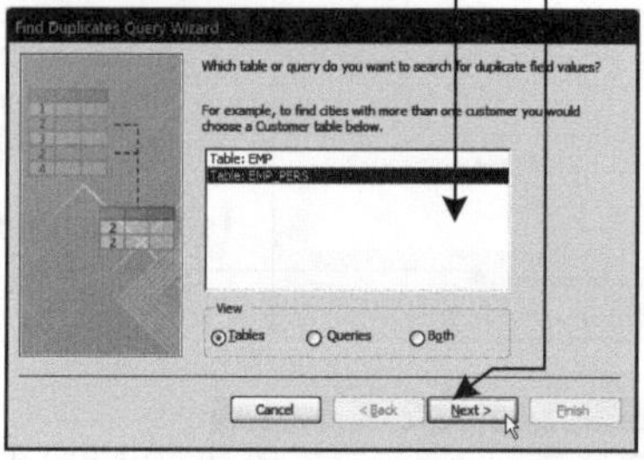

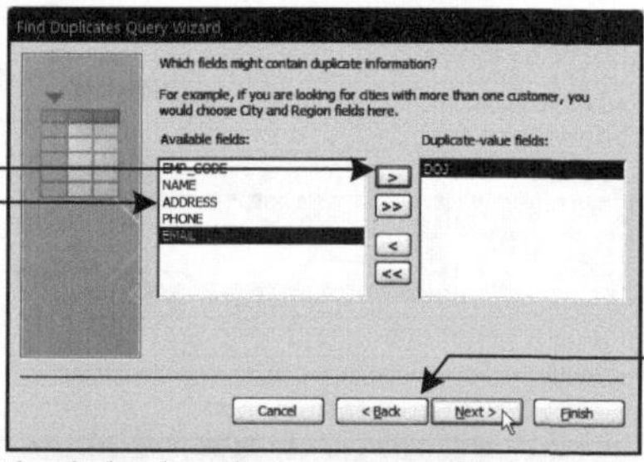

7. In the dialog box that appears, asking you to choose the fields which contains duplicate information.
8. Click a field name.
9. Then click [>] button
10. After that click **Next** button.

You cannot undo the results of a delete query. Therefore, you should back up your database before delete query.

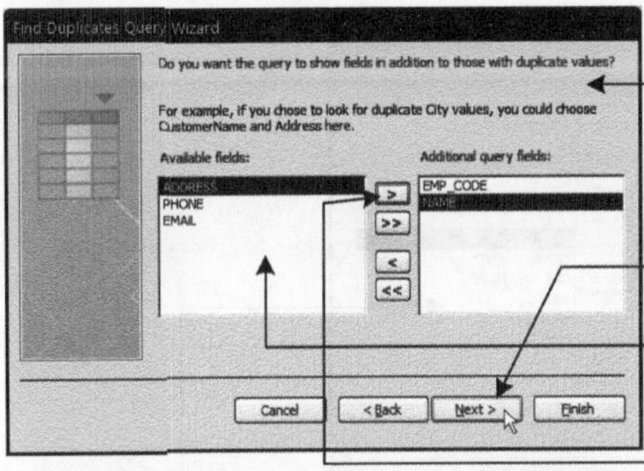

11. In the dialog box that appears, asking whether you want to display any additional field.
12. Click a field name.
13. Then click [>] button.
14. After that click **Next** button.

Another dialog box appears.

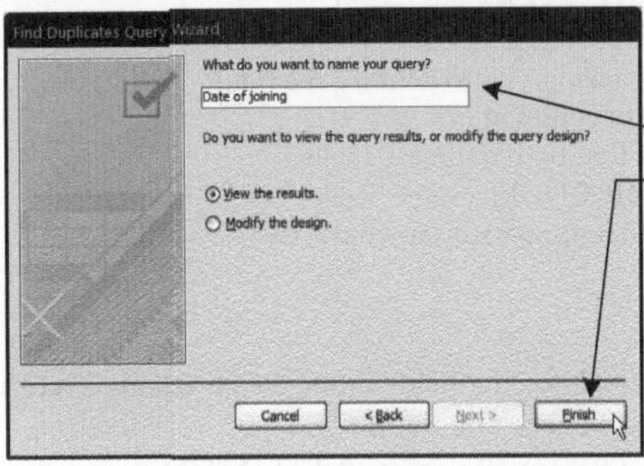

15. In this dialog box, you have to give the name for the query.
16. Then click on the **Finish** button.

Access displays the result of the query in a **Datasheet View** as a separate tab.

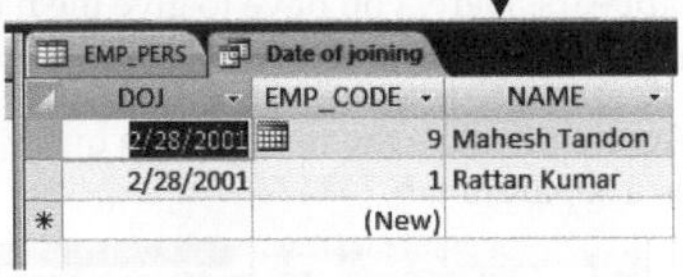

Create an Unmatched Query

Notes:

An unmatched query examines two (or more) tables to look for missing information.

1. Click under the **Create** tab.
2. In the **Others** group, click **Query Wizard.**
3. A New Query dialog box appears. In this dialog box, click **Find Unmatched Query Wizard.**
4. Then click **OK.**
5. In the Find Unmatched Query Wizard dialog box, click the table that you want to search.
6. Then click **Next** button.
7. In the dialog box that appears, asking you to choose a table that contains at least one field that also appears in the table you choose earlier.
8. Click a second table and then click **Next** button.

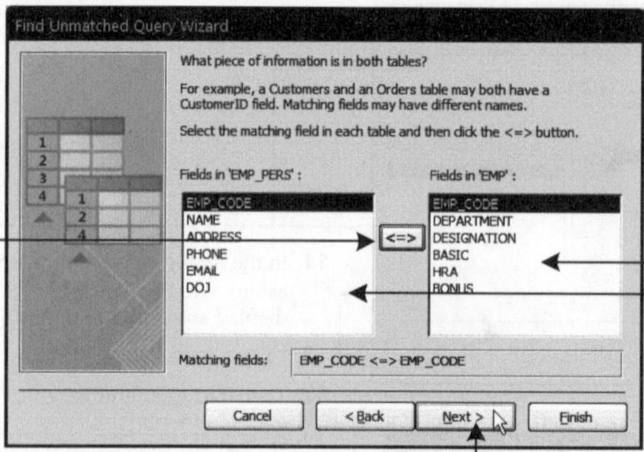

In the dialog box that appears, asking you to identify the field that both database tables have in common.

9. Click on the common field that both database tables share. (In our case, it is EMP_CODE).
10. Click on the [<=>] button that appears between the two fields.
11. Then click **Next** button.
12. Another dialog box appears that asks for the fields From the **Available Fields:** area select the fields which you want in your query.
13. Then click [>] button. The selected fields will move to **Selected Fields:** area.
14. Then click **Next** button.
15. Another dialog box appears. Here, you have to give the name for the query.
16. After giving name, click **Finish**.

Notes:

Criterians are restrictions you place on a query or an advanced filter to identify the specific records you want to work with.

Access displays the result of the query in a **Datasheet View** as a separate tab.

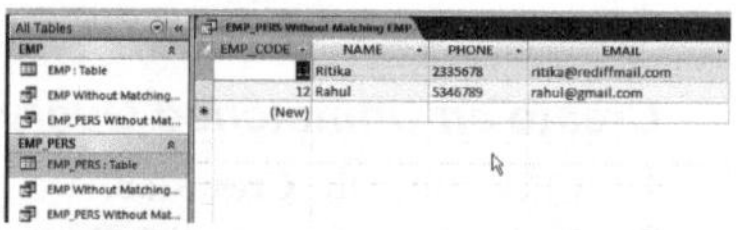

Creating Query using the Design View

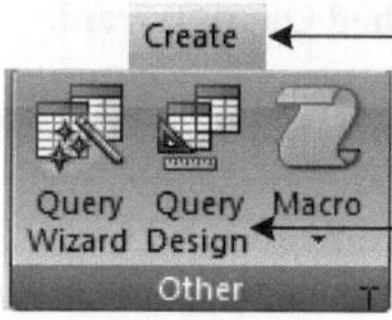

1. Click on the **Create** tab.
2. In the **Others** group, click **Query Design** (*New Query: Object*).

The criterion specifies a condition, based on field values, that expresses what you want to include in the query, such as "show only those records where the surname of Name field is Sharma".

Notes:

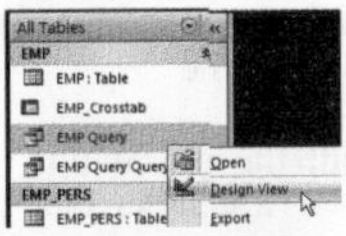

To open/modify an existing query do this:

1. In the ***Navigation Pane****, from the list of queries, right click the query which is to be modified.*

2. Then click ***Design View*** *option.*

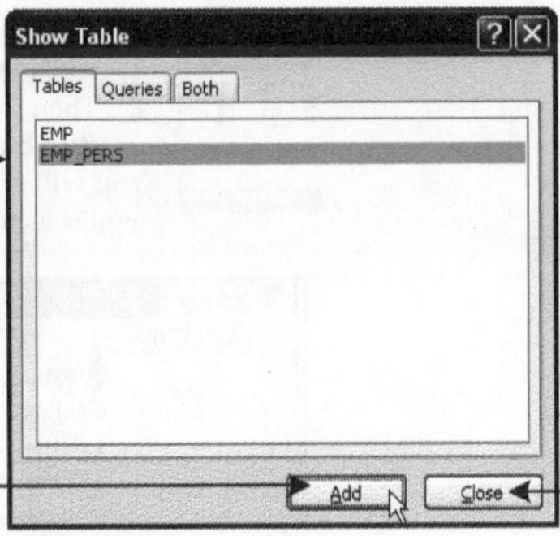

In Show Table dialog box appears that appears, add the tables which you want in the query.

3. Select the **EMP** and **EMP_PERS** table.

4. Click **Add** button.

5. After that click **Close** button.

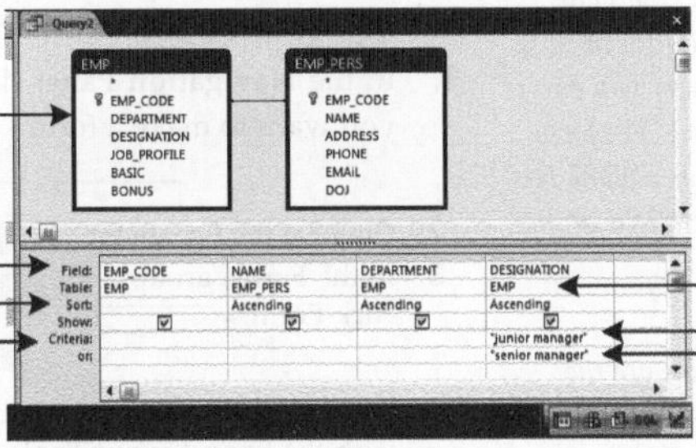

6. Notice that the tables already have proper relations displayed.

7. Drag the fields you want in your query from the tables to the **Field:** row.

8. The **Table:** row automatically gets filled up.

9. From the **Sort:** drop down list box, choose *Ascending, Descending* or *Not Sorted.*

10. In the **Criteria:** row, add any criteria you want in the query report.

11. In the **Criteria:** row and in the Column of DESIGNATION, type the expression "*junior manager*".

12. Alternative conditions can be entered in the **or:** row, say "*senior manager*".

✍ ***The LIKE operator is used to match string pattern. Special characters '*' and '?' are used with LIKE operator to specify a pattern. * is for zero or more character but, ? is for single character.***

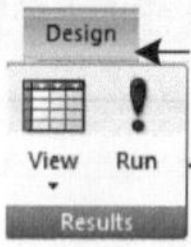

To view the Query Result:

1. Click the under the **Design Tab**.
2. Then in the **Results** group, click on the **Run** button.

You will see all the employees with the information you selected in a Datasheet View as a separate tab.

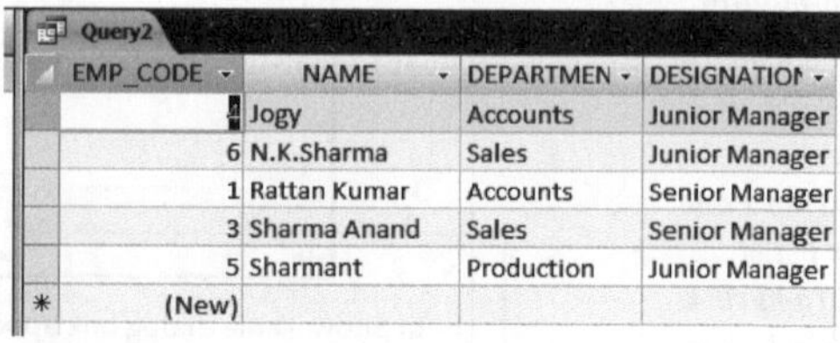

Query2

EMP_CODE	NAME	DEPARTMEN	DESIGNATIOI
	Jogy	Accounts	Junior Manager
6	N.K.Sharma	Sales	Junior Manager
1	Rattan Kumar	Accounts	Senior Manager
3	Sharma Anand	Sales	Senior Manager
5	Sharmant	Production	Junior Manager
(New)			

Notes:

Forms provide you with a "template" that you fill in whenever you enter a record. The form displays a blank box for each field in the table.

Controls are the objects that display data, perform certain actions and create special effects on the form. Text boxes, labels, list boxes, option buttons, push buttons and command buttons are examples of various controls.

Create a Form using the Form Tool

You use Form tool in Access 2007 to create a form with a single mouse-click. When you use this tool, all the fields from the underlying data source are placed on the form.

1. In the **Navigation Pane**, click the table or query for which you want to make a form.
2. Click on the **Create** tab.
3. In the **Forms** group, click **Form**.

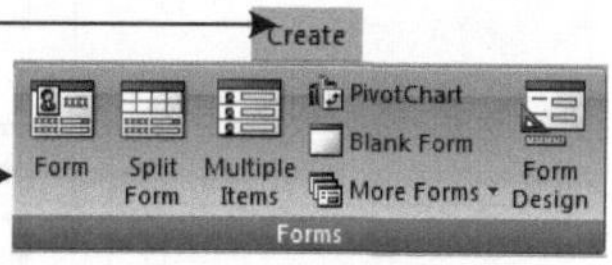

4. Access creates the form and displays it in **Layout view** along with the **Form Layout Tools** i.e. **Format Tab** in the **Ribbon.**

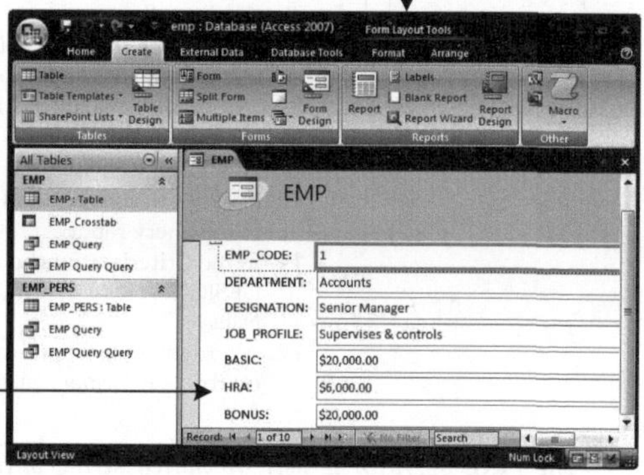

You can make design changes to the form in the layout view while it is displaying data. For example, you can adjust the size of the text boxes to fit the data.

Notes:

When you want to include only selective fields in form, you can use the Form Wizard instead of Form tools.

With the help of Form Wizard, you can use fields from more than one table or query, provided you have specified the relationships among the tables and queries beforehand.

Create a Form using Form Wizard

1. Click under the **Create** tab.
2. In the Forms group, click **More Forms**.
3. Then click **Form Wizard**.

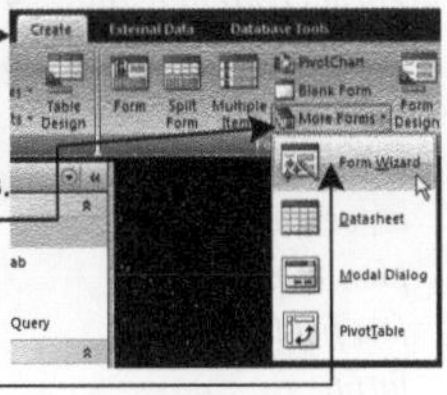

A Form Wizard dialog box appears.

4. In this dialog box, from the **Available Fields:** area, select the fields which you want in your form.
5. Then click [>] button.
6. After that click **Next** button.

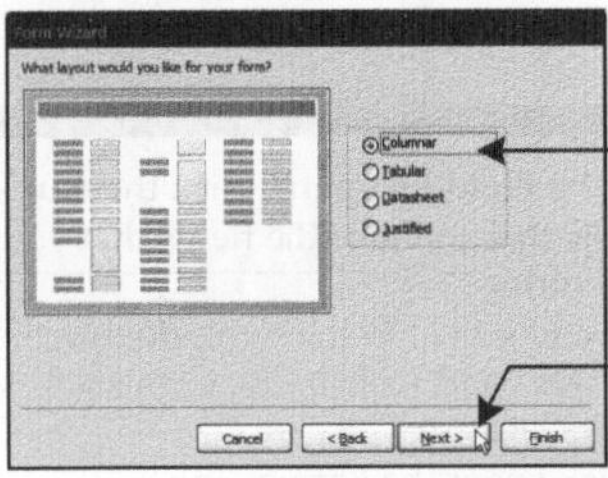

7. In the dialog box that appears, select a layout for the form. The various forms available are *Columnar, Tabular, Datasheet* and *Justified*.
8. Click **Next** button.

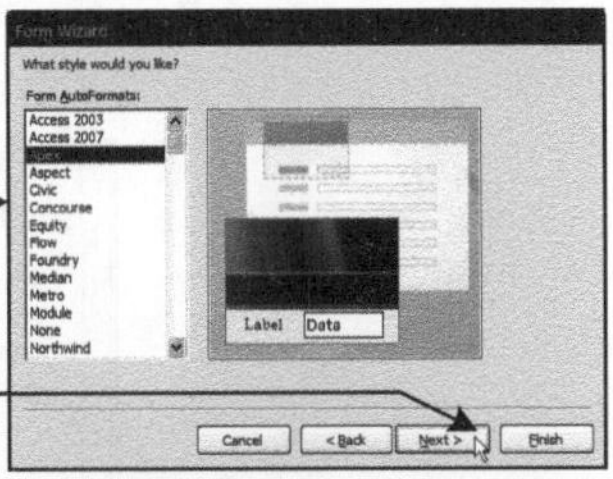

9. In the dialog box that appears, choose a style you want for the form.
10. Click **Next**.
11. In the dialog box that appears provide a *title for the form.*
12. Then click **Finish** button.

The form will open in **form view**.

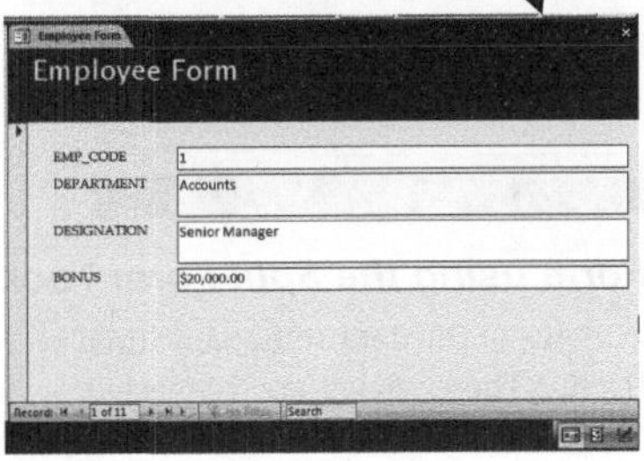

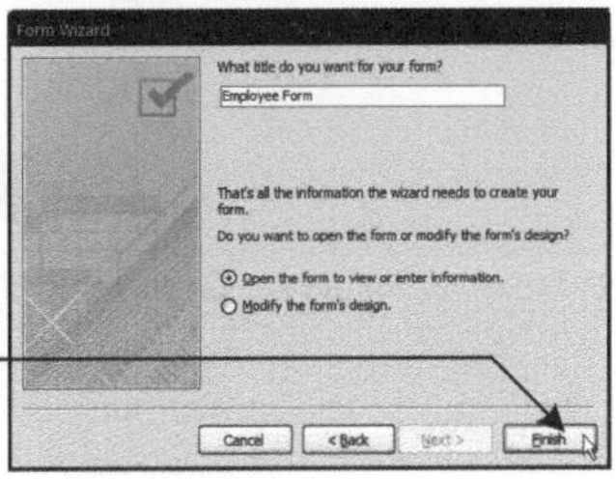

Notes:

Form creation using Blank Form tool can be a very quick way to build a form, especially if you plan to put only a few fields on your form.

Split form feature gives you the benefits of both types of forms in a single form. For example, you can use the datasheet portion of the form to quickly locate a record and then use the form portion to view or edit the record.

Create a Form using Blank Form Tool

1. Click under the Create tab.
2. In the **Forms** group, click Blank Form.

Access opens a blank form in **Layout view** along with the **Field List pane.**

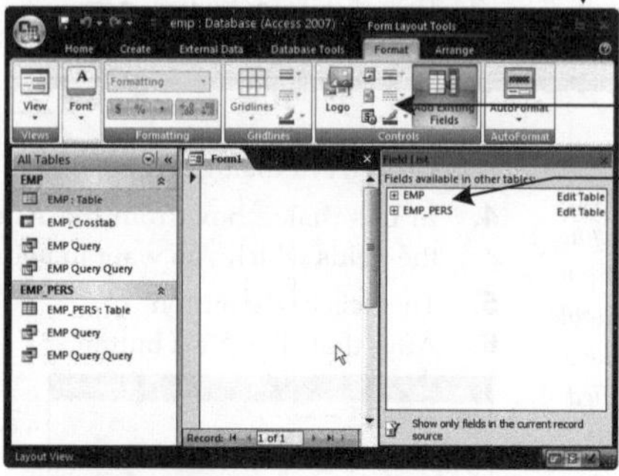

3. In the **Field List** pane, click the plus sign (+) next to the table that contains the fields that you want to include in the form.
4. To add a field to the form, double-click it.

If you want add tools in the form such as logo, title, page numbers, etc.

5. Click under the **Format** Tab.
6. In the **Controls** group, click the tool which you want.
7. After adding tool, the form will look like the following screen.

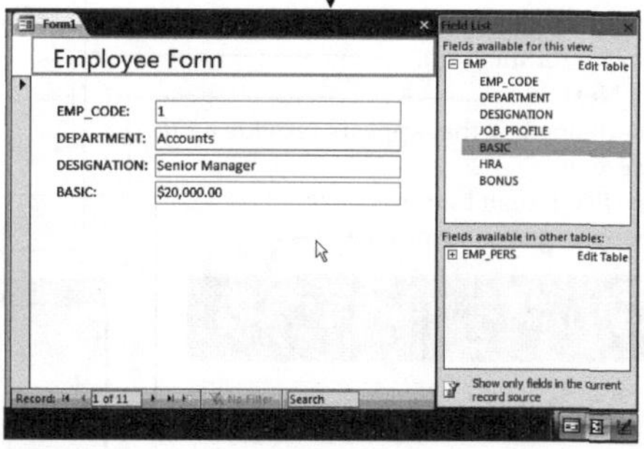

Create a Split Form using the Split Form Tool

Split form gives two views of the data at the same time i.e. *Form view* and *Datasheet view*. These views are connected to same data source and are synchronized with each other at all times.

Notes:

Controls can be of three types:

(a) Bound control: *It is a type of control whose source of data is a field in a table or query.*

(b) Unbound control: *This type of control does not have a source of data such as a field or expression.*

(c) Calculated control: *The source of data of calculated control is an expression, rather than a field.*

*Some controls such as the **bound control** is created when you add a field from the **Field List pane** to your form. But other controls can be created in **Design view** only.*

1. In the **Navigation** Pane, click the table or query for which you want to make a form.
2. Click under the Create tab.
3. In the **Forms** group, click (Split Form) button.

Access creates a form in Layout view along with the Field List pane.

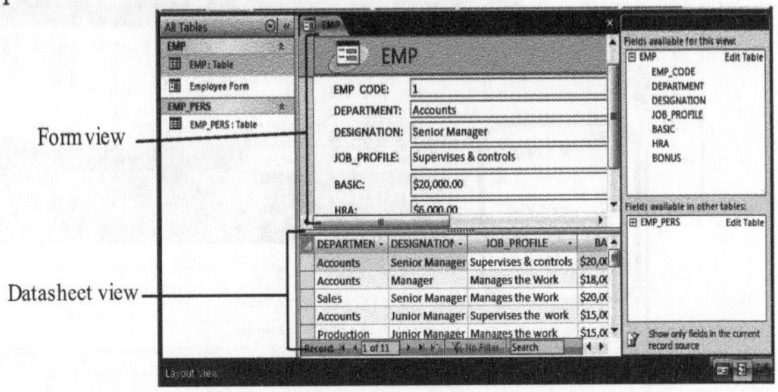

Adding Controls in a Form

Control is a graphical user interface object, such as a text box, check box, scroll bar, or command button that allows users to control the program. It can be used to display data, perform an action, or make the user interface easier to read.

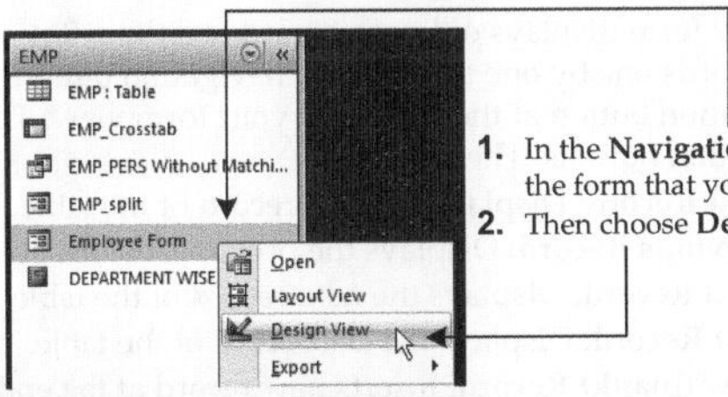

1. In the **Navigation** Pane, right click the form that you want to open.
2. Then choose **Design View**.

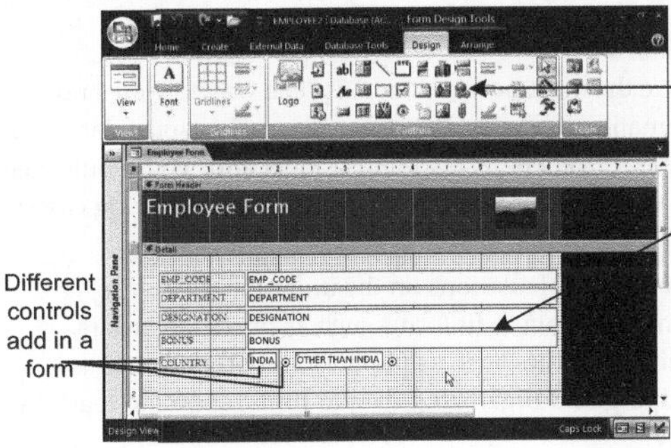

3. Click under the **Design** tab.
4. In the **Controls** group, click the tools of control.
5. Click in the form design grid where you want to position the upper-left corner of the control.
6. Then drag the mouse pointer in the form design grid to create a control of the size that you want.

A form after adding controls appears as seen in this Figure.

Changing the View of a Form

1. In the **Navigation Pane**, click the form for which you want to change the view.
2. Now click under the **Home** tab.
3. In the **Views** group, click arrow next to **View**.
4. Then choose the desired view.

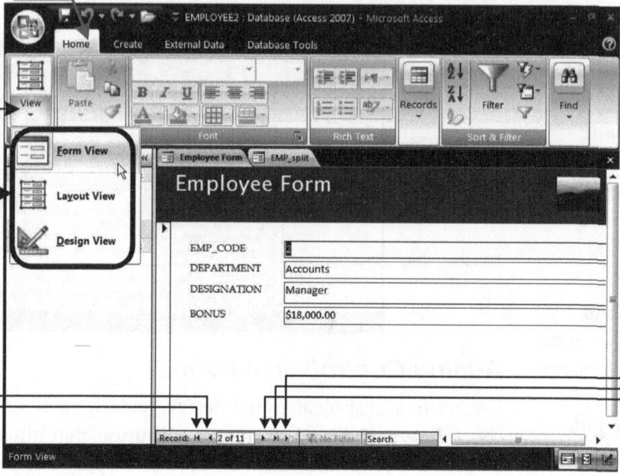

Moving Through Records

Initially form displays only one record at a time. But you can see all the records one by one through the navigation button. You will find navigation button at the bottom of your form view. There are five navigation buttons. These are:

(a) **First Record:** Displays the first record of the table.
(b) **Previous Record:** Displays the previous record of the table.
(c) **Next Record:** Displays the next record of the table.
(d) **Last Record:** Displays the last record of the table.
(e) **New (blank) Record:** Inserts new record at the end of the table.

Notes:

Most common views to work with forms are 

where you view or enter data and in 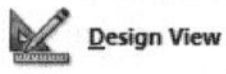

, you can add controls in a form, change properties and layout.

Generating Reports

Reports are the most powerful and flexible way to view and print the information in your database. To make your data more presentable for others to read and understand, you would need to create reports. Reports are very useful in the following cases:

1. Controlling font styles and sizes.
2. Performing calculations on the underlying data.
3. Formatting data to fit forms such as purchase orders.
4. Adding graphics such as pictures and other elements.
5. Grouping and organizing data to form reports to read them easily.

Notes:

Reports let you define how you want your data to appear on the printed page.

*The **Report tool** may not create the final, polished product that you ultimately want. It is however, useful as a means to quickly look at the underlying data. You can then save the report and modify it in **Layout view** or **Design view** so that it will serves your purposes better.*

Create a Report using Report Tool

The Report tool in Access 2007 provides the fastest way for you to create a report, because it generates a report immediately without prompting you for information.

1. In the **Navigation Pane**, click the table or query for which you want to make a report.

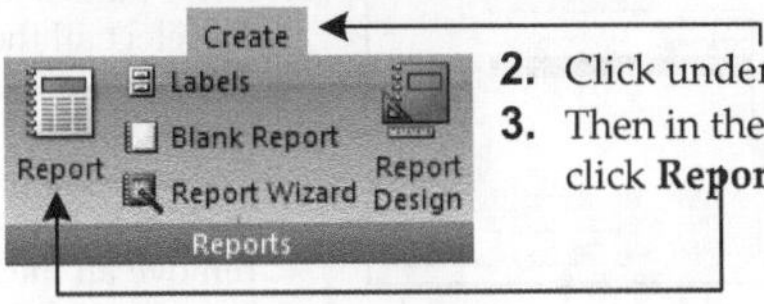

2. Click under the **Create** tab.
3. Then in the **Reports** group, click **Report**.
4. Access generates the report and displays it in *Layout view* along with the **Report Layout Tools** i.e. **Format** Tab in the ribbon.

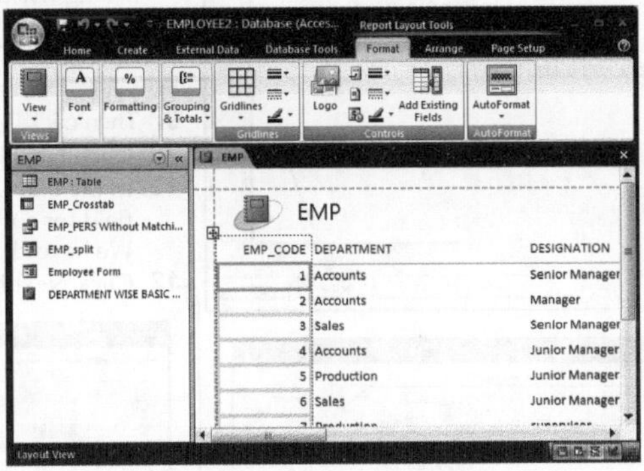

Create a Report using Form Wizard

You can use the Report Wizard to be more selective about what fields appear on your report. You can also specify how the data is grouped and sorted, and you can use fields from more than one table or query, provided you have specified the relationships between the tables and queries beforehand.

1. Click under the Create tab.
2. In the **Forms** group, click Report Wizard button.

A Report Wizard dialog box appears.

✍ ***Creating report using Report Wizard is the easiest way because it guides you step by step through arranging and selecting which data you want to print on a report.***

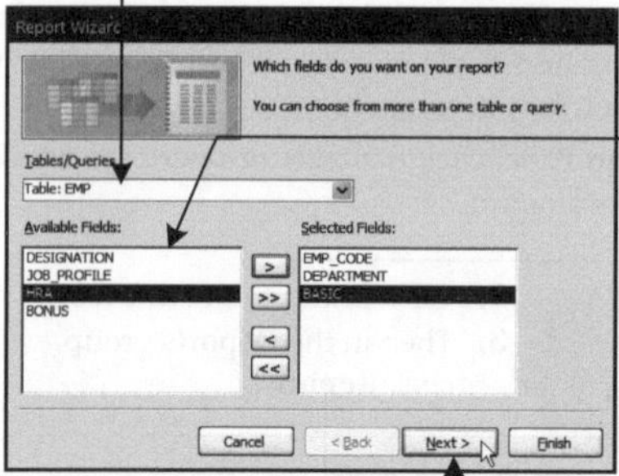

3. In this dialog box, click in the **Tables/ Queries** list box and choose the table or query name that contains the data you want in a report.
4. Then from the **Available Fields:** area, select the fields which you want in your report.
5. After that click [>] button.
   To select all the fields present in the **Available Fields:** area, click [>>] button.
   To remove a field from the **Selected Fields:** area click the [<] button. To remove all the fields, click the [<<] button.
6. Click **Next** button.

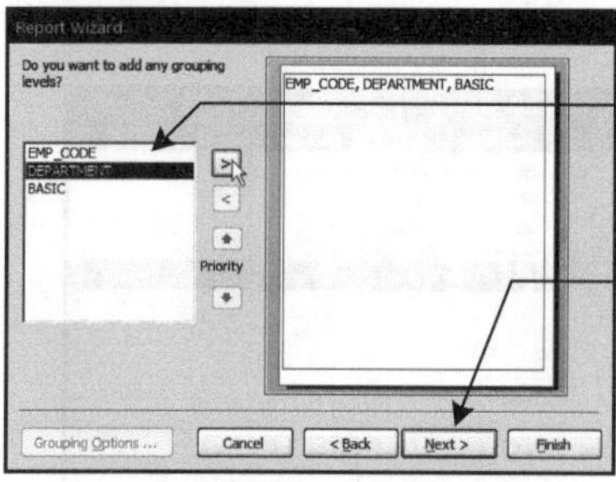

7. Another dialog box that appears, asking whether you want to group your data by a specific field, such as *EMP_CODE, DEPARTMENT*.
8. Click a field name displayed in the box.
9. Then click [>] button.
10. Click **Next** button.
11. In the dialog box that appears, choose a field for sorting your data in report. We have chosen *BASIC* field.
12. Click **Next** button.

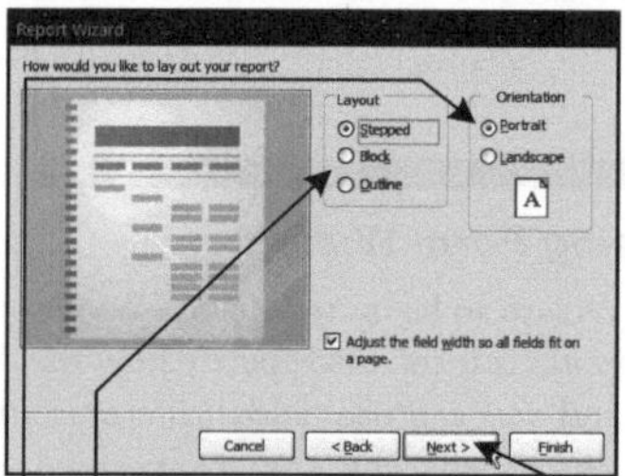

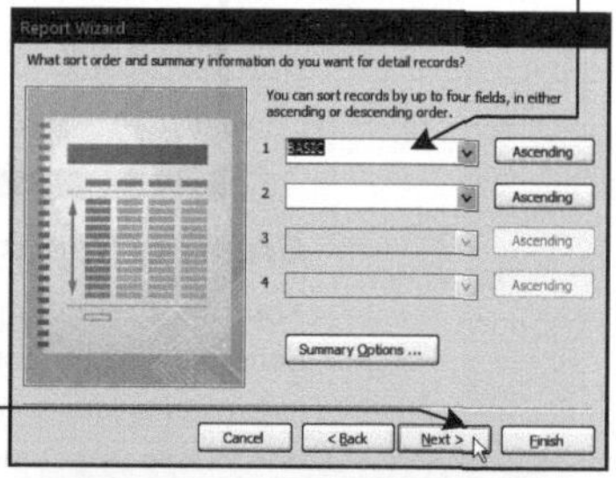

13. In the dialog box that appears, select a layout for the report from the **Layout group**.
14. Select orientation of the page from **Orientation group**.
15. Then click **Next** button.
16. In the dialog box that appears, choose a style you want for the report.
17. Click **Next** button.

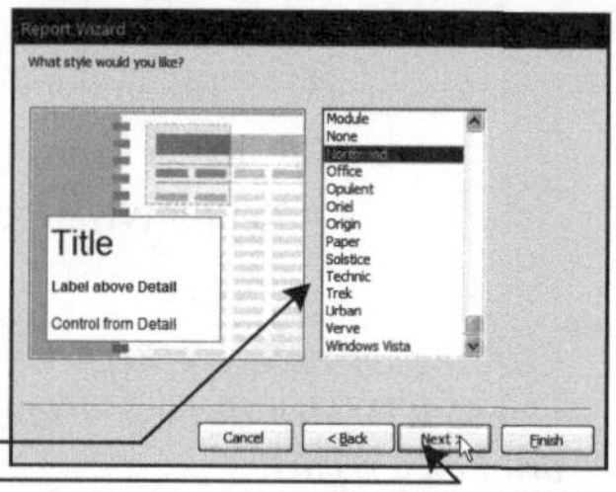

18. In the dialog box that appears provide a title for the report.
19. Then click **Finish** button.

The report will open as shown in following Figure.

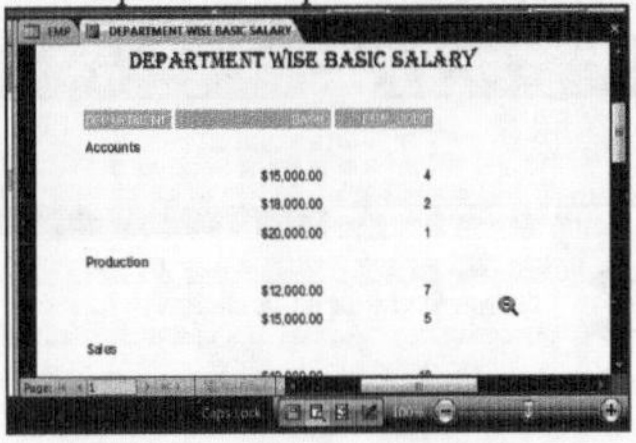

Notes:

Blank Report tool can be a very quick way to build a report, especially if you plan to put only a few fields on the report.

Create a Report using Blank Report Tool

1. Click under the Create tab.
2. In the **Reports** group, click Blank Report.

Access opens a blank report in **Layout view** along with the **Field List pane**

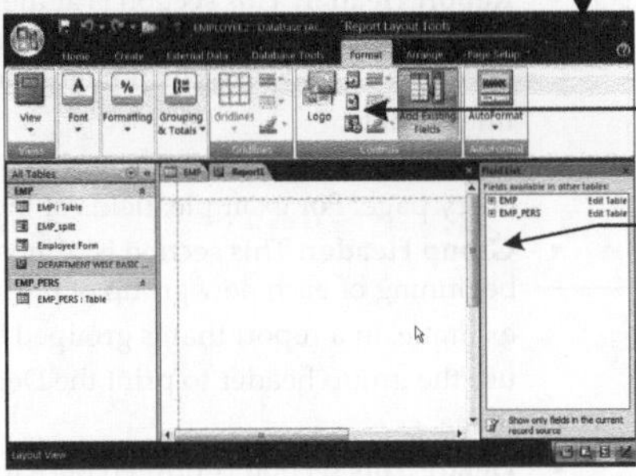

3. In the **Field List** pane, click the plus sign (+) next to the table that contains the fields that you want to include in the report.
4. To add a field to the report, double-click it.

If you want add tools in the report such as logo, title, page numbers, etc.

5. Click under the **Format** Tab.
6. In the **Controls** group, click the tool which you want.
7. After adding tool, the report will look like the following screen.

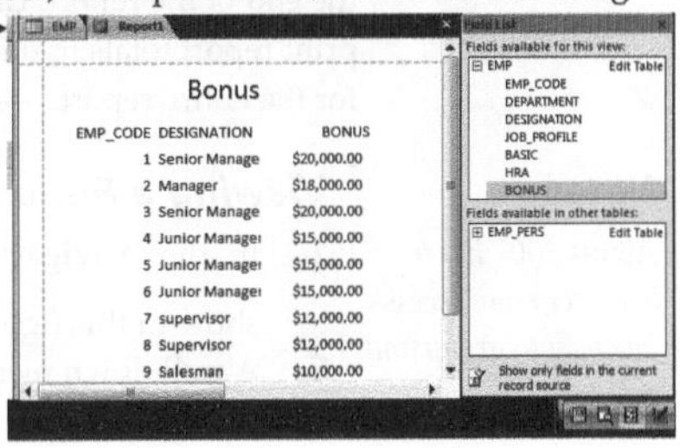

Sections of the Report

In Access 2007, the design of a report is divided into various sections. You can view a report in Design view to see its sections.

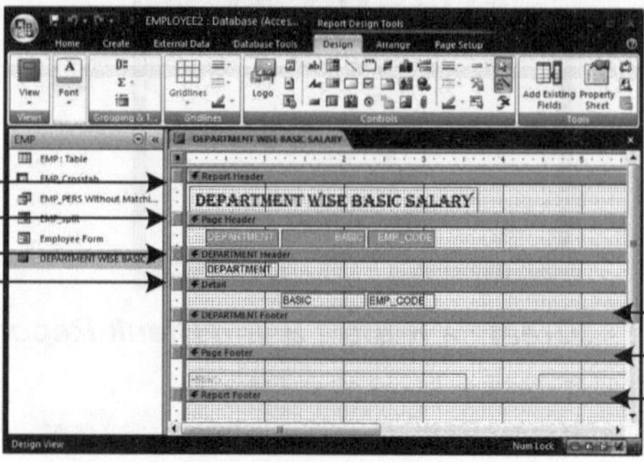

Following are the different sections of the report:

- **Report Header:** This section is at the beginning of the report. It contains information that might normally appear on a cover page, such as a logo, title, or date.
- **Page Header:** This section is printed at the top of every page. For example, fields of the table.
- **Group Header:** This section is printed at the beginning of each new group of records. For example, in a report that is grouped by Department, use the group header to print the Department name.
- **Detail:** This section is printed once for every row in the record source.
- **Group Footer:** This section is printed at the end of each group of records.
- **Page Footer:** This section is printed at the end of every page. Use a page footer to print page numbers.
- **Report Footer:** This section is printed just once, at the end of the report. Use the report footer to print report totals or other summary information for the entire report.

Notes:

Access 2007 has a better & more accessible way to group and sort reports.

Viewing a Report

1. In the **Navigation Pane**, click the downward arrow as show in this figure 

.
2. A pull down menu appears

Notes

*The new **Quick Create feature** automatically generates reports with professional looking designs along with headers and informative footers and totals.*

***Report View** lets you work with reports interactively. By using the new Report view, you can browse a report without having to print or preview it.*

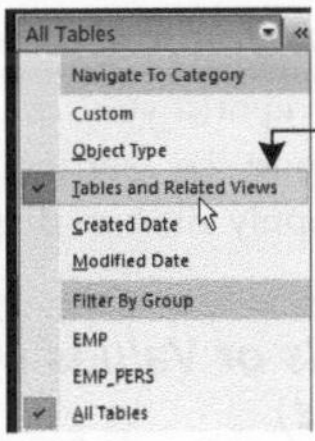

3. In this menu, click **Tables and Related Views.**
4. Access displays a list of all previously saved reports in the navigation pane.
5. Double click a report name which you want to view.

Print Preview a Report

1. Click on the **MS Office** button. Menu appears.
2. Here, point the cursor in **Print** option (no need to click).
3. Now click on **Print Preview** from the option of the print.
4. Access switches to **Print Preview** mode.

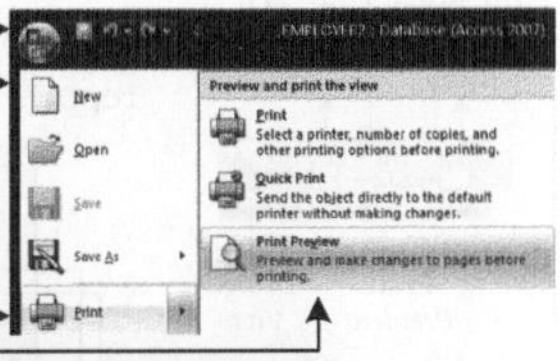

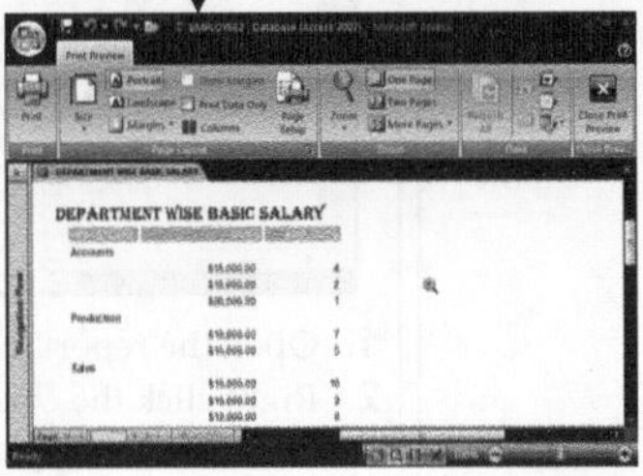

Print a Report

1. Click on the **MS Office** button. Menu appears.
2. Here, click on the **Print** option. A Print Dialog box appears.
3. In Print dialog box, click **OK** button to print the report.

Ensure, the printer is ON and it is online.

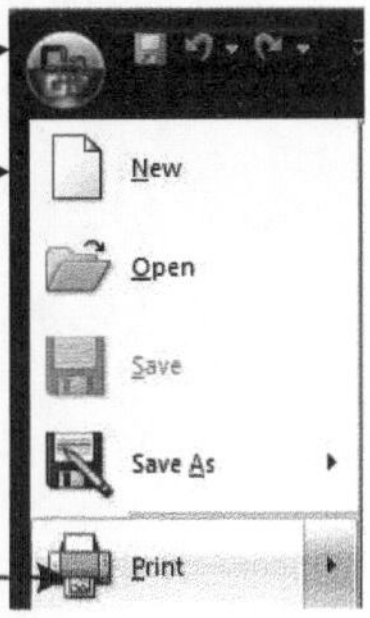

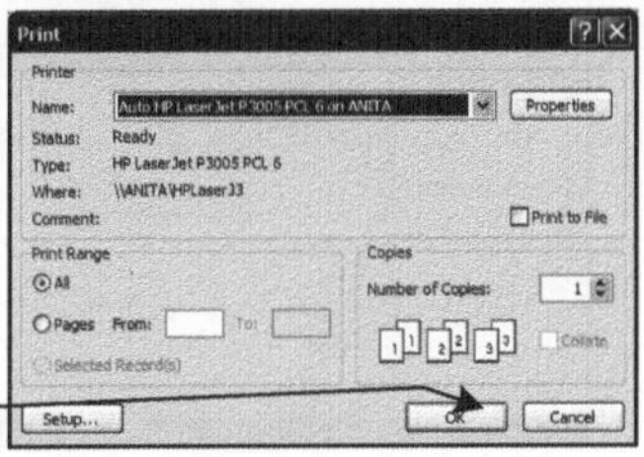

Notes:

For manipulating data in a report first of all you have to switch in ***Layout view****. To switch to the* ***Layout view****, the click* ***Layout view button*** *from the status bar i.e.*

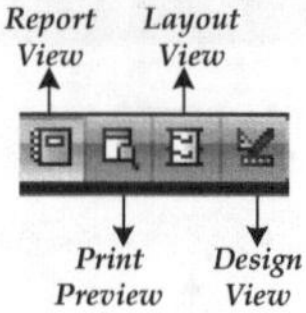

Manipulating Data in a Report

After you create a report, you can manipulate the data displayed in that report i.e. sorting data in ascending or descending order or apply filter to display the data that meet the criteria.

Summing Records or Values (Add the Values Stored in Records)

To make report more useful, use summing facility. By summing records or adding up values stored in fields. Access 2007 can help you to interpret the data better and then displayed it in a report.

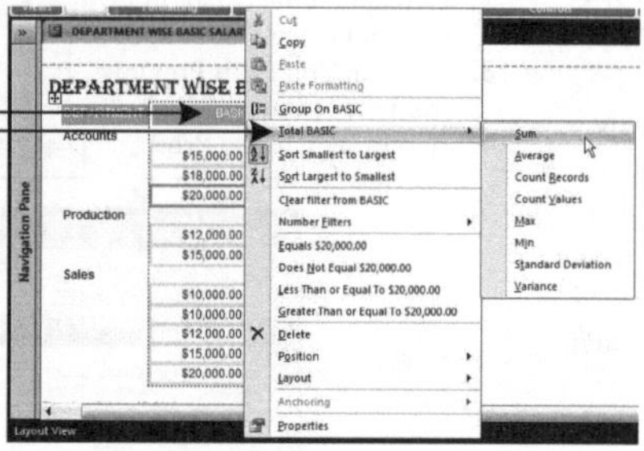

1. Open the report in **Layout view**.
2. Right click the column or field that you want to sum. Access displays pop-up menu.
3. The menu command displays the **TOTAL** command along with the field name you right-clicked, such as *TOTAL BASIC*.
4. Click **TOTAL BASIC**.
5. In sub menu, click on **Sum** command.
6. After sum up, report will look like as seen in the following Figure.

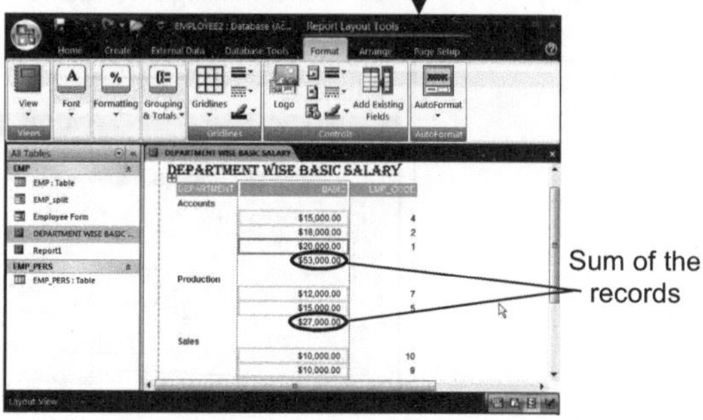

Notes:

Sorting a field rearranges the data in report accordingly to your convenience.

Sorting Data in a Field

Access 2007 can sort data in each field in ascending or descending order.

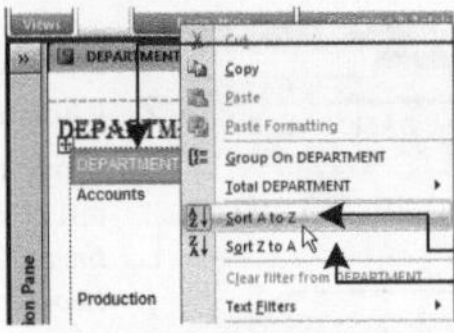

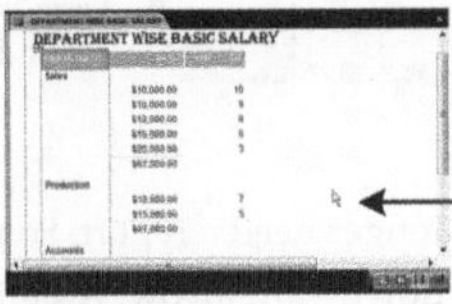

1. Open the report in **Layout view**.
2. Right click the column or field that you want to sort (Here, we have selected *DEPARTMENT* column).
3. Access displays pop-up menu. Choose **Sort A to Z** if you want to sort in ascending order. Choose **Sort Z to A** if you want to sort in descending order.
4. Here, we have select **Sort Z to A**.
5. Access sorts data according to the option we have selected.

Filtering a Data in a Field

Filtering means displaying only that data which meets certain desired criteria.

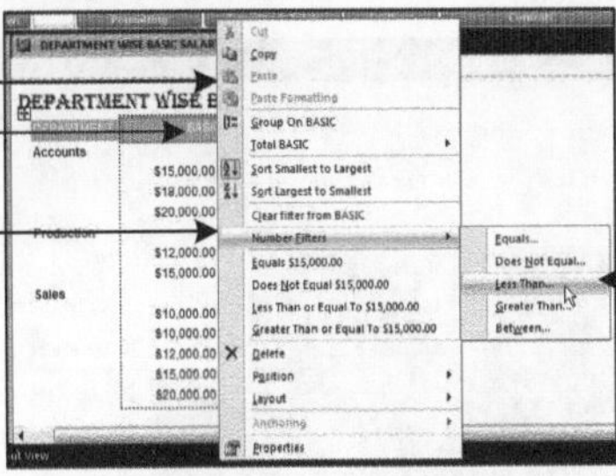

1. Open the report in **Layout view**.
2. Right click the column or field that you want to filter. (Here, we have selected *BASIC* column).
3. Access displays pop-up menu.
4. Click **Number Filters** option from the pop up menu.
5. In sub menu, click **on Less Than...**
6. A dialog box **Custom Filter** appears.
7. Here enter the number and then click **OK**.
8. Report after applying Filter criteria looks like as seen in following Figure.

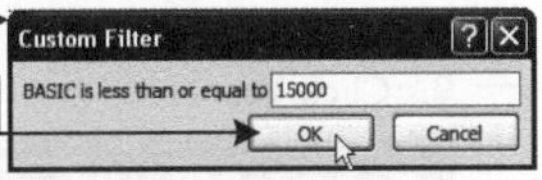

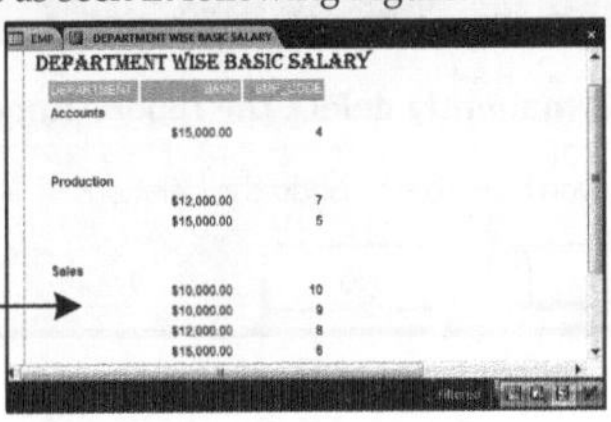

Notes:

*In **Design view**, you can modify the report such as move, resize, add or delete fields in the report.*

Editing a Report

After you created a report, if you want to modify it, then you must switch to the Design view of the report.

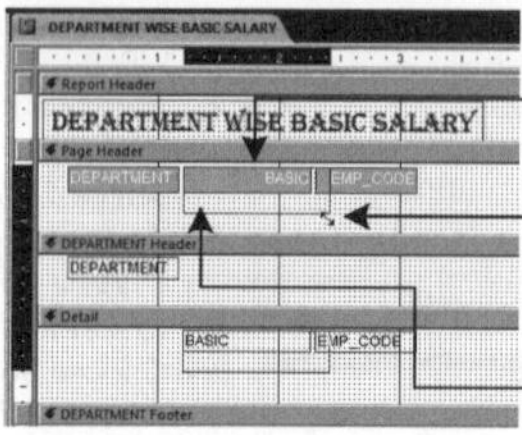

1. Open the report in **Design view**.
2. Click the field you want to resize.
3. Move the mouse pointer over the left or right edge of the field *until the mouse pointer turns into a two-way pointing arrow.*
4. Drag the mouse to resize and expand or shrink the field.

Deleting a Report

Eventually, you may find that you no longer need a report. So you want to delete it.

1. In the **Navigation Pane**, click the downward arrow. A pull down menu appears..
2. In this menu, click **Tables and Related Views**.
3. Access displays a list of all previously saved reports in the navigation pane.
4. Click the report you want to delete.

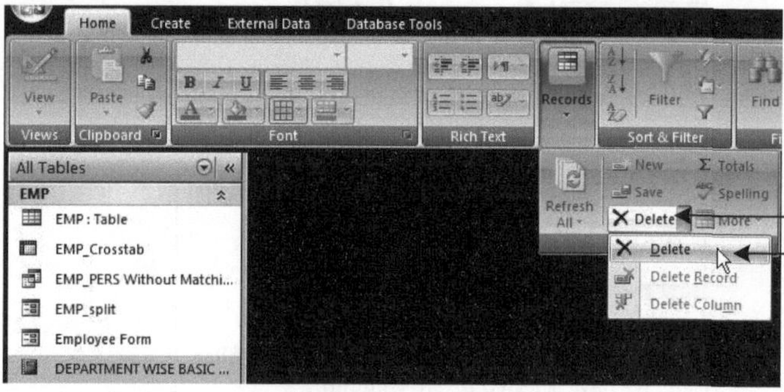

5. Now, click under the **Home** Tab.
6. In the **Records** group, Click arrow next to **Delete**.
7. Click **Delete**.
8. A dialog box appears, asking whether you want to delete report.
9. Click **Yes**.

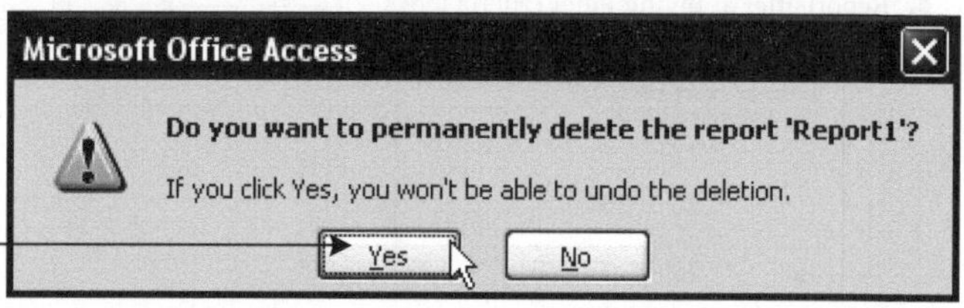

MS PowerPoint 2007

Getting Started

PowerPoint 2007 is a very popular presentation graphics software package. It has set new standards for the working of presentation graphics. PowerPoint 2007 helps you bringing *ideas* and *information* that you want to convey to your audience with no difficulty.

Notes:

Presentations

You can make presentation in the form of slides, handouts or speaker's notes.

Slides

Slides are individual "pages" of a presentation.

It may contain text, graphs, clipart, etc. You can even print slides for overhead projector transparencies.

Handouts

Handouts consist of printed versions of your slides—either two, three, or six slides per page.

Starting PowerPoint 2007

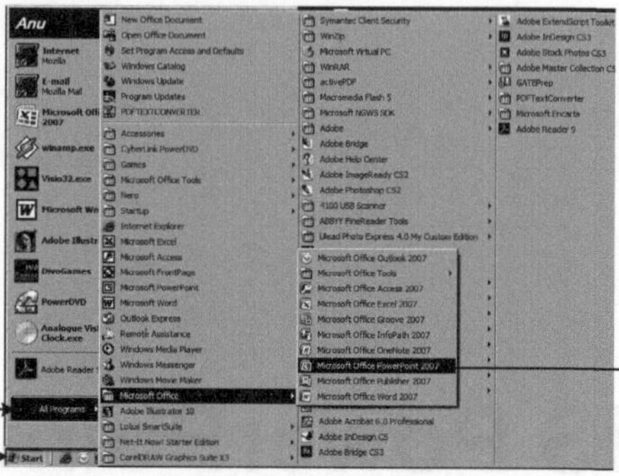

1. Click the **Start** button on the Taskbar.
2. Highlight **All Programs**, click **Microsoft Office**.
3. A sub menu appears, click **Microsoft Office PowerPoint 2007.**

When you first start PowerPoint 2007, it displays a blank presentation showing a single slide.

Understanding the Screen Elements

The main elements of the PowerPoint 2007 window are given below:

Title bar: The *Title bar* is at the top of the screen. It shows the title PowerPoint and the name of presentation. If you have not yet saved any presentation then it displays the default name for the presentation which is *Presentation1*.

Ribbon: Ribbon is displayed just below the title bar. In Ribbon, Commands are organized in logical groups, which are collected together under tabs.

Quick Access Toolbar: This toolbar is located by default at the top of PowerPoint 2007 window. By default, this toolbar displays the Save, Undo and Repeat buttons.

Minimize button: Shrinks the application window to a bar on the taskbar. You can click its button on the taskbar to reopen it.

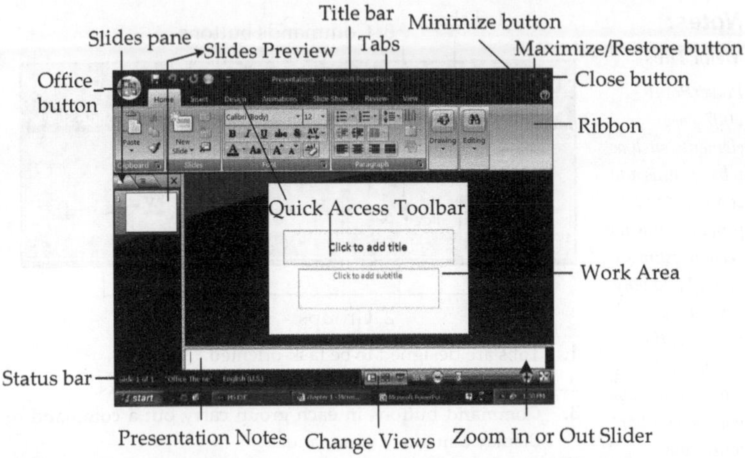

Notes:

PowerPoint 2007 comes with new themes. Themes offer you a wide range of options when you are formatting your presentations. Themes simplify the process of creating professional presentations. Just select the theme that you want, and PowerPoint 2007 does the rest.

Maximize button: A box at the right of a title bar that fills available space with the document or application.

Restore button: A double box at the right of a title bar that restores an application or document into a sizable window.

Close button: A box at the right of a title bar (X) that closes the window or dialog box.

Work area: Where active PowerPoint slide(s) appear. It shows it in Normal view, but other views are available that make the work area appear differently.

Status bar: It gives the information about the presentation and provides shortcuts for changing the view and the zoom.

PowerPoint 2007 Interface

There is a new look for PowerPoint 2007. There is also a new user interface that replaces menus, toolbars, and most of the task panes from previous versions of PowerPoint. The new user interface is designed to help you to be more productive in PowerPoint; more easily find the right features for various tasks and also is more efficient.

Ribbon

The primary replacement for menus and toolbars in PowerPoint 2007 is the Ribbon. Designed for easy browsing, the Ribbon consists of tabs that are organized around specific scenarios or objects. The controls on each tab are further organized into several groups. The Ribbon can host richer content than menus and toolbars can, including buttons, galleries, and dialog box contents.

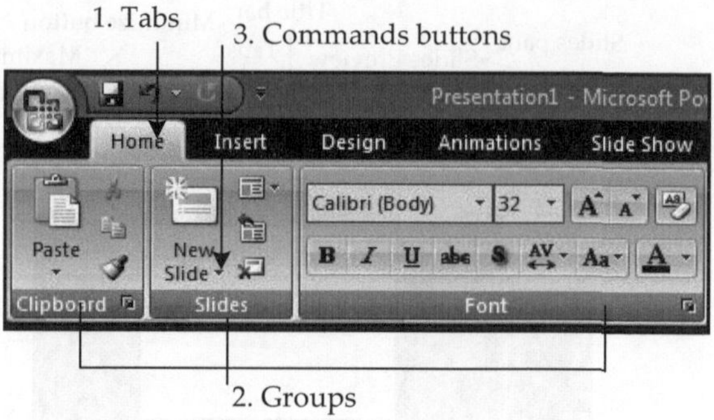

1. Tabs are designed to be task-oriented.
2. Groups within each tab break a task into subtasks.
3. Command buttons in each group carry out a command or display a menu of commands.

Contextual Tools

Contextual tools enable you to work with an object that you select on the page, such as table, picture, or drawing. When you click the object, the pertinent sets of contextual tab appear in color next to the standard tabs.

1. Select an object in your presentation.
2. The name of the applicable contextual tools appears in an accent color, and the contextual tabs appear next to the standard set of tabs.
3. The contextual tabs provide controls for working with the selected item.
4. A standard tab available on the Ribbon.

Program Tabs

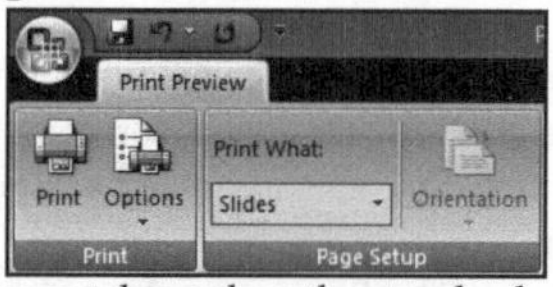

Program tabs replace the standard set of tabs when you switch to certain authoring modes or views, including *Slide Master, Handout Master, Notes Master*, and, in this example, *Print Preview.*

Notes:

Menu Tabs

PowerPoint 2007 uses elements such as tabs, groups and commands that provide paths for accomplishing tasks. Following elements are more like the menus and toolbars that you may be familiar with from previous versions of PowerPoint.

Office Button:

This button is located at the upper-left corner of the PowerPoint window and opens the menu. This command is related to managing documents such as creating, saving, and printing that are available from the menu.

Creating PowerPoint Template

Creating a presentation from one that already exists is usually simpler. The templates include complete presentations with all their details that you can change, as well as presentations with placeholders.

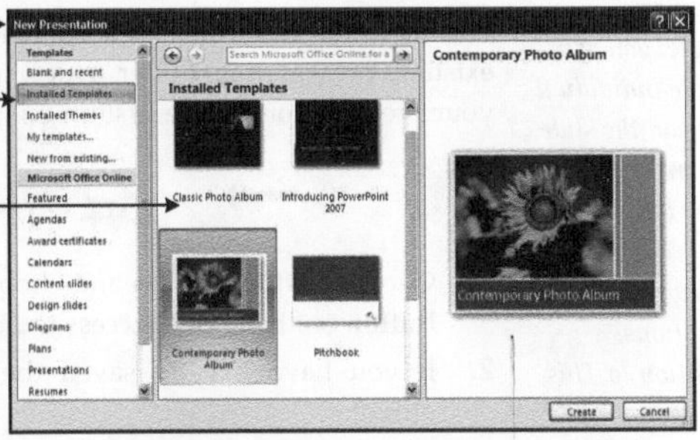

1. Click the **Office** button and choose **New**.
2. The **New Presentation** dialog box appears.
3. Click the **Installed Templates** in the left pane.
4. In the centre pane, you can see a different types of templates with all formatting, such as title, subtitle background, themes colors, themes font etc. Select the desired template you want to apply.
5. In the preview box, you see a sample presentation for which the template is designed.

6. You can see the selected template as default presentation title name.
7. Now you can change or insert your own text and graphics with placeholders.

Notes:

Home tab: *When you click it, this tab is active. Buttons related to working with document contents are organized in this tab. It has six groups: Clipboard, Slides, Font, Paragraph, Drawing and Editing. Only the button representing commands that can be performed on the currently selected document element are active.*

Insert tab: *Click this button for related items you can insert. They are organized on this tab. It has five groups: Tables, Illustrations, Links, Text, Media Clips.*

Design tab: *Click this tab which will show buttons that are related to items. You can give design to your slides. They are organized on this tab. It has three groups: Page Setup, Themes, Background.*

Notes:

Animations tab: *Click this tab which will show buttons that are related to items. You can give animations to your slides. For example, you can animate individual objects on the slide. They are organized on this tab. It has three groups: Preview, Animations, Transition to This slide.*

Slide Show: *Click this tab which will show buttons that are related to items. In this tab, you can view, take up the full computer screen, like an actual presentation. For example you can see how your graphics animated effects will look during the presentation. It has three groups: Start slide show, Set Up and Monitors.*

Saving the Presentation

When working on a presentation, it is very important that you save it at regular intervals so that in case there is system failure, you do not lose much of your work.

PowerPoint has two commands to save your file **Save** and Save **As** command.

The **Save** command is used to save the current presentation file.

The **Save As** command is used when you want to save an existing presentation under a new name or you are saving your presentation for the first time.

1. Click the **Office** button and choose Save or click the **Save button** on the **Quick Access** toolbar.
2. If you have already saved the file, click the **Save As** option.

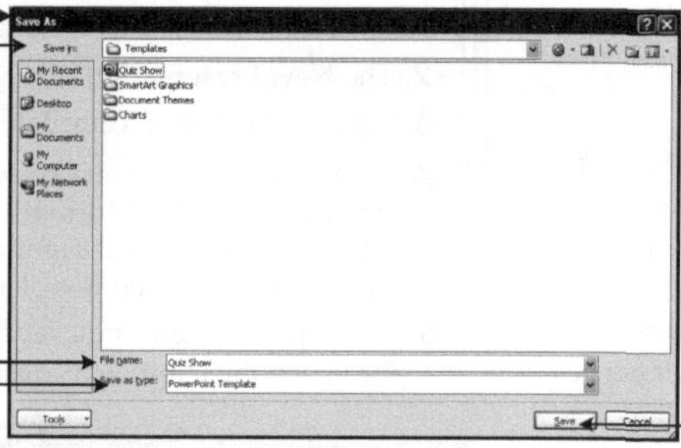

3. The **Save As** dialog box appears.
4. Choose the desired folder or drive you want to save in the **Save in:** drop-down list.
5. Enter the name for your file in the **File name:** drop-down list.
6. In the **Save as type:** list, click the file format that you want to save the file in. For example, if you select PowerPoint template, it adds the template to your list of available templates.
7. Click the **Save** button.

The Save As option gives you various file formats so that the presentation can be given without the presence of PowerPoint software package on your machine.

Notes:

Review tab: *Click this tab which will show buttons that are related to items. In this tab you can view and add comments to your presentation and you might prefer to check spelling all at once when you finish your document. It has three groups: Proofing, Comments and Protect.*

View tab: *Click this tab which will show buttons that are related to changing the view during presentation. It has six groups: Presentation views, window, macros, Show/Hide, Zoom, Color/Grayscale.*

Creating a New Template based on an Existing Presentation

You can create a template in almost the same way as you create a presentation. If you have a template that already has most of the features you want, you will save time by creating a new presentation based on that existing template.

1. Click the **Office** button and the choose **New**. The **New Presentation** dialog box appears.
2. Under **Templates**, click **New from existing...** option.

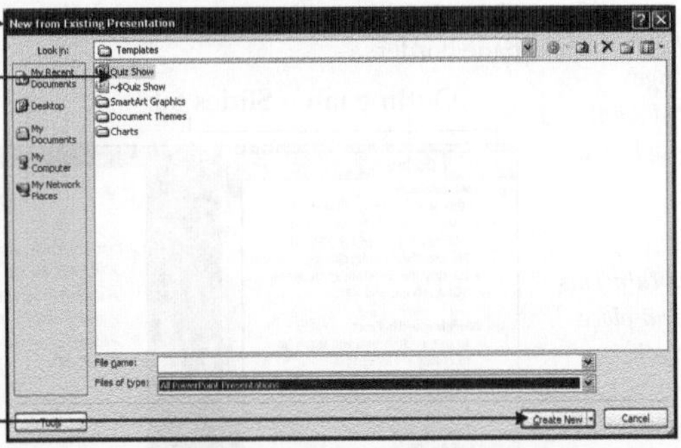

3. The **New from Existing Presentation** dialog box appears.
4. Select a template that is similar to the one that you want to create, and then Click **Create New**.
5. Make the changes you want to apply such as themes colors, fonts and other formats.
6. Click the **Save As** button to save the template.
4. The **Save As** dialog box appears. Give the new name to template file in the **File name:** drop-down list.
5. Select the PowerPoint Template in the **Save as type:** drop-down list, and then click **Save** button.

PowerPoint Views

PowerPoint offers four ways (*views*) to look at your presentation. Each view enables you to work on a different aspect of the presentation. The changes made in one view are also reflected in all other views.

The AutoContent Wizard is not available in PowerPoint 2007. Instead, you can create your presentation by using templates. PowerPoint 2007 templates include different themes and layouts, including most of those that existed in the AutoContent Wizard. Templates give you a starting point and make it easier to complete your presentation quickly.

Notes:

Outline tab: *Use the outline tab to organize and develop the contents of your presentation. You can type all of the text of your presentation and rearrange bulleted points, paragraphs and slides.*

Slides tab: *This is a great place to view the slides in your presentation as thumbnail-sized images while you edit. The thumbnails make it easy for you to navigate through your presentation and to see the effect of any design changes.*

Slide Pane:

The Slide pane displays a large view of the current slide. In this view, you can add text and insert tables etc.

Normal View

Normal view is the main editing view, where you write and design your presentation. The view has four working areas:

- Outline tab
- Slides tab
- Slide pane
- Notes pane

These panes let you work on all aspects of your presentation in one place. You can adjust the size of different panes by dragging the pane borders.

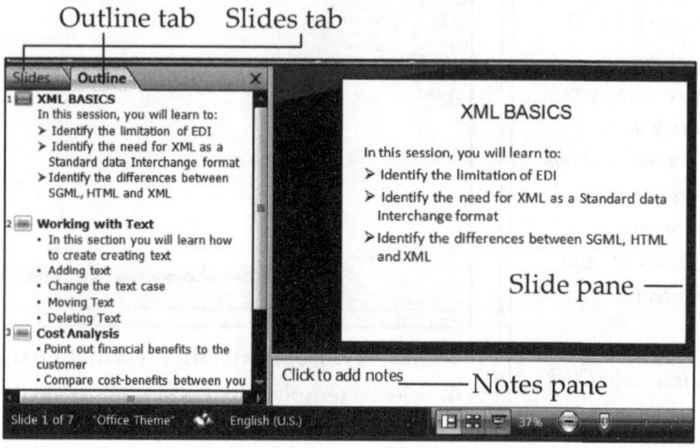

Notes pane: The notes pane lets you add speaker notes or information you want to share with the audience. If you want to have graphic in your notes, you must add the notes in notes page view.

Slide Sorter View

The slide sorter view is a view of your slides in thumbnail form. In this view, you can see the design consistency and the flow of your presentation. If need be, you can easily reorder the slides, copy or delete the slides.

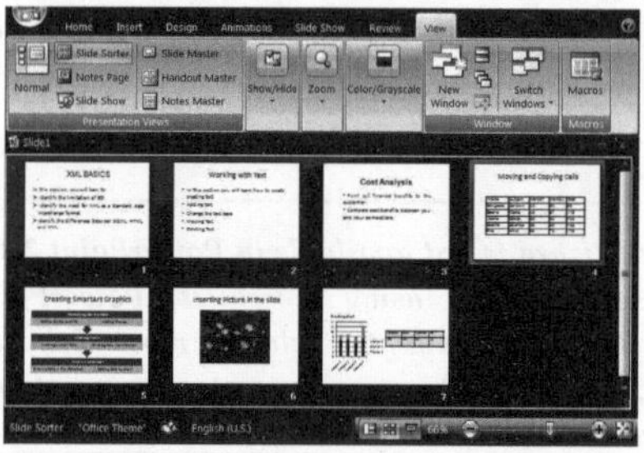

Notes Page View

This view helps you to prepare the speaker notes used while you are making the presentation to your audience. Notes pages view produces a smaller version of the slide on the top part of a page and leaves the lower part free for notes or key points.

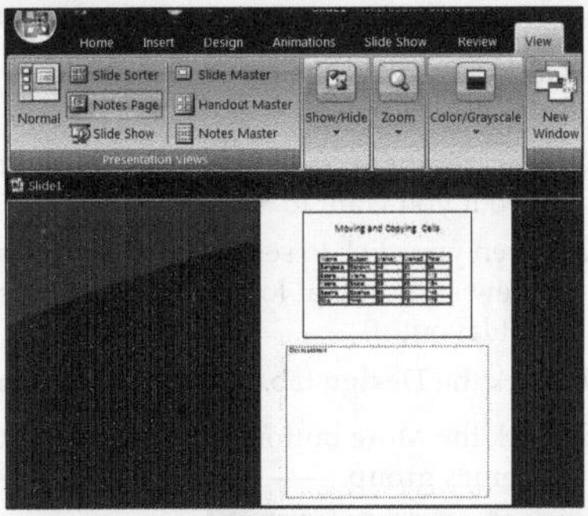

Notes:

A document theme is a set of formatting that include a set of theme colors, fonts and theme effects (including heading and body text fonts, lines and fill effects).

Slide Show View

This view of PowerPoint shows the progress of the presentation from slide to slide just like a real slide show. In this view, all *menus, toolbars, rulers,* the *status bar, scrollbars,* and the Windows *taskbar* are removed from the screen.

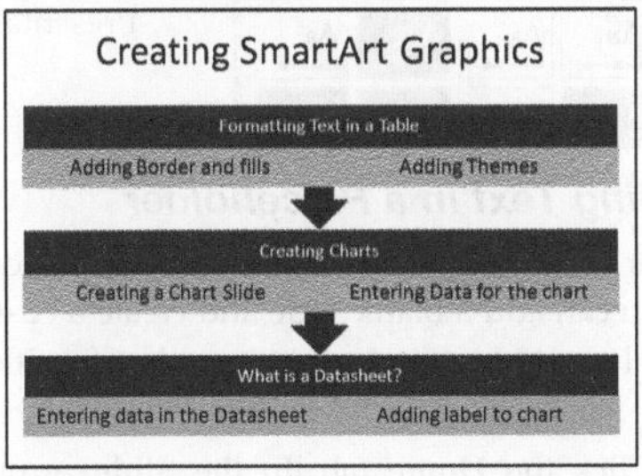

A theme is a set of unified design elements that provide a look for your document by using colors, fonts and graphics. You can use predefined themes that come with PowerPoint, or you can define your own.

PowerPoint Layouts and Themes

A layout determines where text, graphics, charts and other elements appear on an individual slide. A theme determines the look of an entire presentation's colors, fonts, and overall format.

1. Click the **Home** tab, in the **Slides** group. Click the **New Slide** down pointing arrow.

Notes:

To display a blank PowerPoint presentation, click the New button on the ***Quick Access Toolbar*** *or press* ***Ctrl + N*** *keys together.*

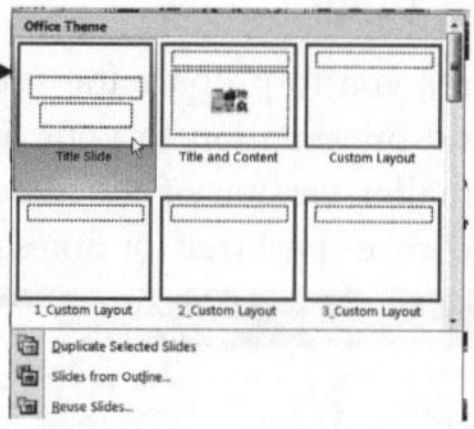

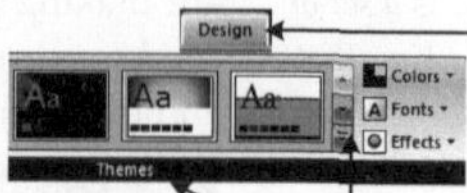

2. PowerPoint opens a layout list. Click the desired layout you want to apply.
3. When you click to select a layout, PowerPoint inserts a new slide at that location in your presentation with that layout.
4. Click the **Design** tab, in the **Themes** group.
5. Click the **More** button at the lower right corner in the **Themes** group.

To enter text in a Presentation, there are ***two ways****: Inserting a new slide with text placeholder. Inserting text in an existing slide.*

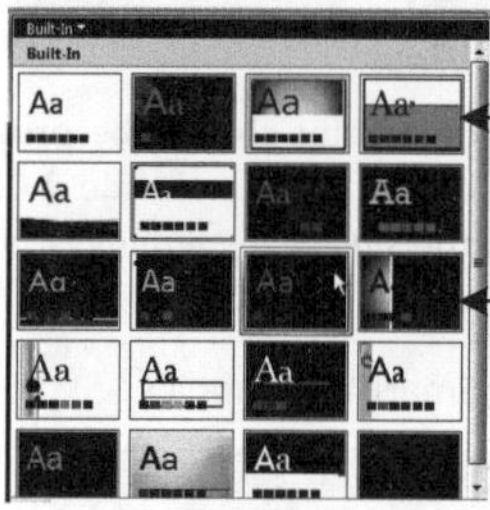

6. A list of Built-in themes options appears.
7. Select a desired style you want to apply in your Presentation.

You might want to open more than one presentation to copy and paste from one to another.

Adding Text in a Placeholder

PowerPoint 2007 comes with predefined layouts you want to use, or you can add a blank slide and create a custom layout. Many of these layouts contain text placeholders for title, body and bulleted list.

1. Click the **Home** tab. In the **Slides** group click **New Slide** down pointing arrow. A list of layout slides appears.

Depending on your screen's resolution and the details in a presentation's slide, you might need to zoom in or out by dragging the Zoom slider in PowerPoint's lower-right corner.

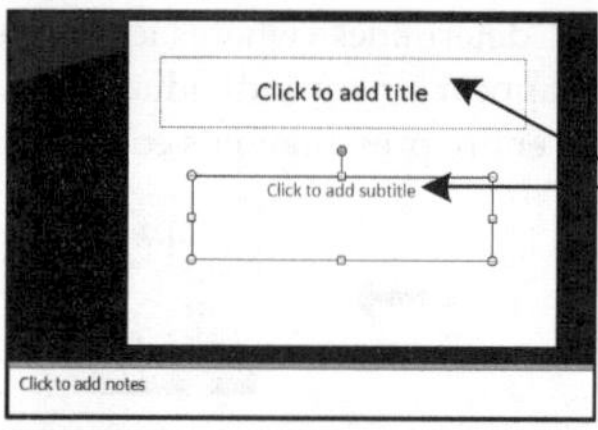

2. Click anywhere within a placeholder to select it. The border indicates that the current placeholder is selected.

Notes:

Closing the Presentation: *When you finish giving or editing a presentation, close the presentation by clicking Office button and selecting Close.*

3. The sample text disappears and an insertion point appears inside the placeholder, indicating that you can enter or type text.
4. In a title or subtitle placeholder, the insertion point may be centered.
5. In a bulleted-list placeholder, the sample text disappears and the bullet remains, with the insertion point positioned where the text will begin.
6. Type the text for the slide inside the selected placeholder and press **Enter** key.
7. When you finish entering text, deselect the object by clicking a blank area of the slide of the gray border around the slide.

Editing Text on a Slide

*To select all the text in a placeholder, click inside the placeholder and then clicking select and then **Select All** in the **Editing** group on the **Home** tab.*

You can make changes to the text in any text object simply by clicking the object. An insertion point appears, indicating that the text is ready for editing. Then you can start making changes to the text. Before you can change existing text, you have to select it by using the following techniques:

- Select an individual word by double clicking it. The word and the space following it are selected.
- Alternatively, position the insertion point at the beginning of the text you want to select, hold down the **Shift** key, and either press an arrow key to select characters one at a time.

Copying Text

*The keyboard shortcut key to copy text is **Ctrl + C.***

You can copy text that appears in one place to another place. Copying of text occurs with the assistance of the Windows Clipboard.

1. Select the text you want to copy.
2. In the **Home** tab, click copy icon on the **Clipboard** group
3. Move to the place in your presentation where you want to insert this text.
4. Click the **Paste** down pointing arrow and choose **Paste command** on the **Clipboard** group.

*The keyboard shortcut key to paste text is **Ctrl + V.***

Moving Text

*The keyboard shortcut key to cut text is **Ctrl + X.***

Moving text operation is similar to the copy text operation except that text is moved i.e. it is deleted from the original location and copied to a new place.

1. Select the text you want to move.
2. Click the **Cut** button on the **Home** tab.
3. Click the **Paste** button on the **Home** tab.

Notes:

If you delete text accidentally, you can undo your action by clicking the Undo button on the Quick Access toolbar.

You can also align text in the Paragraph Launcher dialog box in the alignment section.

*The shortcut key to decrease font size is **Ctrl + <**.*

*The shortcut key to increase font size is **Ctrl + >**.*

Right type and size of font creates good impression on your audience.

Deleting Text

You can delete characters, words, or all the text in a text box. using one of the methods:

- The **Del** key erases the character to the right of the cursor.
- The **Backspace** key erases the character to the left of the cursor.

Formatting Text

Formatting means applying characteristics and effects to text in order to enhance its appearance. The formatting you apply to the text in a presentation is very important because it affects the way your words are received by your audience.

Aligning Text in a Slide

Alignment is the way text is placed between the margins of a page or a text box on a slide.

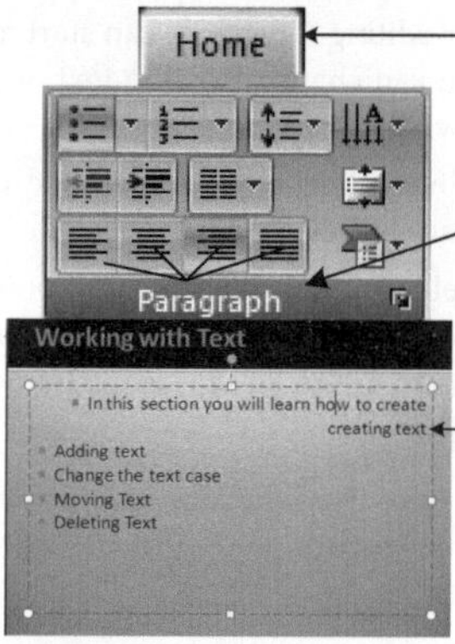

1. Click the **Home** tab.
2. Select the text that you want to align the text.
3. Click the desired alignment you want to apply in the **Paragraph** group.

Changing the Font Size, Style and Effects in Font dialog box

Font size is measured in *points,* which is a height measurement; each point is 1/72 of an inch.

1. Select the text you want to change.

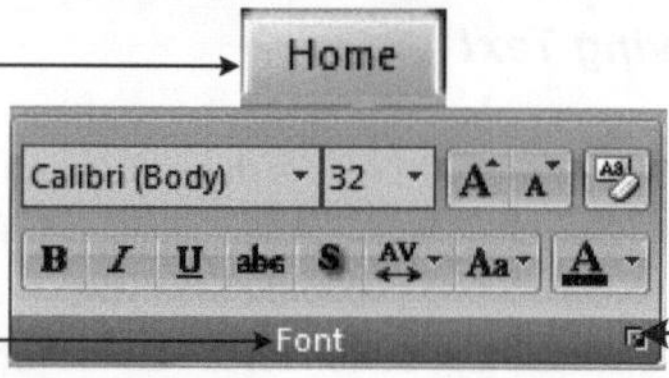

2. Click the **Home** tab and choose **Font** group.
3. Or click the **Font lanuncher** dialog box.

Notes:

You can also change the text color by clicking the Home tab of font group. Then click the Font color drop-down arrow. The font color palette appears. Move the mouse pointer over the color, you can see the effect changes in the text. Choose the desired color you want to apply the text.

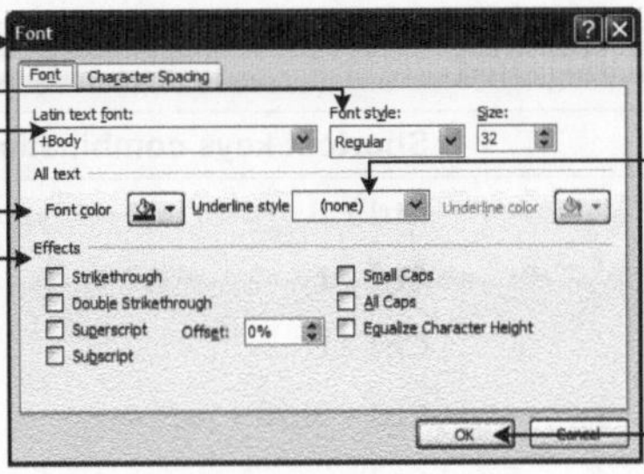

4. The **Font** dialog box appears.
5. Click the desired **text font:** drop-down list.
6. Click the desired **Font style:** drop-down list.

The options in Font style has the following choices:

Regular: The normal way the text appears.
Bold: The text appears bold or highlighted.
Italic: The text appears Italic.
Bold Italic: The text appears bold and Italic highlighted

7. **Font color:** Specifies the color of the selected text.
8. **Underline style:** Specifies whether selected text is underlined and the underline style. Click none to remove underlining.
9. The Effects section has the options:
   Strikethrough: Draws a line through the selected text.
   Superscript: The text appears raised like x^2y
   Subscript: The text appears lowered like H_2O
10. Click the desired options you want to check and then click OK button.

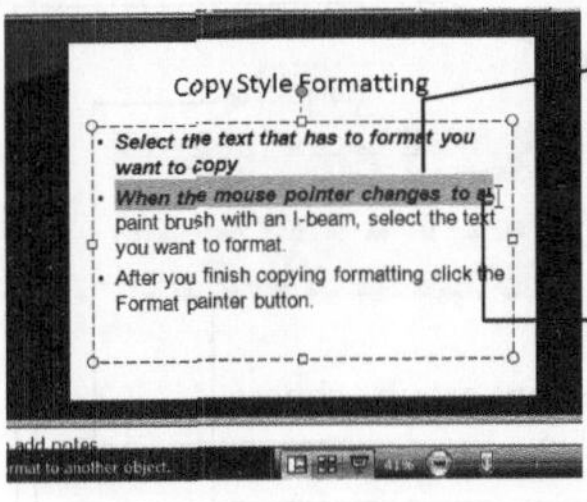

1. Select the text that has the format you want to copy.
2. Click the Home tab, and choose **Format painter** button.
3. When the mouse pointer changes to a paint brush with an I-beam, select the text you want to format.
4. After you finish copying formatting, click the **Format painter** button or press **Esc** key to restore the normal I-beam pointer.

Applying Character Formatting using the keyboard

Most of the character formatting can also be applied using the keyboard shortcut.

1. Select the text you want to format and use the shortcut key combinations for the desired formatting effects.

Format	Shortcut keys combination
Bold	**Ctrl + B**
Italic	**Ctrl + I**
Underline	**Ctrl + U**
Superscript	**Ctrl + Shift + +**
Subscript	**Ctrl + =**
Copy Formatting	**Ctrl + Shift + C**
Paste formatting	**Ctrl + Shift + V**
Remove formatting	**Ctrl + Spacebar**
Change case of letters	**Shift + F3**
Change the font	**Ctrl + Shift + F**
Change the font size	**Ctrl + Shift + P**
Increase the font size	**Ctrl + Shift + >**
Decrease the font size	**Ctrl + Shift + <**

Using the Change Case Command

PowerPoint provides the facilities to change capitalization of any text by using the **Change Case** command.

Notes:

To resize a placeholder, drag one of its corner borders.

Move Placeholder

1. Click inside placeholder.

2. Drag with mouse to desired position.

1. Select the text for which you want to change capitalization.

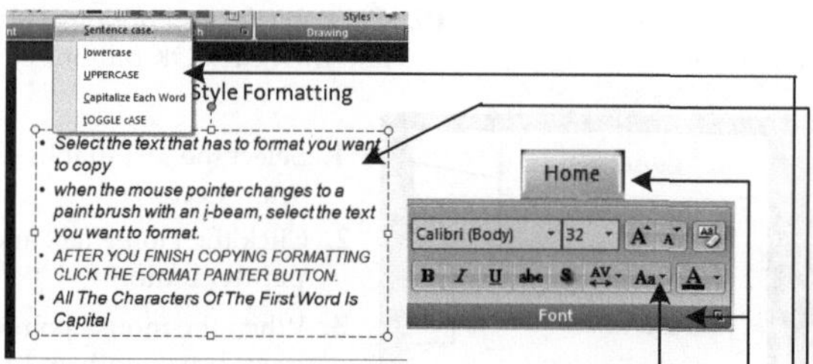

2. Click the **Home** tab. In the **Font** group, choose **Change Case** command icon.
3. Click the down pointing arrow.
4. Select the desired option you want to apply to the text.
5. The different types of Change case command is applied in the text.

Bullets and Numbering

1. Select the text or paragraphs you want to add bullet.

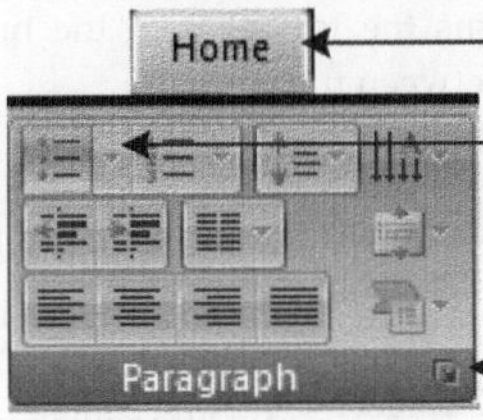

2. Click the **Home** tab, in the **Paragraph** group.
3. Click the down arrow to choose the Bullets and Numbering dialog box.

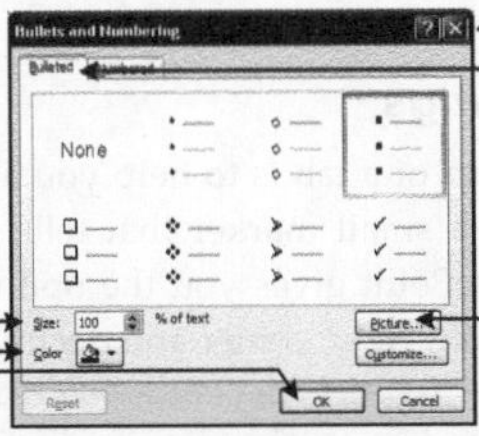

4. The **Bullets and Numbering** dialog box appears.
5. Click the **Bulleted** tab you want to modify.
6. You can select the **Picture...** button you can use the picture file to use as a bullet.
7. In the **Size:** spin box, enter the bullet size you want as a percentage of the font size.
8. In the **Color:** spin box, choose the color of the bullet you want.
9. Click OK button to accept the changes.

Formatting Paragraphs

A Paragraph can have the following characteristics:

Alignment, Tab and Indents, Line spacing and Space before and after the paragraph.

Alignment

You can change alignment for specific text with buttons in the Paragraph group in the Home tab.

Left alignment: aligns the text at the left margin and makes a zigzag right margin.

Right alignment: aligns the text to the right margin and makes a zigzag left margin.

Notes:

Size Placeholder

1. Click inside placeholder.

2. Drag sizing handles to increase/decrease size.

Remove bullets and Numbering

1. Select the text you want to remove bullets and numbering.

2. In the Paragraph group of Home tab choose the bullets down arrow.

A list of bullet palette list appears, choose None. Or

3. You can press Backspace to remove bullet or numbering from an item in the list.

Change Text Alignment

1. Select text or click in text paragraph.

2. Click desired alignment button in the Paragraph group.

Center alignment: centers text between the left and right margins on the center line. In this case both the margins are zigzag.

Justified: aligns the text at both the margins by increasing the spacing between the words.

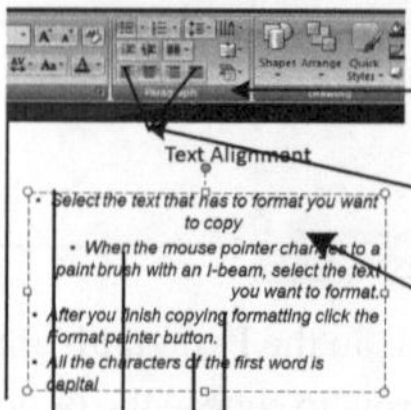

1. Click the **Home** tab of **Paragraph** group.
2. Click the desired alignment you want to apply.
3. Different alignment applied in the Slide.

Center alignment
Right alignment
Justify
Left alignment

Notes:

*The **Keyboard shortcut** to apply bold formatting to selected text, press **CTRL+B**.*

*The **Keyboard shortcut** to apply Italic formatting to selected text, press **CTRL+I**.*

*The **Keyboard shortcut** to apply Underline formatting to selected text, press **CTRL+U**.*

To Clear a tab stop, drag the tab marker off the ruler. Or

To remove all the tab stops.
1. In the Paragraph dialog box, click Tabs.
2. In the Tabs dialog box, Clear All.

Tab settings

The function of a tab is to help you align text in your documents. The tab is a small marker that tells the text where you want to stop. PowerPoint gives you the option of choosing four different tab stops: left, right, center and decimal tabs.

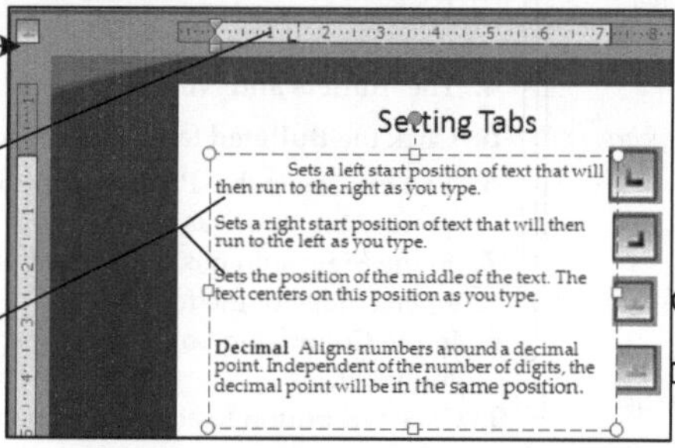

1. Choose the type of tab you want by clicking in the tab selection box at the left of the horizontal ruler until the tab type appears.
2. Move the pointer to the ruler bar and click the point at which you want to add the tab.
3. For example, to set different tabs appears in the slide.

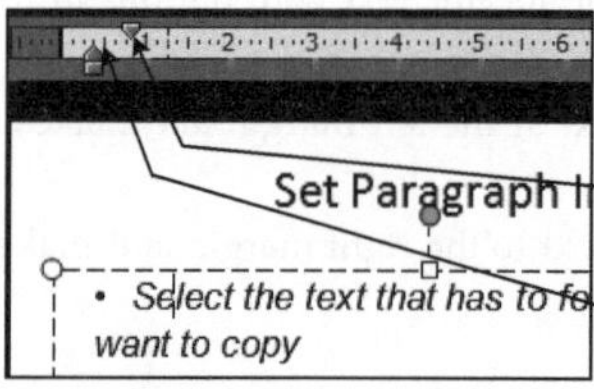

4. Select the text you want to set an indentation.
5. If the ruler is not displayed, click **View** tab and choose Ruler in the **Show/Hide** group.
6. To set the indent for the first line of a paragraph, drag the upper indent marker.
7. To set the left indent for other lines in a paragraph, drag the lower indent marker.

Notes:

Change Line Spacing

1. Click Line Spacing button.

2. Click desired spacing at drop-down list.

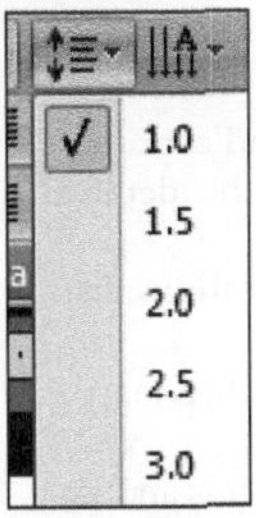

The Shortcut key to open a Spelling dialog box is F7.

***Grammar** checking is available only in Outlook 2007 and Word 2007.*

Line Spacing

PowerPoint takes care of the spacing of your text automatically. Type the text, and PowerPoint puts it where it needs to go. Sometimes, however, you may want to change the spacing PowerPoint has set for you. You might want to fit one or more lines of text on a slide.

1. In the Slide pane, click anywhere in the paragraph you want to add space between lines.
2. In the **Home** tab, click the **Paragraph Launcher** dialog box.

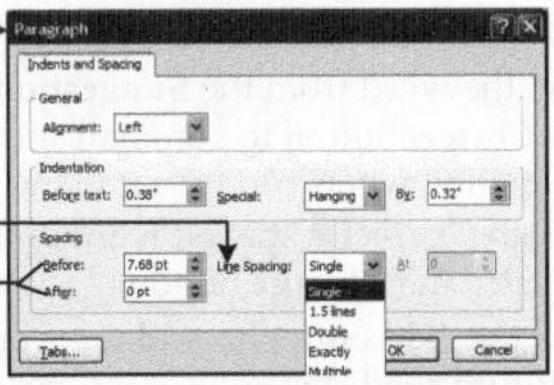

3. The Paragraph dialog box appears.
4. Select the desired **Line Spacing** options in the Spacing section.
5. In the spinner box,click up-arrow or down-arrow for adding space Before or After the paragraph.
6. After you make changes in the dialog box click OK button.

Using Spelling Checker

PowerPoint's spelling checker checks the spelling of the entire presentation all slides, outlines, notes pages, and handout pages. The spelling checker in PowerPoint compares all the words in your document with a dictionary file, in the way any MS Office application does.

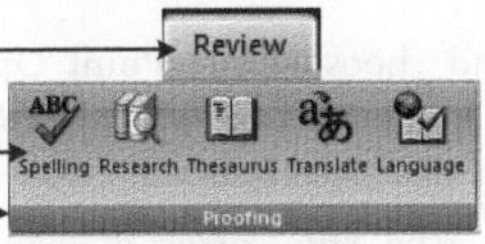

1. Click the **Review** tab. In the **Proofing** group, click **Spelling** icon.

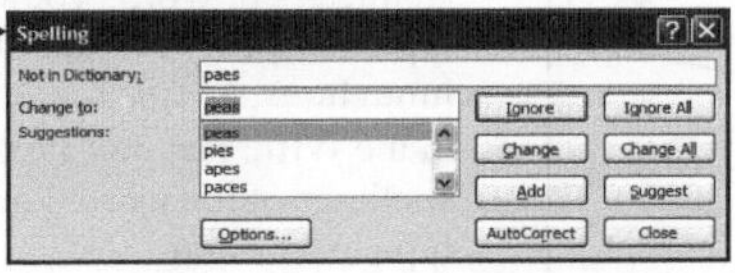

2. The **Spelling** dialog box appears.

Notes:

Use Thesaurus

1. Click desired word.

2. Click Review tab.

3. Click Thesaurus button.

4. Position mouse pointer on desired replacement word in Thesaurus task pane, click down-pointing arrow at right of word, and then click Insert.

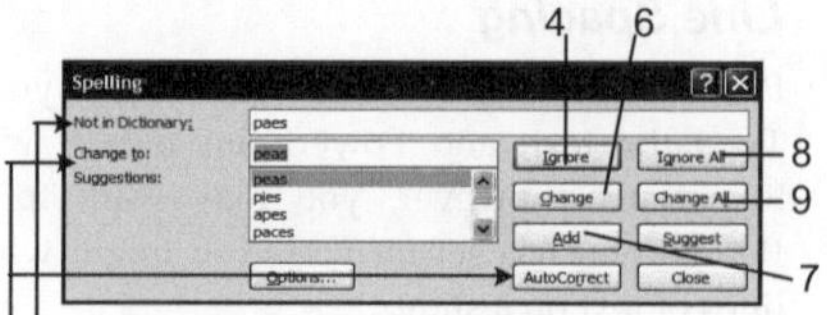

3. The spelling checker highlights the first unrecognized word in the presentation file and displays the word in the **Not in Dictionary:** box.

4. Click the **Ignore** button to leave the word as it is and go on to the next word.

5. Select the word from the **Suggestions:** list and click the AutoCorrect button to automatically correct the identical misspelling when you type it in the future.

6. Click the correctly spelled word in the **Suggestions:** list and click the **Change** button.

7. Click the **Add** button to add the word to the dictionary for future spell checks.

8. Click the **Ignore** button to leave the word as it is and go on to the next word.

9. Click the correctly spelled word in the **Suggestions** list and click the **Change All** button to correct all identical misspellings throughout the document.

10. Click **Close** button after the spelling is completed.

Using AutoCorrect

AutoCorrect is a feature that automatically corrects common typing errors. The common typing errors involved in entering the word *the* or *When* (*teh*, *WHen* for example) are automatically corrected.

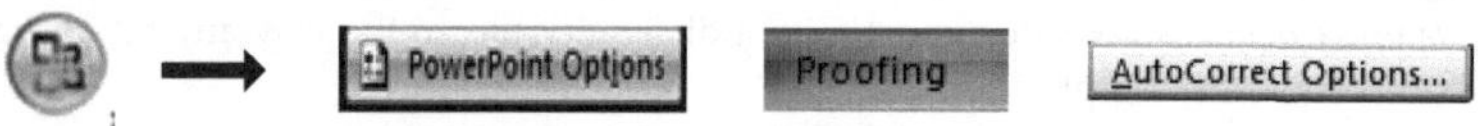

1. Click the **Office** button, and choose **PowerPoint Options**. The PowerPoint Options dialog box appears. In the left pane, click **Proofing** page options. In the right pane, click AutoCorrect Options... button.

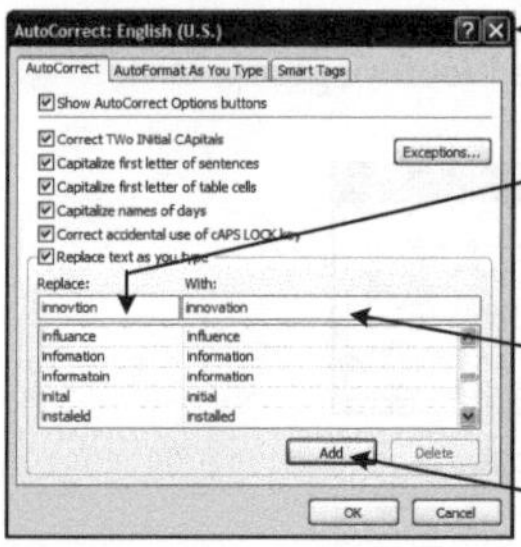

2. The **AutoCorrect** dialog box appears.

3. In the **Replace:** text box, enter the characters or words you want to type misspell. For example, type innovtion.

4. In the **With:** text box, type the correct spellings of the word. For example, type innovation.

5. Click **Add** button. And then click the OK button.

Inserting A Table Slide

PowerPoint includes a Table feature you can use for displaying columns and rows of data. Insert a table in a slide with the Table button in the Insert tab or with the **Insert Table** button in a Content placeholder.

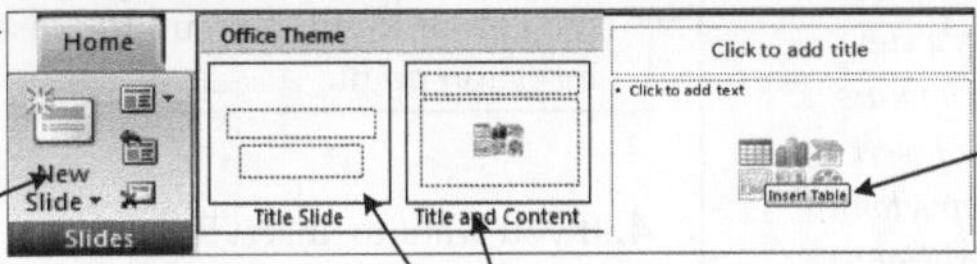

1. Click the **Home** tab.
2. Click **New Slide** down pointing arrow in the **Slides** group.
3. A list of slides appears.
4. Click the **Title and Content** Slide. A new slide appears.
5. Click the Table place holder. **Insert Table** dialog box appears.

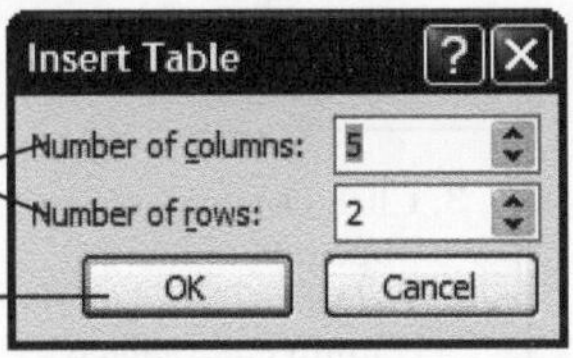

6. In the Insert Table dialog box, enter the number of columns and the number of rows you want to insert in the table. Or you can type the number of rows and columns.
7. After you specify the number of rows and columns, click OK to create the table.

Editing a Table

Once you have created a table and entered text or numbers, you can modify its structure by adding, deleting, moving and copying cells, columns and rows. You can also change the width of columns, height of rows and merge or split cells to accommodate typed text in the cells.

Adding Columns and Rows

1. Click anywhere in the column next to where you want the new column to appear.
2. In **Table Tools** contextual tab, click **Layout** tab.

Notes:

Entering Text in Table

When you create a new table, an empty table appears within a gray frame on the slide. When you insert a table, the insertion point flashes in the first cell in the upper left corner of the table. The text you type appears at the insertion point. After entering the text in the table and to exit the editing mode, click anywhere outside the table.

Selecting Columns and Rows

In Table Tools Contextual tab, click Layout tab. In Table group click Select drown pointing arrow and choose desired choice you want to select.

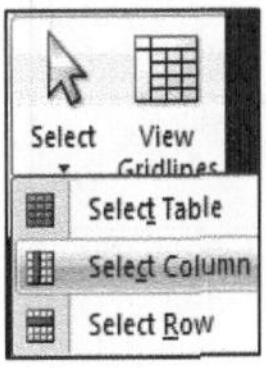

Notes:

To insert column

Right click the mouse, choose Insert, a sub menu appears, choose Insert Columns to the Left or Right.

To insert Row

Right click the mouse choose Insert, a sub menu appears, choose Insert Rows Above or Below.

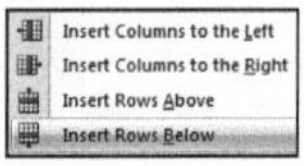

To move the selected text using drag and drop*—Position the mouse pointer over the selected text, press and hold down the left mouse button and drag the text to the destination cell.*

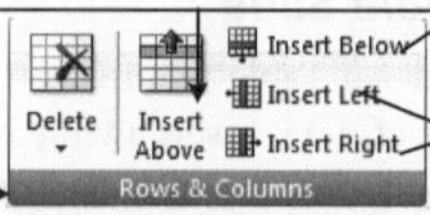

Row Insert option

Column Insert option

3. In **Rows & Columns** group choose Insert Columns to the Left or Right. A column is inserted to the left of the insertion point.

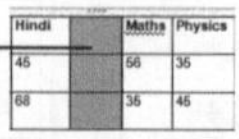

4. If you want to Insert Row choose Insert Below or Above. A Row is inserted to the above of the insertion point.

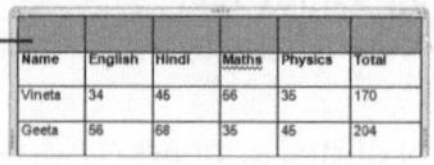

Deleting Columns and Rows

1. Select the columns/rows you want to delete.
2. In **Table Tools** contextual Tab, click **Layout** tab, in **Rows & Columns** group.

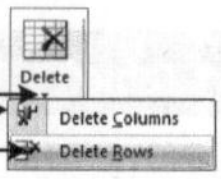

3. Click Delete down pointing arrow, a lists of option appears.
4. To Delete Columns choose **Delete Columns**. The column gets deleted.
5. To Delete Rows choose **Delete Rows**. The Row gets deleted.

Copying and Moving Cells

Once you select the contents of a cell, you can copy or move these to another location using drag and drop. Alternatively, use the **Cut**, **Copy** and **Paste** commands from the **Home** tab or from the shortcut menu that appears when you select a cell and click the right mouse button.

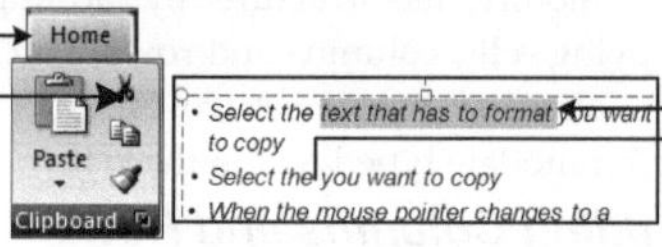

1. Select the text you want to move (to Cut).
2. Click **Home** tab and choose **Cut** option.
3. The selected text gets deleted.

Notes:

To copy the selected text using drag and drop—Position the mouse pointer over the selected text, press and hold the key, press and hold down the left mouse button and drag the text to the destination cell.

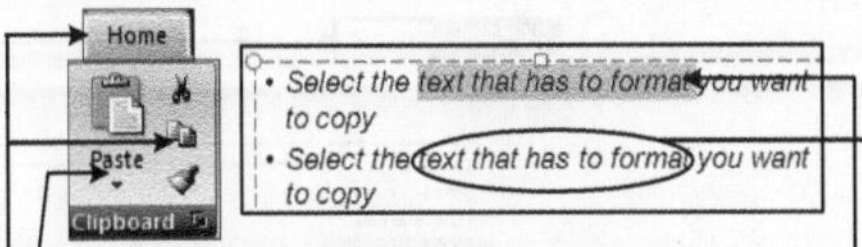

1. Select the text you want to copy.
2. Click **Home** tab and choose **Copy** option.
3. Click **Paste** option. The selected text gets copied.

Changing Column Width

You can also change the size of the columns by adjusting the width of the columns.

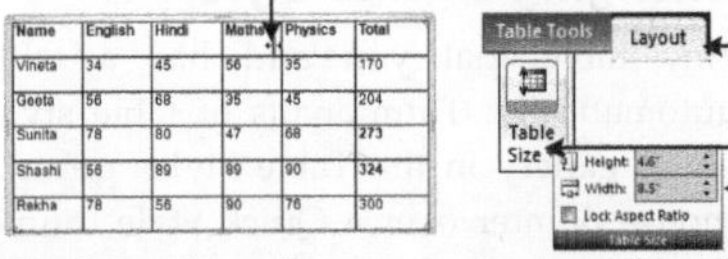

When you delete the contents of a cell, you do not delete the cell. To delete the cell, you must merge the cell with another or delete the column or row.

1. Position the pointer anywhere on the column's right border until the pointer changes to a double line and arrow.
2. Drag the column border to the left or right to decrease or increase the column width. A dashed line indicates the target column width.
3. Release the mouse button. The column width is changed to the new size you specified by dragging.
   Or
4. In **Table Tools** contextual tab, click **Layout** tab. Click Table Size down arrow.
5. Select the **Column Width** up and down arrow, to set the width of the selected cells.

To add a row at the end of a table, click the last cell of the last row, and then press TAB.

Changing Row Height

You can change the size of *rows* of a table by adjusting the height of the rows.

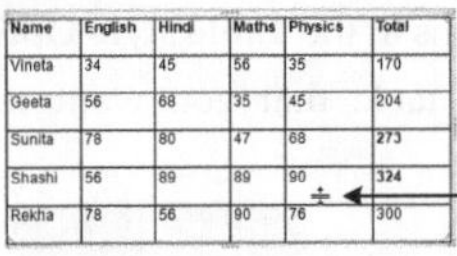

1. Position the pointer anywhere on the row's right border until the pointer changes to a double line and arrow.
2. Drag the row border to the left or right to decrease or increase the row height. A dashed line indicates the target row height.

Notes:

To maintain the same ratio between the height and width of the table when you resize it, select the ***Lock Aspect Ratio*** *check box.*

To merge cells

1. Select the cells you want to merge.

2. Click the ***Layout*** *tab.*

3. Click ***Merge*** *down pointing arrow and choose* ***Merge cells*** *in the Merge group.*

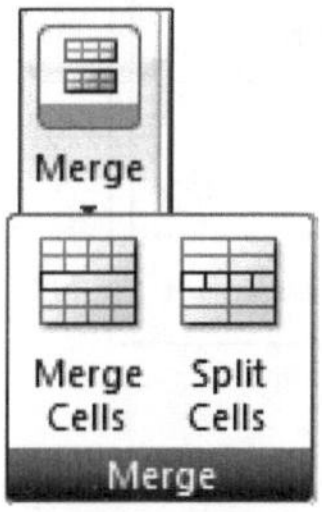

To Split cells

1. Select the cell that you want to split.

2. Click Split Cells options in Merge group.

3. The cell is split into two cells of equal width.

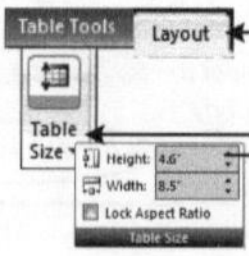

3. Release the mouse button. The column width is changed to the new size you specified by dragging.
Or

4. In **Table Tools** contextual tab, click **Layout** tab. Click **Table Size** down arrow.

5. Select the **Row Height** up and down arrow, to set the height of the selected cells.

Changing a Table Style

Any table that you add has a table style applied to it automatically. Thumbnails of table styles appear in the Quick styles gallery in the Table Styles group. When you place your mouse pointer over a Quick Style thumbnail, you can see how the Quick Style affects your table.

Table style

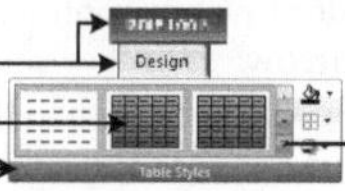

1. In **Table Tools** contextual tab, click **Design** tab.

2. In the **Table Styles** group, click the table style that you want.

3. Click the **More** button, a Style gallery opens.

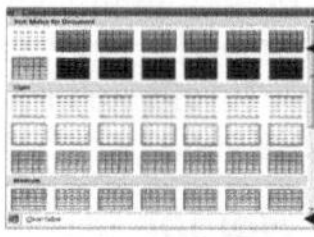

4. Click the desired style you want.

5. To clear the table style, click the **More** button and then click **Clear Table.**

Change Table Style Options

You can apply a table style to specific parts of your table by selection options in the **Table style Options** group.

1. Click the table that you want to change the table style option.

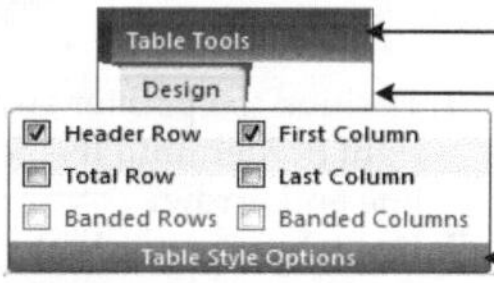

2. In **Table Tools** contextual tab, click **Design** tab.

3. In **Table Style Options** group, there are six option.

Notes:

*You can use the **Eraser** to delete borders between table cells. Under **Table Tools**, on the **Design** tab, in the **Draw Borders** group, click **Eraser**, or press and hold SHIFT while the pointer is a pencil , and then click the borders that you want to delete.*

- To emphasize the first row of the table, select the **Header Row** check box.
- To emphasize the last row of the table, select the **Total Row** check box.
- To have alternating striped rows, select the **Branded Rows** check box.
- To emphasize the first column of the table, select the **First Column** check box.
- To emphasize the last column of the table, select the **Last Column** check box.
- To have alternating striped columns, select the **Branded Column** check box.

4. Select the desired options you want to apply in the table and click the options check box.

Adding Border and Fills

PowerPoint establishes default borders around cells and the table itself, on the current presentation template. You can change borders separating cells, columns and rows or around the entire table.

1. Select the entire table, or the cells, columns, or rows around which you want to specify the border.

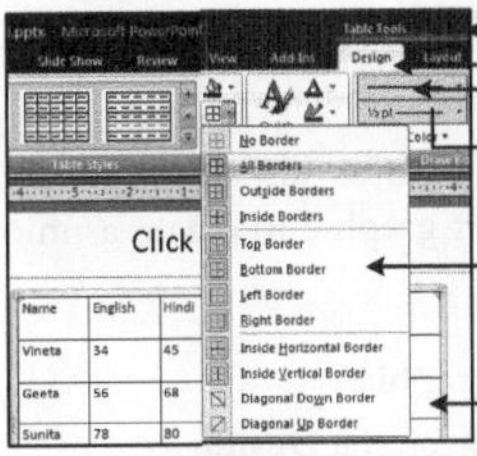

2. Under **Table Tools**, on the **Design** tab, click **Borders** down arrow. The actual name of this button changes depending on what was last selected.
3. The borders drops down to show all the different border types. Click the border you want.
4. The selected portion of the table changes to reflect the new border type.
5. If you want to change the border line style, click down arrow and choose **Pen** Style in **Draw Borders** group.
6. Click the **Border Weight** and pen color in the **Draw Borders** group. Click the desired style you want to apply.

Creating a SmartArt Graphic

A SmartArt graphic is a visual representation of information that you can quickly and easily create, choosing from among many different layouts, to effectively communicate your message or ideas. When you create a SmartArt graphic, choose a type of SmartArt graphic, such as Process Hierarchy, Cycle or Relationship. It is similar to SmartArt graphic. Each type contains several different layouts. After you choose a layout, it is easy to change the layout for your SmartArt graphic.

Notes:

To both move a table and create a duplicate of it, press and hold **Ctrl** *while you drag the table.*

1. Click the **Insert** tab, in **Illustrations** group, Click **SmartArt** option.

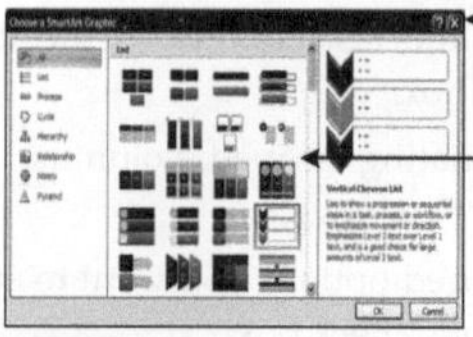

2. **Choose a SmartArt Graphic** dialog box appears.
3. Click the type of layouts that you want.

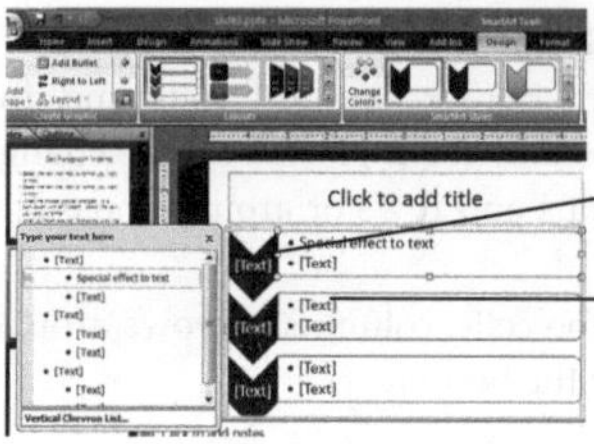

4. Enter your text by doing one of the following:
   - Click in a shape in your SmartArt graphic, and then type the text.
   - Click [Text] in the Text pane, and then type your text.
   - Copy text from other program, click [Text], and then paste into the Text pane.

Apply a SmartArt Style to a SmartArt graphic

A SmartArt Style is a combination of various effects, such as line style, bevel, or 3-D, that you can apply to the shapes in your SmartArt graphic to create a unique and professionally designed look.

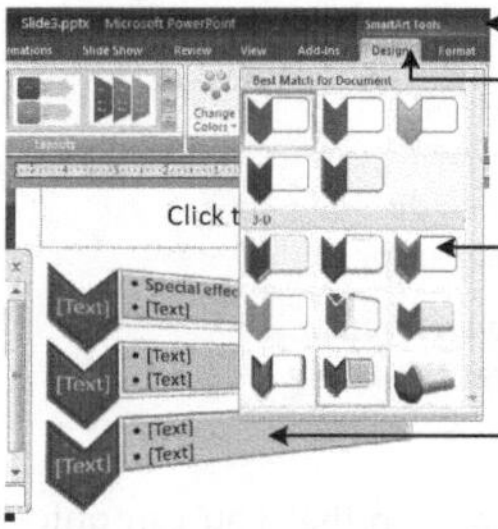

1. Click your SmartArt graphic.
2. Under **SmartArt Tools**, on the **Design** tab, in the SmartArt Styles group.
3. A list of SmartArt styles appear.
4. The selected styles applied in the slide.

Change the Colors of an Entire SmartArt Graphic

You can apply color variations that are derived from the theme colors to the shapes in your SmartArt graphic.

Notes:

You can use only Office PowerPoint 2007 to save your SmartArt graphic in a graphics file format such as .gif, .jpg and .png.

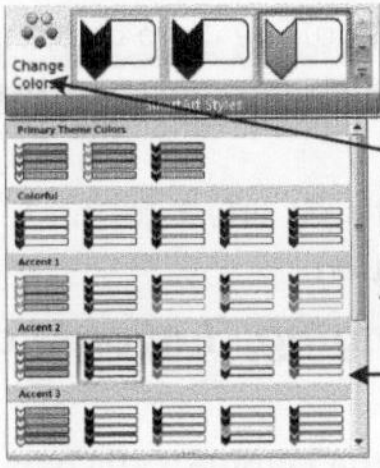

1. Click your SmartArt graphic.
2. Under **SmartArt Tools**, on the **Design** tab, in the **SmartArt Styles** group.
3. Click **Change Colors** down arrow.
4. A list of **Theme Colors** appears. Select the desired colors you want to apply.

Organization Chart

An *organization chart* is a graphical representation of the structure of an organization. By using a SmartArt graphic in PowerPoint 2007, you can create an organization chart and include it in your presentation. To create an organization chart quickly and easily, you can type or paste text in the organization chart.

If you want to create an organization chart, use the ***Organization Chart layout****. When you use this layout, additional functionality, such as the assistant shape and the hanging layouts, becomes available.*

1. Click the **Insert** tab, in the **Illustrations** group, click **SmartArt**.
2. The **Choose a SmartArt Graphic** dialog box appears. Click **Hierarchy**, click an **Organization chart layout**, and then click OK.

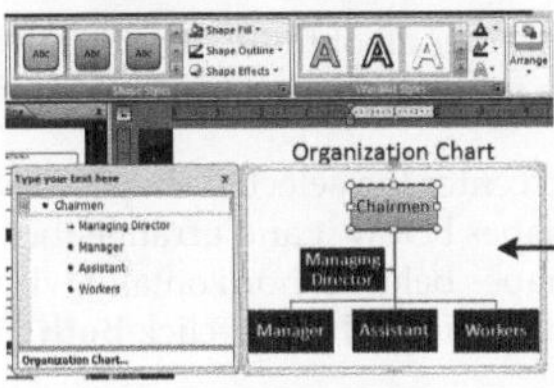

3. An Organization chart appears in the Slide.

Formatting the Organization Chart

Different components of an org chart which can be formatted are **Text Fill**, **Text outline** and **Text Effects**. While formatting the text, you can change fill, outline, effects of the text in the organization chart.

The keyboard shortcut key to insert a new SmartArt graphic is ***Alt + N + M*** *keys pressed together.*

1. Select the text you want to format.

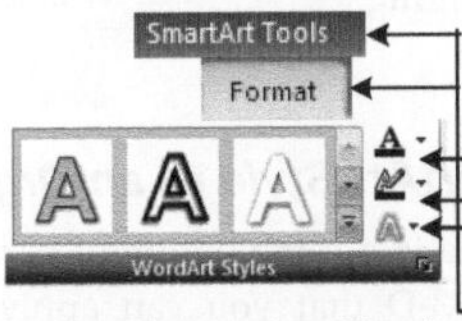

Text Fill
Text Outline
Text Effects

2. Under **SmartArt Tools** on **Format** tab, in **WordArt Styles** group.

Text Fill: Specify Text fill drop down menu and choose the desired text fill such as a solid color, gradient, picture or texture.

Notes:

The keyboard shortcut to switch between the Text pane and your SmartArt graphic is ***Ctrl + Shift +F2*** *pressed together.*

Add a Picture fill to a Shape

1. Click the shape in the ***SmartArt*** *graphic that you want to add a picture fill to.*

2. Under ***SmartArt Tools****, on the* ***Format tab****, in the Shape Styles group, click the arrow next to* ***Shape Fill****.*

3. Click ***Picture****, locate the folder that contains the picture that you want to use, click the picture file, and then click* ***Insert****.*

Text Outline: Specify text outline drop down menu and choose the desired text outline such as color, width and line style for the outline of the text.

Text Effects: Specify a visual effect to the text, such as shadow, reflection or 3-D rotation.

Changing the Hanging Layout of Organization Chart

A hanging layout affects the layout of all shapes below the selected shape.

1. Click the shape in the organization chart that you want to apply as hanging layout.
2. Under **SmartArt** Tools, on the **Design** tab, in the **Create Graphic** group, click **Layout** down arrow and then do one of the following options:

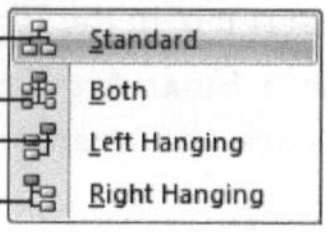

- To center all of the shapes below the selected shape, click **Standard**

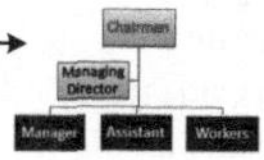

- To center the selected shape above the shapes below it and arrange the shapes below it horizontally with two shapes in each row, click **Both**.

- To arrange the selected shape to the right of the shapes below it and leftalign the shapes below it vertically, click **Left hanging**.

- To arrange the selected shape to the left of the shapes below it and rightalign the shapes below it vertically, click **Right Hanging**.

Apply a SmartArt Style to an Organization Chart

A SmartArt Style is a combination of various effects, such as line style, bevel, or 3-D that you can apply to the shapes in your SmartArt graphic to create a unique and professionally designed look.

1. Click the SmartArt graphic whose SmartArt Style you want to change.

Notes:

Restore defaults layout and color:

*1. Click the **SmartArt graphic** to select it.*

*2. Under **SmartArt Tools**, on the **Design** tab, in the **Reset** group, click **Reset Graphic**.*

Insert Image

1. Click Insert tab.

2. Click Picture button.

3. At Insert Picture dialog box, navigate to desired folder.

4. Double-click desired picture file.

2. Under **SmartArt Tools**, on the **Design** tab, in the **SmartArt Styles** group, click the **SmartArt Style** that you want.
3. Click the **More** button to see the more Styles. Select the desired styles you want to apply.
4. When you place your pointer over a thumbnail, you can see how the SmartArt Style affects your SmartArt graphic.

Using Clip Art Gallery

Clip Art gallery is a collection of graphic files in PowerPoint that you can insert in presentations. It has built a gallery of clip art images into the Clip Art gallery.

1. Select the slide that contains a Clip Art slide.
2. Click the Clip Art icon in the slide. A clip art task pane appears.

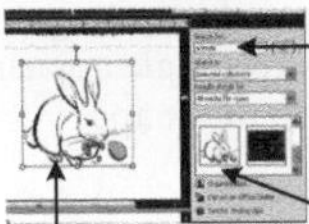

3. Select the current entry in the **Search for:** box or click in the box if there is no entry, type animals, and then click **Go**.
4. The task pane displays animals list.
5. Click the selected picture, once it appears at the center of the slide or select the picture, it appears a small arrow at the right of the side of the picture. Click the arrow and then Insert.
6. When you are finished using the Clip Gallery, click the Close button on the Clip Gallery title bar.

Add WordArt

WordArt is a gallery of text styles that you can add to your documents to create decorative effects, such as shadowed or mirrored (reflected) text. In PowerPoint 2007, you can also convert existing text into WordArt.

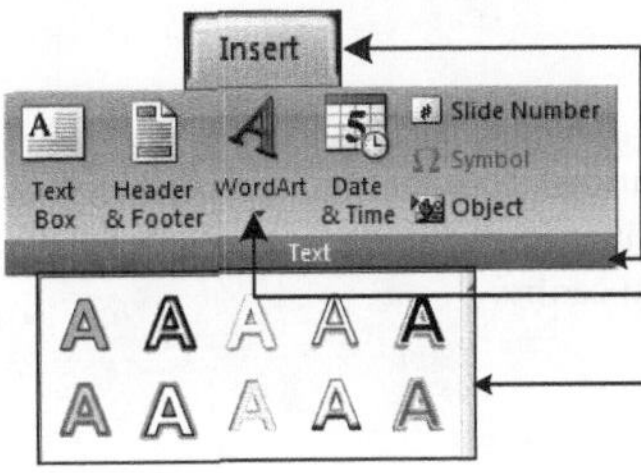

1. Select the slide on which you want to add a special effect.
2. Click the **Insert** tab, in the **Text** group.
3. Click **WordArt**, click down arrow and choose the WordArt style that you want.
4. Enter your text.

Notes:

To create a perfect square or circle (or constrain the dimensions of other shapes), press and hold SHIFT while you drag.

Drawing with Shapes

PowerPoint Shapes are familiar shapes that you are likely to use very often. These shapes are fully adjustable in size. Many shapes include additional adjusting handle, which allows you to adjust many characteristic features. Shapes provides the following categories of tools: Lines, Block arrows, Rectangles, Stars and Banners, Basic shapes and Action buttons.

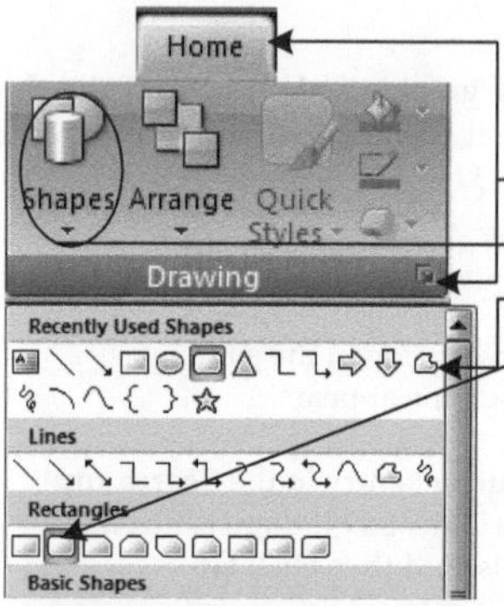

1. Click the **Home** tab, in the **Drawing** group.
2. Click **Shapes** down arrow.
3. A list of shapes gallery opens.
4. Click at **Rounded Rectangle** in the gallery.
5. After select the shape the mouse pointer changes to plus sign, drag the rounded rectangle. A rectangle appears. And you apply style to the shape.

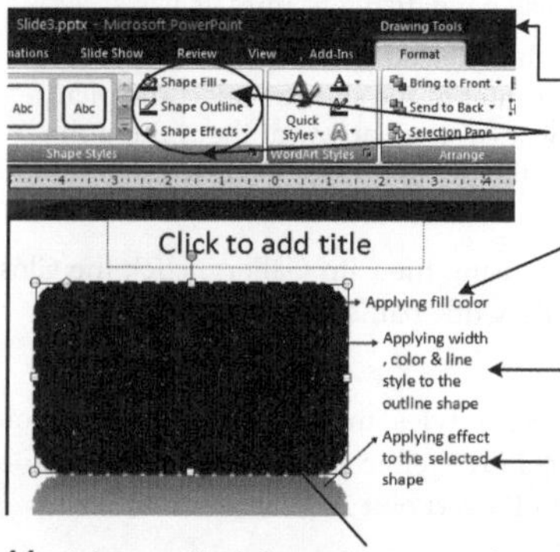

6. Select the shape and click **Drawing Tools**.
7. In **Shape Styles** group. You can add **fill**, **outline** and **effect** to the shape.
8. Applied shape fill color to the selected shape with a solid color, gradient, picture or texture.
9. Applied shape outline to specific color, width, and line style for the outline of the selected shape.
10. Applied shape effects to apply a visual effect to the selected shape such as shadow, reflection etc.
11. After applied the style to your shape appears as shown above.

Rotating and Flipping Objects

You can change the position of shapes by rotating or reversing them. Reversing a shape is also referred to as creating a mirror image or flipping. You can rotate a single object or a group of objects around its own centre.

Notes:

Flipping an Object

Flipping means to turn an object by 180°, either horizontally or vertically (leading to a lateral/vertical inversion respectively).

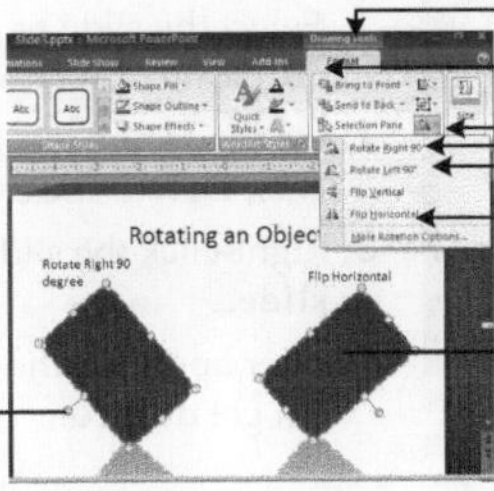

1. Select the drawing object, by clicking mouse pointer on it
2. Under **Drawing Tools** in the **Format** tab of **Arrange** group.
3. Click **Selection Pane** down arrow and choose one of the following options:
   - To rotate the shape 90 degrees to the right, click Rotate Right 90°
   - To rotate the shape 90 degrees to the left, click Rotate Left 90° Or
   - **Flip Horizontal:** Mirrors the object left to right (lateral inversion)
   - **Flip Vertical:** Rotates the object 180 degrees top to bottom (vertical inversion)
4. Drag the rotation handle in the direction that you want to rotate the shape.
5. When the object is in the desired angle position, release the mouse button. The object appears in its new rotated position

To resize the shape, click it, and then drag its sizing handles (sizing handle: One of the small circles or squares that appears at the corners and sides of a selected object. You drag these handles to change the size of the object.).

Duplicating and Deleting Slides

To add a slide that contains the content of an existing slide in a presentation, you can duplicate the slide. You can duplicate i.e. copy or delete selected slides in slide sorter view also.

*To indent the new shape, press **Tab** from within the Text pane. To negative indent, press **Shift +Tab**.*

1. Select the slide or slides you want to duplicate.
2. Click the **Home** tab, in the **Slides** group, click **New Slide** down arrow and choose **Duplicate Slides**. Or
3. Right-click the slide and choose **Duplicate slide.**
4. The selected slide gets duplicated.

Notes:

Delete the ***WordArt***

1. Select the ***WordArt*** *that you want to remove, then press* ***Delete*** *key.*

Charts that you create will be embedded in PowerPoint 2007, and the chart data is stored in an Excel 2007 worksheet that is incorporated in the PowerPoint file.

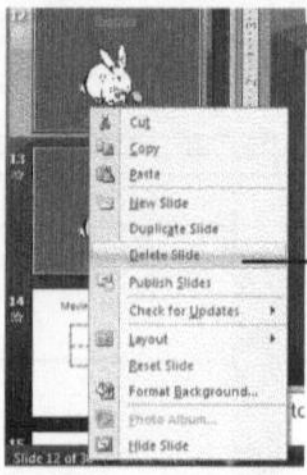

1. Select the slide or slides you want to duplicate.
2. On the **Home** tab, in the **Slides** group, click **Delete slide** Or.
3. Right-click the slide and choose **Delete slide.**
4. After applying the command, the slide will get deleted.

Creating Charts in PowerPoint

PowerPoint creates or modifies a chart using MS Graph. This a graphing program shared by all components like *Word, Excel, PowerPoint.* So if you know how to create graphics in one of the components, you can use the same technique in other components also.

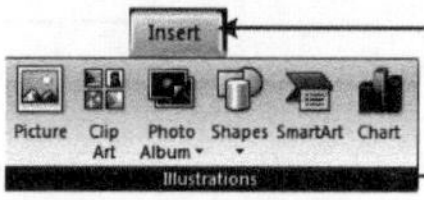

1. Click the **New Slide** in the **Slides** group. The new slide appears. The center of the slide contains *table, chart, Media Clips, SmartArt* etc. Or
2. Click the **Insert** tab, on the **Illustrations** group, click the **Chart** icon.

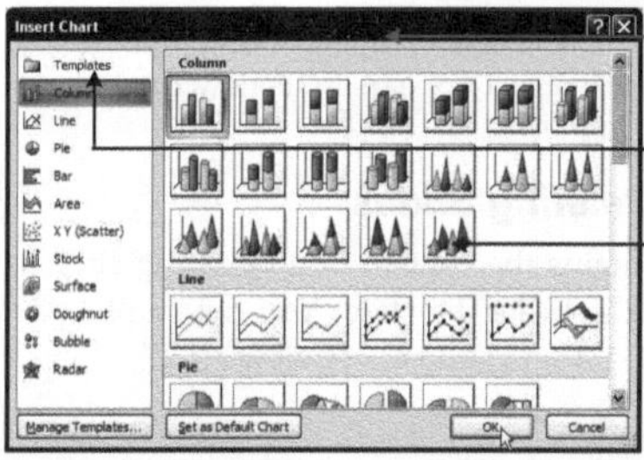

3. The **Insert Chart** dialog box appears.
4. Select the chart type under **Templates**.
5. For example, if you click the **Column** chart type, there are different types of columns in the column section. Select the desired chart type. Click OK.

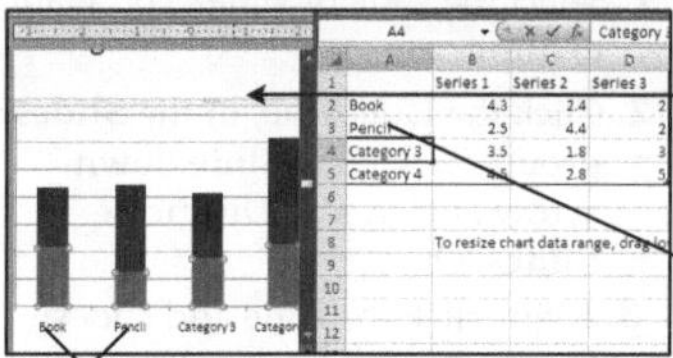

6. A sample chart appears in the Excel worksheet and the datasheet window containing the sample data for the chart appears.
7. In Excel to replace the sample data, click a cell on the worksheet, and then type the data that you want.
8. When you enter data in Excel you can see the data as well chart also simultaneously appearing in the PowerPoint.

Notes:

Edit axis or axis title

If a chart or axis title is not linked to a worksheet cell, do the following:

1. On a chart, click the chart or axis title to activate it, and then click it again to place the cursor in the text.

2. Type the new text

3. Press Enter.

*You can also right-click the title, and then click **Edit Text** on the shortcut menu.*

To add the background styles gallery to the Quick Access Toolbar, right-click a thumbnail, and then click Add Gallery to Quick Access Toolbar.

9. In Excel, click the MS Office Button and then click Save As.
10. In the Save As dialog box in the save in: list, select the folder or drive that you want to save the worksheet.
11. In the File name: box, type a new name for the file.
12. Click Save.
13. In Excel, Click the Office button and then click Close.

Changing Data in an Existing Chart

If you create a chart for your presentation and then the data used in the chart changes, you can update the data so that the chart is accurate.

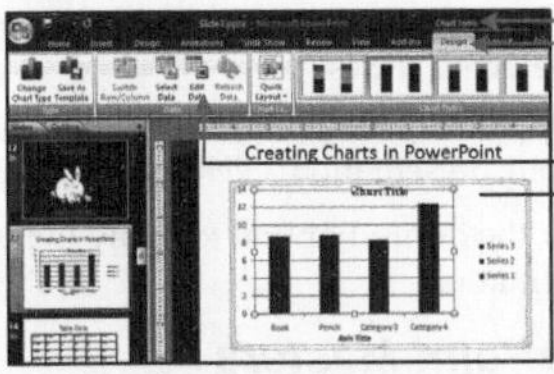

1. Select the chart that you want to change.
2. Under **Chart Tools**, on the **Design** tab, in the **Data group**, click **Edit Data**.
3. Excel opens in a split window and displays the worksheet that you want to edit.
4. To edit the contents of a title or data in a cell, in the Excel worksheet, click the cell that contains the title or the data that you want to change, and then type the new information.

   For example, if you want to change the default data (contain Category1), type it, you will see the chart in PowerPoint automatically getting changed.
5. If the chart is linked, save the worksheet. Or if the chart is embedded, PowerPoint saves the embedded chart automatically.
6. After applying changes in Excel, click **MS Office Button** and then click **Close**.

Adding Background Colour

You can not only add different colours and fill effects to the drawing objects, but also apply the same styles to the background of all the slides.

1. Click the slide or slides that you want to add a background style.

Notes:

To add the background styles gallery to the Quick Access Toolbar, right-click a thumbnail, and then click ***Add Gallery to Quick Access Toolbar****.*

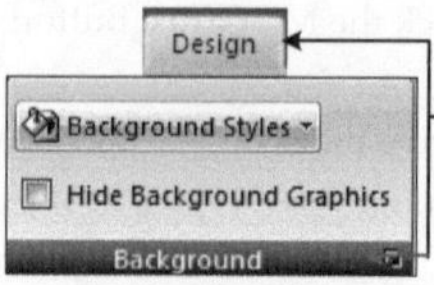

2. Click the **Design** tab, in the **Background** group, click the **Background Styles**.

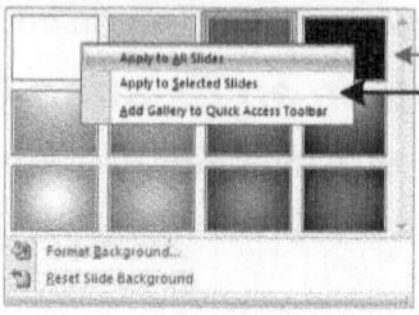

3. It displays a background gallery.

   Right click the background style that you want, and then do one of the following:

- To apply the background style to the selected slides, click **Apply to Selected** slides.
- To apply the background style to all of the slides in your presentation, click **Apply to All** slides.

4. Click the desired option to apply the background style in presentation.

PowerPoint Masters is a special slide that allows you to define all the formatting attributes and to add any common graphical object that will appear in your presentation.

PowerPoint Masters

PowerPoint Masters is an important concept. It is a concept for customizing presentation and giving it the design consistency.

PowerPoint 2007 has the following Masters:

1. Slide Master
2. Handout Master
3. Notes Master

The Shortcut keys to insert a new ***Slide Master*** *is by pressing* ***Ctrl + M*** *keys together.*

Adding a Slide Master

A slide master is a part of a template that stores information, including placements of text and objects on a slide, text and object placeholder sizes, text styles, backgrounds, color themes, effects, and animation.

To resize a placeholder, drag one of its corner borders.

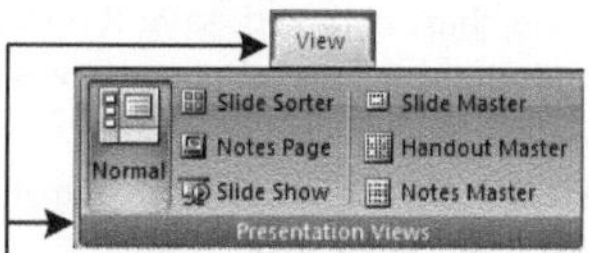

1. Click the **View** tab, in the **Presentation Views** groups, click **Slide Master**.

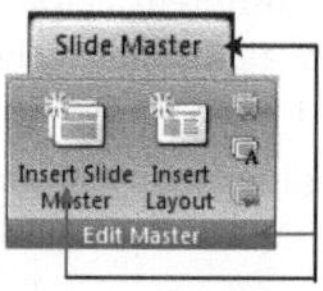

2. On the **Slide Master** tab, in the **Edit Master** group, click **Insert Slide Master**.

Notes:

Applying a Theme to a slide Master

*1. Click **View** tab, in the **Presentation Views** groups, Click **Slide Master.***

*2. On the **Slide Master** tab, in the **Edit Theme** group, click the arrow below Themes, and then click a desired theme.*

3. If you want to remove an unwanted, default placeholder, click the border of the placeholder, and then press delete.

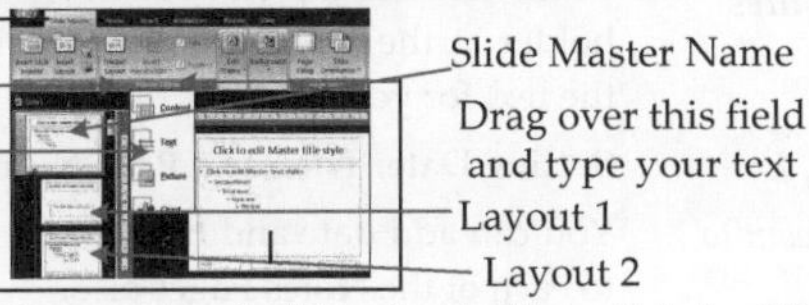

4. If you want of add a placeholder, click the **Slide Master** tab.
5. In the **Master Layout** group, click the arrow next to **Insert Placeholder**, and then click the type of placeholder you want.
6. Click the Office button and then click Save As.
7. In the **File name:** box, type a file name.
8. In the Save as type: list, click PowerPoint Templates, and then click **Save** button.

Using Notes Pages

Notes Pages— These pages are like the script for your presentation. In this script, you have image of slides along with the words you want to speak for the specific slide.

Notes Pages act like a manuscript for your presentation. You would write the text you want to discuss during the course of a presentation, for each slide.

You can also type and format your notes as you work in Normal view, but to see how your notes pages will be printed and to see the full effect of any text formatting, such as font colors, switch to **Note page view**.

Creating Notes

Notes Pages act like a manuscript for your presentation. You would write the text you want to discuss during the course of a presentation, for each slide. You can also type and format your notes as you work in Normal view, but to see how your notes pages will be printed and to see the full effect of any text formatting, such as font colors, switch to **Note page view**.

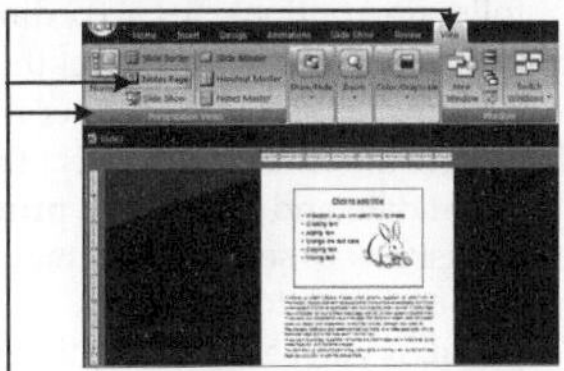

1. Click the **View** tab, in the **Presentation View** click **Notes pages.**

Notes:

Print the Notes Pages

1. Open the presentation for which you want to print notes.

2. Click the Office button, click the arrow next to Print, and then click Print preview.

*3. In the **Print Preview** tab on the **Page Setup** group, click the arrow under the **Print What:** drop-down list and then choose **Notes pages**.*

*4. To specify the orientation, click the arrow under orientation and then click **Portrait** or **Landscape**.*

*5. Click **Print**.*

In the **Notes Page View**, you see the entire Notes page as it will print. There is a picture of the slide at the top and a text place holder at the bottom. Click the place holder to begin entering the text for your Note.

Setting Date, Time and Page Numbers in Notes Pages

You can add date and time, headers, footers and page numbers to each of the Notes Pages also.

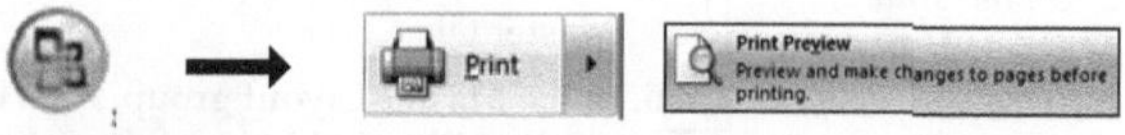

1. Click the **Office button** and choose **Print**. A sub menu appears. Click **Print Preview**.
2. The **Print Preview** tab appears with **Print** group.
3. Click **Options** down arrow. Select **Header and Footer...** .

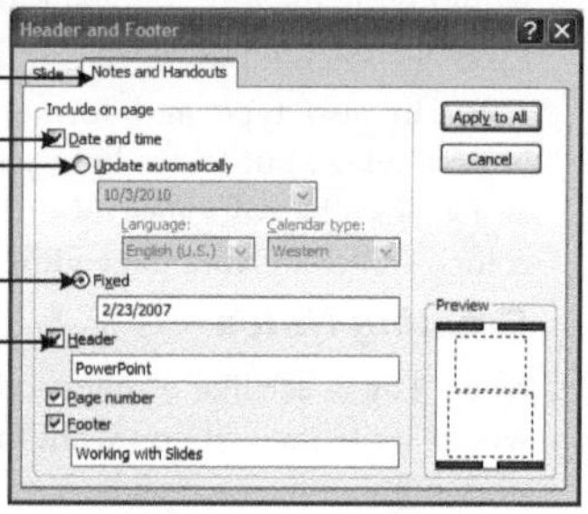

4. The Header and Footer dialog box appears. Now click the **Notes and Handouts** tab property sheet.

   The **Header and Footer** dialog box offers the following options. Set accordingly.
5. **Date and time:** If you select this option, the date and time appear in the upper right corner of the page.
6. **Update automatically:** Select this option to print the actual date and time when printouts are made. Use the list box to select the format you would like the date and time to appear in.
7. **Fixed:** If you select this option, when you want to specify the specific date to be printed in text box.
8. **Header:** The header appears on the top left corner of the page. Enter the text for the header in the box below this option.

Notes:

The header, footers, page numbers and the date on each handout will be printed if you have selected any of these items on your Notes Pages. The same is automatically applied to your Handouts.

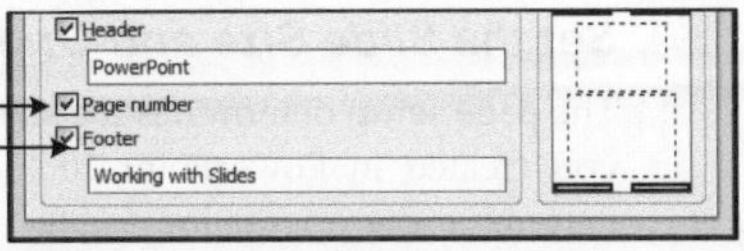

9. **Page Number:** The page numbers are shown as numerals only and appear in the lower-right corner of the page.
10. **Footer:** The footer appears in the lowerleft corner of the page. Enter the text for the footer in the box below the option.
11. Click **Apply to All** to use the selected settings.

Using Handouts for Printing

*The **Preview** box, located in the **Header and Footer** dialog box, displays the header and footer information in the location that the slide, handout, or notes page will display it.*

Handout lets you include two, three, six or nine small images of the slides in your presentation. You can select the format when you print them. You can print your entire presentation the slides, outline, notes and audience handouts. You can also print specific slides, handouts, notes pages, or outline pages.

1. Open the presentation you want to print.
2. Click the **Office** button, click the arrow next to Print, and then click **Print Preview**.

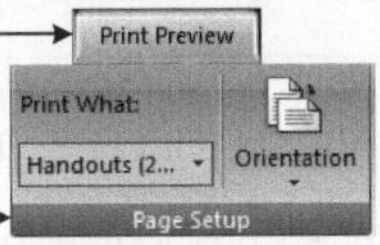

3. In the **Print Preview** tab on the **Page Setup** group, click the arrow under the **Print What:** drop down list and then choose Handouts (3 slides per page).

The Handouts (3 Slides Per Page) format provides lines for the audience to take notes.

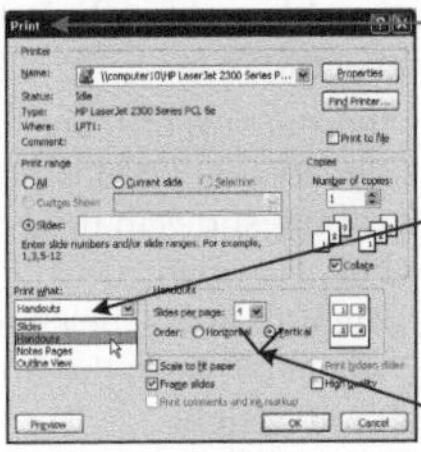

4. Click the **Print** command in the **Print** group, or press **Ctrl + P** keys together. The **Print** dialog box appears.
5. In the **Print what:** box, click the item you want to print.

   If you select Handouts, you can then select a number of slides per page. And also indicate whether the order should be horizontal or vertical.
6. Select any other options you want to apply.
7. After applying the option in the handouts section, click OK.

Set the Slide Size and Orientation for Printing

The page setup determines the size and orientation of the slides you created in PowerPoint 2007. In setting up the page you determine the orientation for the slides, the size of the slides, the starting number of the slides, the orientation for the notes, handouts and outline.

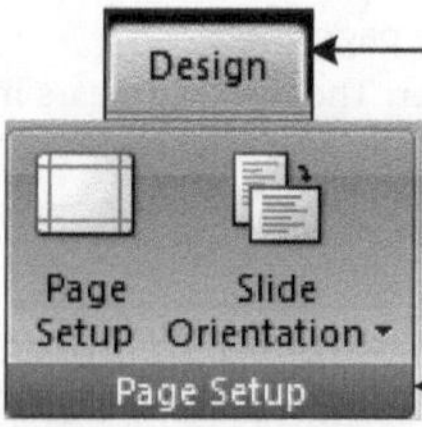

1. Click the **Design** tab, in the **Page Setup** group. Click **Page Setup**. The **Page Setup** dialog box appears.

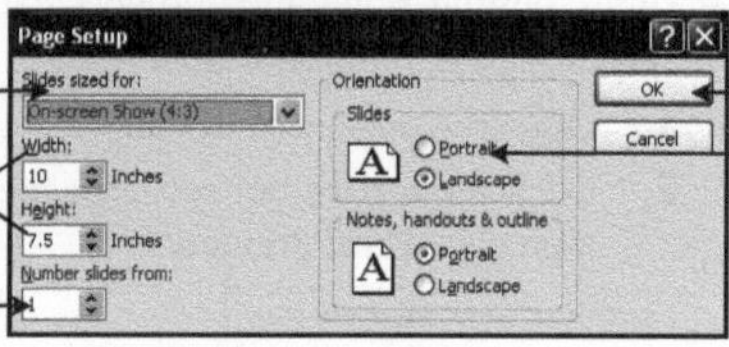

2. Select slide size from the **Slides sized for:** drop-down list in the **Page Setup** dialog box.
   The six preset slide sizes are:
   - On-screen Show
   - 35mm Slides
   - Letter Paper
   - Overhead Banner
   - A4 Paper
   - Custom
3. If you select custom option, then you specify the custom width and height in the **Width:** and **Height:** edit boxes.
4. To specify the starting number for the slides, enter the number you want to start the numbering of the slides in the **Number slides from:** edit box.
5. To set the orientation for the slide in the slides box, select between the **Portrait** and **Landscape** options.
6. Finally click OK.

Custom Shows

Use a basic custom show to give separate presentations to different groups in your organization. For example, if your presentation contains a total of five slides, you can create a custom show named "Custom 1" that includes just slides 1, 3

Notes:

All slides in a presentation must be set to one type of orientation.

*Another way to select the slides to print is to switch to Slide Sorter or Outline view. For this, press and hold down the **Shift** key as you click each slide or slide icon. When you open the **Print** dialog box, click the Selection option in the **Print Range** section.*

*To select multiple sequential slides, click the first slide, and then hold down **Shift** key while you click the last slide that you want to select. To select non-sequential slides, hold down **Ctrl** key while you click each slide that you want to select.*

Notes:

To preview a custom show, click the name of the show in the Custom Shows dialog box, and then click Show.

*To create a graceful ending to a slide show you can add a black slide at the end of presentation. Click **Office button**, click PowerPoint Options button. The PowerPoint Options dialog box appears. Click Advanced Page, under **Slide Show** click **End** with black slide check box. If you do not include the black slide option, then PowerPoint will reappear first slide after the last slide.*

and 5. You can create a second custom show named "Custom 2" that includes slides 1, 2, 4 and 5. When you create a custom show from a presentation, you can always run the entire presentation in its original sequential order.

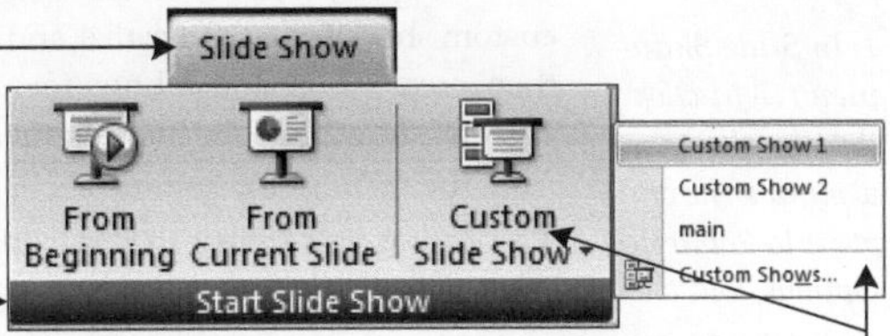

1. Click the **Slide Show** tab, in the **Start Slide Show** group.
2. Click the arrow next to **Custom Slide Show**, and then click **Custom Shows...** .

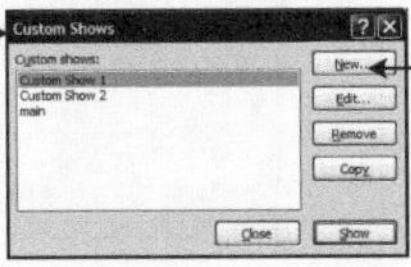

3. **Custom Shows** dialog box appears.
4. Click **New... button.**

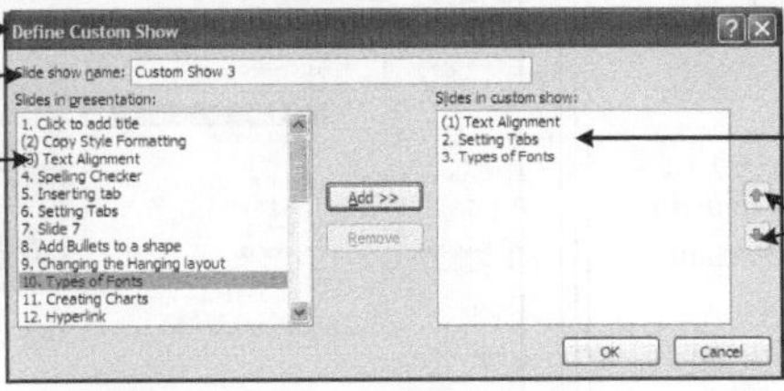

5. The **Define Custom Show** dialog box appears.
6. Under **Slides in presentation:** click the slides that you want to include in the custom show and then click **Add >>**
7. To change the order in which slides appear, under **Slides in custom show:** click a slide, and then click one of the arrow to move the slide **up** or **down** in the list.
8. Type a name in the **Slide show name:** box and then click OK. To create additional custom shows with any slides in your presentation, repeat steps 1 through 5.
9. To Preview a custom show, click the name of the show in the Custom shows dialog box, and then click Show button.

Notes:

Write on slides during a presentation

*1. In **Slide Show view**, right-click the slide that you want to write on, point to Pointer Options, and then click a pen or highlighter option.*

2. Hold down the left mouse button and drag to write or draw on your slides.

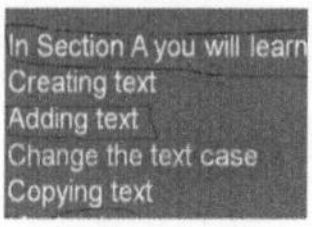

*If you want to print your notes in color, select a color printer. Click the **Office Button**, click the arrow next to **Print**, and then click **Print Preview**. Under Print, click Options, point to **Color/Grayscale** and then click **Color**.*

Hyperlinked Custom Shows

Use a hyperlinked custom show to organize content in a presentation. For example, create a **main** custom show about your company's new overall organization, you can then create a custom show for *department A* and name it as **custom show1** and then create a custom show for *department B* and name it as **custom show2** within the organization and link to these shows from the main presentation.

1. Repeat step from 1 to 5 as explained in **Custom Show**.
2. To create a hyperlink from the main show, select the text or object that you want to represent the hyperlink.

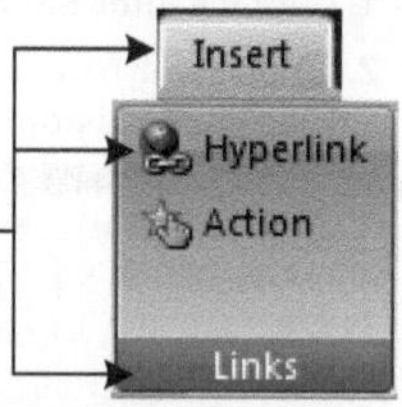

3. On the **Insert** tab, in the **Links** group, click **Hyperlink**.

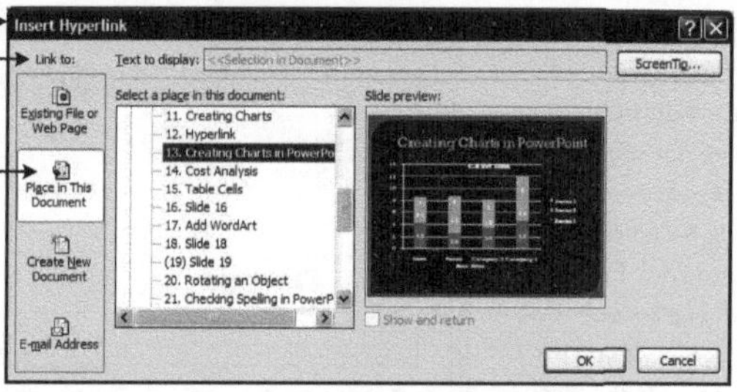

4. The **Insert Hyperlink** dialog box appears.
5. Under **Link to:** click **Place in This Document**.
6. Do one of the following:
   - To link to a custom show, in the **Select a place in this document:** list, select the custom show that you want to go through and then select the Show and return check box.
   - To link to a location in the current presentation, in the **Select a place in this document: list**, select the slide that you want to go to.
7. To **Preview** a custom show, click the name of the show (*main*) in the **Custom shows** dialog box and then click **Show** button.

Notes:

The shortcut key to ***Insert Hyperlink*** *press* ***Ctrl + K*** *keys together.*

Remove Slide Transition from your presentation

1. In the pane that contains the ***Outline*** *and* ***Slides*** *tabs, click the* ***Slides*** *tab.*

2. On the ***Home*** *tab, click a slide thumbnail.*

3. On the ***Animations*** *tab, in the* ***Transition To This Slide*** *group, click* ***No Transition.***

Add Transitions between Slides

Slides transitions are the animation-like effects that occur in the slide show view, when you move from one slide to the next. You can control the speed of each slide transition effect. You can also add sound.

1. Select the slide(s) you want to add a transition effect.

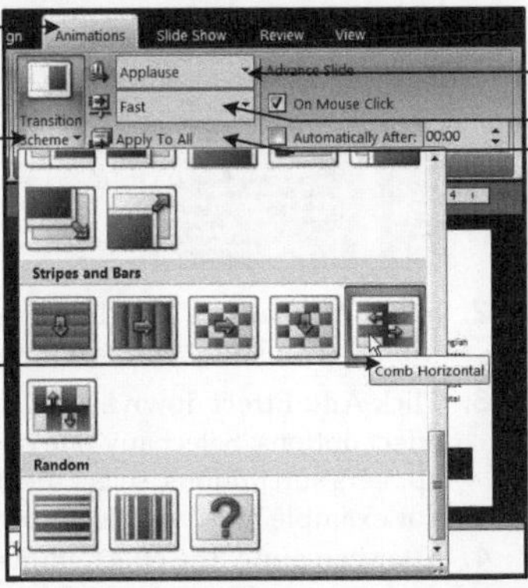

2. Click the **Animations** tab. In the **Transition to This slide** group, click **Transition schema** down arrow and then select the effect that will be applied during the slide show. For example here we select **Comb Horizontal** under stripes and Bars.

3. To set the slide transition speed in the Transition to this group, click the arrow next to **Transition Speed** and then select the speed that you want. Choose the speed of transition from *Slow*, *Medium* or *Fast*.

4. If you Apply to all slides, click **Apply to All** in the **Transition to This Slide** group.

5. Select the **Sound** option to give sound transitions to your slide show from the Sound drop-down list in the Transition to This Slide group.

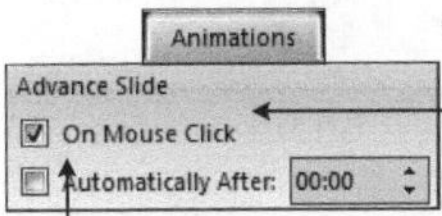

6. The Advance section has two options for transition:

- On mouse click check box if you want the transition to take place on clicking the mouse.
- Automatically after in this case the transition takes place automatically after the time you specify in the seconds box.

Notes:

Delete a sound

1. Click the slide that contains the sound that you want to delete.

2. In Normal view, click the sound icon  *or CD icon*  *, and then press DELETE.*

To delete multiple sounds, repeat steps 1 and 2 for each slide that contains sound files that you want to delete.

Hide a slide

1. In the pane that contains the Outline and Slides tabs, click the Slides tab.

2. Right-click the slide that you want to hide, then click ***Hide Slide.***

3. The hidden slide icon  *appears with the slide number inside, next to the slide that you have hidden.*

7. After applying all options, you can see the effect in the Slide show. Click the **Slide Show** tab, in the **Start Slide Show** group, click From Beginning icon. Click the next button (i.e.→) to go to the next slide.

Custom Animation Effects

1. Select the slide you want to apply custom animation effects.

2. In the **Animations** tab, click **Custom Animation** icon. The **Custom Animation** task pane appears.
3. Click **Add Effect** down arrow. You can see the effect options. Select any one option, again it appears sub options, select the desired options. For example here we select **Spin** effect to animate.
4. After you apply the effect, immediately it animates the selected effect option in the slide.
5. In the **Modify:** (selected option) list box, you can see the options applied in the list.
   In Start: drop down list, select the desired options, such as *On click, With previous, After Previous.*
   In **Direction:** drop down list, select the desired amount. (i.e it will depend upon the selection of the effect option)
   In **Speed:** drop down list, select the desired options, such as *Very slow, Slow, Medium, Fast, Very Fast.*
6. Click **Play** button. You can see the preview in the current slide. It shows both the options applied in the slide list.

Set Up a Slide Show Option

1. Click **Slide Show** tab in the **Set Up** group, choose **Set Up Slide Show** icon.
2. The **Set Up Show** dialog box appears.

Notes:

Starting the Slide Show

*1. Click **View** tab in the presentation views and choose Slide Show icon. (press **F5** or **Shift** + **F5** keys together.*

Or

*2. Click **Slide Show** tab in the **Start Slide Show group**, choose Slide Show from beginning.*

*3. In the **Slide show**, you go to next slide, press **N** or click the **Backspace** key to go to the previous slide.*

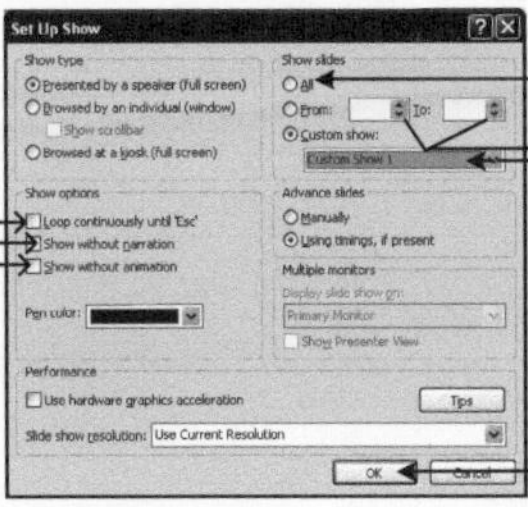

3. To Show all slides in your presentation, Click **All** in the Show slides section.
4. To show a specific group of slides from your presentation, enter a starting and ending slide in **From:** and **To:** edit boxes.
5. To start a custom slide presentation that derives from another presentation, click Custom Show: drop down list and then click the presentation that you want to view as a custom show.
6. Click the check box, to play a sound file or animation continuously, select the **Loop continuously until press Esc** key.
7. To show a presentation without playing an embedded narration, select the show **without narration** check box.
8. To show a presentation without playing an embedded animation, select the Show without animation check box.
9. Select the desired option you want to set in the Set Up Show dialog box, then click OK button.

Outlook 2007

Getting Started

MS Outlook 2007 is an application package of MS Office. This is a powerful tool of *Personal Information Management* (PIM) program that helps a person in organizing his schedule, keep track of contacts and communicate with others. Many people have several appointments to keep and tasks to accomplish in a day.

Outlook helps them by maintaining schedule and by organizing the information in a structured and readable manner. By having this facility, one can keep a track of meetings, e-mail messages, and notes with a particular contact. This organization consists of Outlook's Calendar, Contacts, Tasks and Notes. Contact information can be found via Find option, which can be accessed from the calendar, e-mail, and other Outlook components. PIMs gives an opportunity to individuals and workgroups to organize, find, view and share information in a convenient way.

Notes:

*The Shortcut key to hide the **Navigation Pane:***

*Press **Alt + F1** keys together.*

A ribbon does appear in some parts of Outlook, such as when you create a new email message.

You can drag the edge of any window pane in Outlook to widen or shrink the columns of information.

Starting Outlook 2007

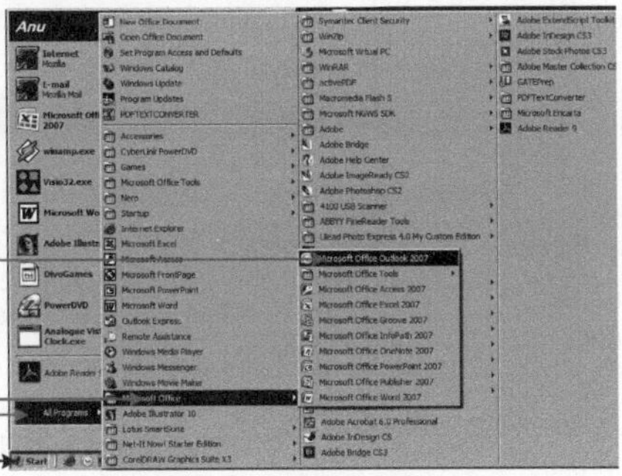

1. Click the **Start** button on the Taskbar.
2. Highlight **All Programs**, click **Microsoft Office**.
3. A sub menu appears, click **Microsoft Office Outlook 2007.**

Outlook 2007 Window Screen

The Outlook window opens in a default page. It is similar to other Windows programs. It has a title bar, a menu bar, a toolbar, a status bar, and Minimize, Maximize/Restore, and Close buttons. A Mail contains Personal Folder and Favorite Folders with All Mail Items. The icons in the vertical Outlook Bar, to the left of the To-Do bar contains Date Navigator, Appointments and Task list. These are explained below.

Title Bar: Displays the name of the program you are currently using (Outlook) and the item you are currently working with.

Menu Bar: The Menu Bar is the horizontal bar below the title bar that contains the names of command dropdown menus. You can click a Menu Bar name to display that Menu's list of commands.

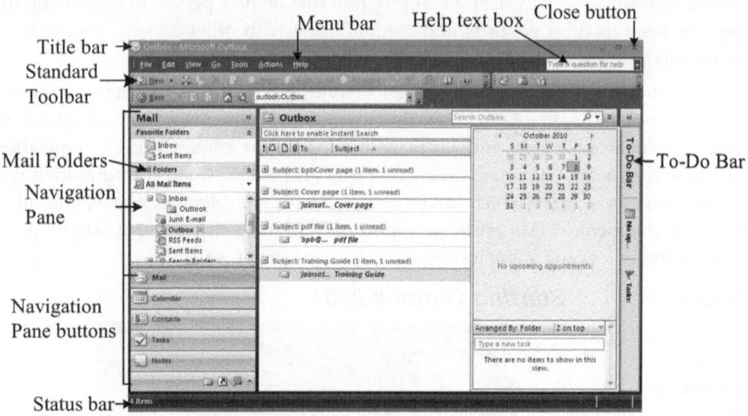

Notes:

Show a toolbar

1. Right-click the menu bar or any toolbar.

2. Click the name of the toolbar that you want to show on the shortcut menu

Hide a toolbar

Right-click the toolbar, and then clear the check box next to the name of the toolbar that you want to hide.

Standard toolbar: Contains buttons for common commands such as creating new items, printing items, and getting help. The buttons on the Standard toolbar change depending on what you are working on.

Help text box: Type a question about Outlook here and press the <Enter> key to search Outlook Help for answers. The Outlook Help window displays the results.

Close button: Click the close button in the Title bar to exit the Outlook program.

To-Do Bar: Keep tabs on your calendar, appointments, and tasks all in one place. The To-Do Bar can also be displayed in a minimized format.

Status bar: Displays messages and feedback.

Navigation Pane Buttons: Click a button to see the folders and tools for a certain category—i.e. *Mail, Calendar,* or *Contacts.*

Navigation Pane: It contains buttons and icons you can click to move among Outlook's folders and tools. The pane's contents change when you click a different Navigation Pane button—i.e. Mail, Calendar, or Contacts.

Mail folders: Displays all your mail folders, including the Inbox, Outbox, Junk E-mail, Drafts, and Sent Items folders.

Scroll bars: Use the vertical scroll bars to view different parts of the panes.

Notes:

To minimize or expand the Navigation Pane in the window, click the Minimize Navigation Pane or Expand the Navigation Pane button at the top of the Navigation Pane.

Display the To-Do Bar

*Select **View** menu and choose **To-Do Bar** and then select **Normal**.*

*To minimize the **To-Do Bar**, click the Minimize the **To-Do Bar** button, which is located at the top of the **To-Do Bar**.*

HTTP accounts work similar to IMAP in Outlook 2007.

Creating an E-mail Account

To send and receive e-mail messages with Office Outlook, you need to add your e-mail account information to it. Outlook 2007 supports Microsoft Exchange Server 2000, POP3, IMAP and HTTP e-mail servers. Your Internet service provider (ISP) or e-mail administrator can provide you with the configuration information that you need to manually set up your e-mail account in Outlook 2007.

Adding an E-mail Account in Outlook

The Internet Connection Wizard makes short work of setting up your online mailbox by walking you through each step for every e-mail account you have set up.

Before you get going, make sure you know e-mail address along with the following information. [You may need to contact your ISP, (Internet Service Provider), to get it.]

First, information about the e-mail servers:

- The type of e-mail server you use: POP3 (most e-mail accounts), HTTP (such as Hotmail), or IMAP
- The name of the incoming e-mail server
- For POP3 and IMAP servers, the name of the outgoing e-mail server (generally SMTP)

Second, information about your account:

- Your account name and password
- Find out if your ISP requires you to use Secure Password Authentication (SPA) to access your e-mail account

Let us look at the steps which we need to follow for setting up an email account in Outlook Express.

1. Click the **Tools** menu and choose **Accounts Settings...** .

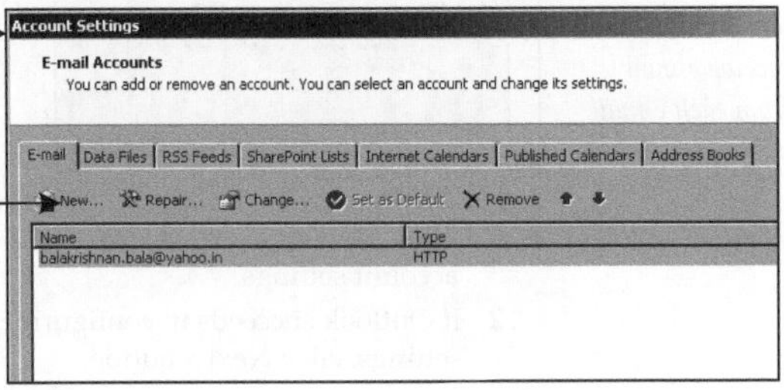

2. The **Account Settings** dialog box appears.
3. The **New...** option.

Notes:

*The shortcut key to open the New mail message is **Ctrl + N** keys pressed together.*

You can set up multiple e-mail accounts in Outlook and route all the messages to one Inbox folder or to different folders depending on the rules you set up. Click Tools menu and choose Rules and Alerts option. The Rules and Alerts dialog box opens, you can use to tell Outlook which folders is place email in when you receive e-mail from each e-mail account.

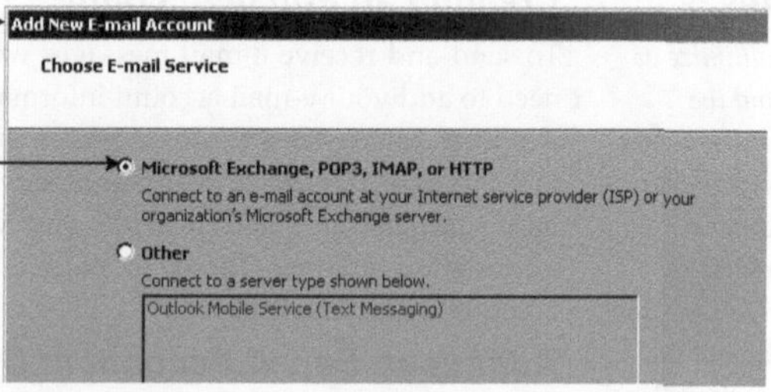

4. The **Add New E-mail Account** dialog box appears.
5. The default setting that has the Microsoft Exchange Server, POP3, IMAP, or HTTP radio button is selected.
6. Click Next > button.

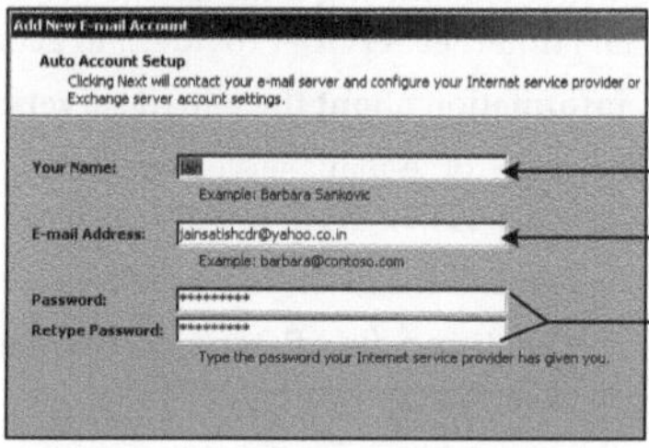

7. Type the name in the **Your Name:** list box.
8. Type E-mail Address in the **E-mail Address:** list box.
9. Type **Password:** and **Retype Password:** list box.
10. Click Next > button.

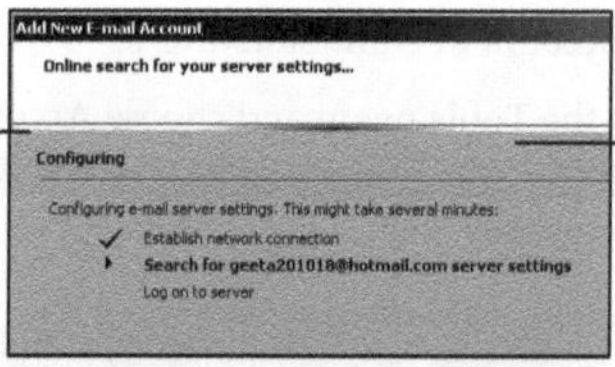

11. Another dialog box appears, letting you know that Outlook is trying to automatically detect the e-mail account settings.
12. If Outlook succeeds in configuring e-mail account settings, click **Next >** button.

If Outlook fails to set up the e-mail, there is one more thing it will try, so click Next if you get this message: An encrypted connection to your server is not available. Click Next to attempt using an unencrypted connection.

Notes:

If Outlook is successful, three check marks will appear to the left of the Add New E-mail Account dialog box appears that displays text boxes for entering your server settings.

To send and receive e-mail, you need to be connected to a mail server. You can think of the mail server as the post office. It is the computer with the network connection that receives your messages and directs your outgoing messages to other computers on a network. The computer is used to create your messages and read the messages you have received. This is known as the mail client.

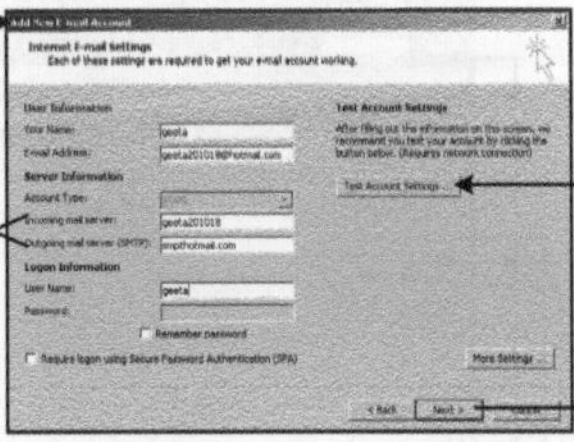

13. The **Add New E-mail Account** dialog box appears that displays text boxes for entering your server setting.
14. Type in your **incoming** and **outgoing** mail server settings.
15. Click the **Test Account Settings...** button. Outlook attempts to connect to the internet and send a message to your e-mail account to verify that everything is working.
16. Click Next > button.

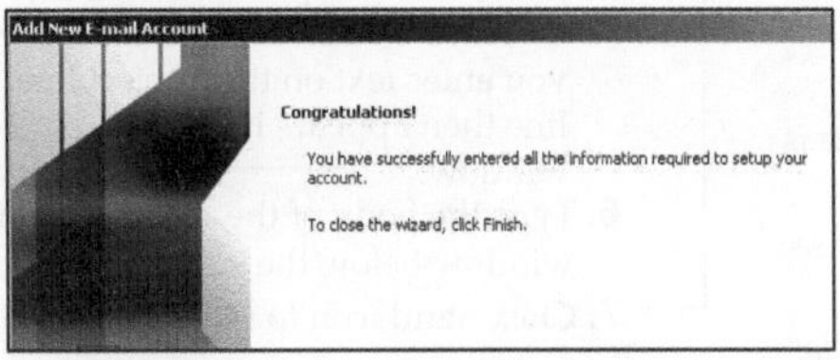

17. Another dialog box appears to inform you that you are done setting up your e-mail account.
18. Click Finish.

Creating and Sending E-mail Messages

One of the most common tasks for Outlook users is sending and receiving e-mail. The mail message window, like other item windows in Outlook 2007, features the new Ribbon in place of menus and toolbars.

To create a new e-mail message and type the e-mail address, do the following:

1. Click the **File** menu and choose **New**. A sub menu appears. Click **Mail Message**.

The Shortcut key to open an e-mail message window is Ctrl + N keys pressed together. Or Click the New down arrow in the Standard toolbar and then click Mail Message.

Notes:

*If you send an e-mail to a recipient inside your Contacts folder, type the recipient name's first few letters and pressed **Ctrl + K** keys together Outlook fills in the name and e-mail for you.*

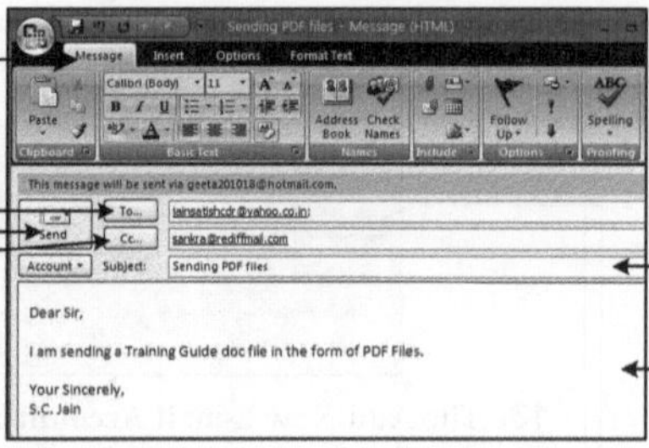

2. Outlook opens an Untitled Message window.
3. Enter the receipient addresses in the **To...** text box. If you enter multiple recipient addresses are entered separated by a semicolon and one space.
4. If you want to send a copy of the message to someone besides the recipient, enter the address in the **Cc...** text box.
5. The new message window's title bar appears. It displays Untitled - Message (Plain Text) until you enter text on the Subject line. The subject line then appears in the title bar of the message window.
6. Type the body of the message in the message window below the subject line.
7. Click **Send** icon to send the message.

*Keeping your **Inbox** folder sorted by date is important so that you will see new email messages at the top of your Inbox.*

Replying to an E-mail Message

Replying to an e-mail is like answering a letter—it acknowledges your receipt of the message and allows you to respond.

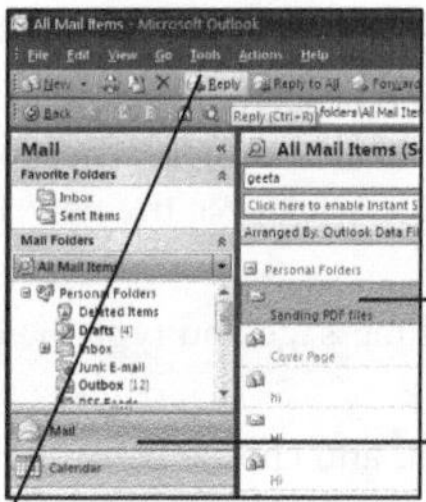

1. Click the **Mail** button in the **Navigation** pane and double click the message that you want to reply to.
2. Click the message that you wish to reply to.
   Outlook displays the contents of that message in a pane on the right side of the Outlook window.
3. Click the **Reply** button in the Standard toolbar.
4. Outlook displays a message window with the recipient's e-mail address and subject line already typed in along with a copy of the original message.
5. Click in the message text box and type the message.
6. Click the **Send** icon.

*The Shortcut key to Reply a message is **Ctrl + R** keys pressed together.*

Notes:

The Shortcut key to Forward a message is ***Ctrl + F*** *keys together.*

Mail messages can be forwarded to multiple recipients.

You must have at least one valid e-mail recipient in the ***To, Cc,*** *or* ***Bcc*** *box.*

If you want to forward two or more messages, select the first message, hold Ctrl,keys and then select each additional message. Each message will be forwarded as attachments in a new message. Type the subject of the message in the ***Subject*** *box.*

Forwarding an E-mail message

Sometimes you may receive a message, but rather than reply to it, you want to send it (forward it) to someone else. Forwarding a message essentially copies a message and sends it to someone else whom the original sender may not even know.

1. Click the **Mail** button in the **Navigation** pane and double-click the message that you want to forward.
2. Click the **Forward** icon.
3. A message window appears that contains your chosen message.
4. Click in the To… text box and type an e-mail address
5. Click in the message window and type any additional text you want to send along with the forwarded message.
6. Click the **Send** button.

Using a stored e-mail address to create a new e-mail message

If you have stored names and e-mail addresses, you can retrieve an e-mail address so you do not have to type it again. To retrieve e-mail address, follow these steps:

1. Click the **Mail** button in the **Navigation** pane and double-click the message that you want to forward.
2. Click the **File** menu and choose **New**. A sub menu appears. Click **Mail Message**.
3. The message window appears. Click the **To** Button.
4. The **Contacts** dialog box appears.

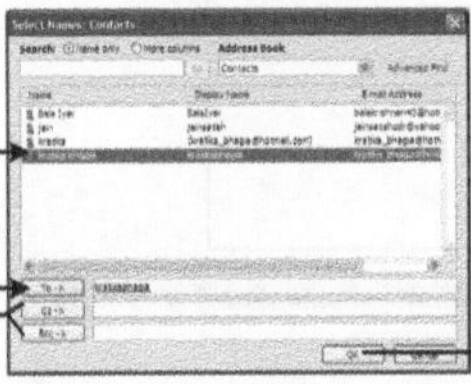

5. Click the name to select it.
6. Click the To button to chosen e-mail address to the **To** text box.
7. Click additional e-mail addresses and then click the **Cc** or **Bcc** button.
8. Click OK.
9. Outlook automatically enters your chosen e-mail address in the **To** text box.
10. Click in the **Subject** text box and type a description of message.

11. Click in the message text box and type your message.
12. Click the **Send** icon to send your message.

Forwarding E-mail Message

If you have received an e-mail message that you would like to share with someone else, you can forward the message to them.

1. Open the message you want to forward icon in the Standard toolbar.
2. A message window appears that contains your chosen message.
3. In the **To** text box, type the username or e-mail address of the person you are forwarding the message to.
4. Click the message window and type any additional text you want to send along with the forwarded message.
5. Click the **Send** icon.

Attaching a file to a message

One of the most useful features of e-mail is the ability to attach one or more files to a message. You can attach pictures, documents, PDFs and more in Outlook.

1. To create a new e-mail message, type a subject and type an e-mail address.

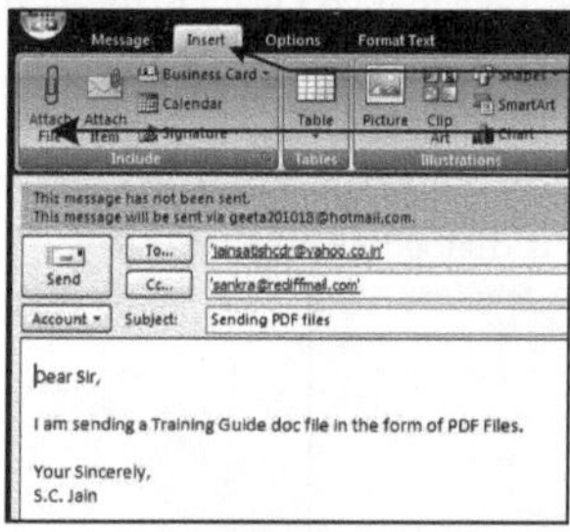

2. Click the **Insert** tab.
3. Click the **Attach File** icon.

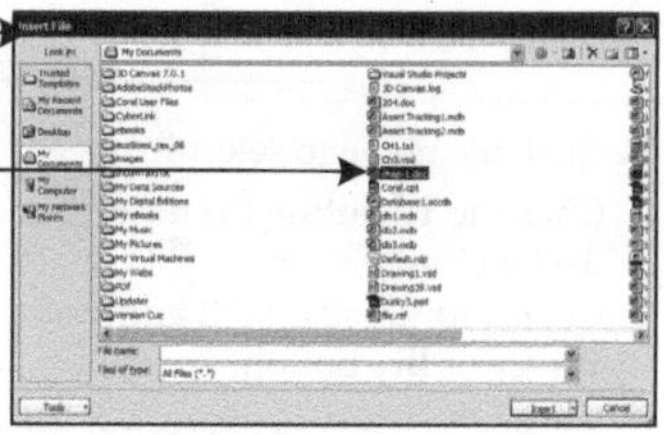

4. The **Insert** dilaog box appears.
5. Select the file you want to attach to your message and then click **Insert**.

Notes:

If the message's original sender sent the e-mail to blind carbon copy(Cc) recipients, they will not receive your reply.

You can forward only one message at a time.

Attachments in the original e-mail are not forwarded with the new text message.

Be careful when attaching files to messages. Many ISPs put a limit on the maximum size of an e-mail message, such as 25 MB. Try to keep any file attachments small if the recipient has a slow Internet connection, downloading a large file attachment can take a long time.

Notes:

*If you hold down the **Ctrl** or **Shift** key while clicking a file, you can select multiple files at once.*

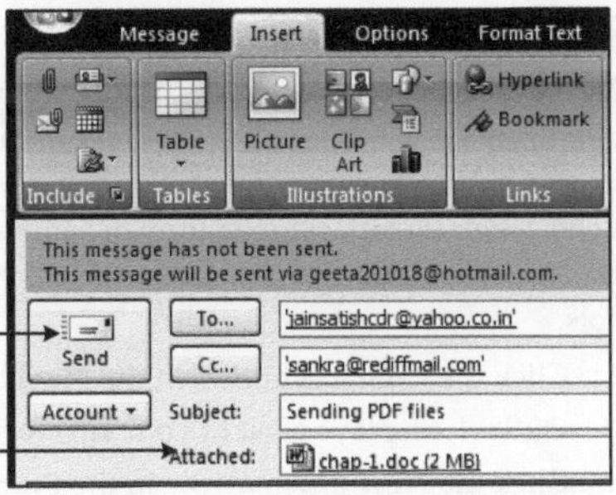

6. It displays an attached option with text box in the message window.
7. Select and right-click any file in the Attachment text box, a pop-up menu appears, choose Remove if you do not to attach a file to a message.
8. Click the **Send** icon.

Rather than select multiple files to attach to a message, you can compress or Zip multiple files into a single compressed file by using a separate program like WinZip

Deleting E-mail Messages

To delete an e-mail message: from the message window or from the **Inbox.** If you accidentally delete a message, you also have some capability of retrieving it.

Delete a message through message dialog box

1. Double-click the e-mail in the **Inbox** folder you want to delete.
2. A message window opens.
3. On the **Message** tab, in the **Actions** group, click **Delete. Or**
4. From the **Office button** click **Delete** option.
5. Your message is deleted and sent to the **Deleted** Items folder.

Retrieving Deleted Messages

If you have accidentally deleted a message that you want to keep, you can retrieve it if your Deleted Items folder has not been emptied yet. You may be able to retrieve some messages that have been emptied from your Deleted Items folder.

*The Shortcut key to open the **Distribution List** is **Ctrl + Shift + L** keys pressed together.*

1. From the **Folder** list, select **Deleted** Items. Items in the **Deleted Items** folder will appear.
2. Select the message you want to keep.
3. Drag the message to the **Inbox** folder.
4. The message is moved from the **Deleted Items** folder to the **Inbox** folder.

Storing Contact Information

The Contacts list contains information about people and organizations you interact with. The Contacts list lets you enter as much or as little information about your contacts as you want, such as their names, phone numbers, and addresses. You can then use the information in the Contacts list with the other Outlook tools.

1. Click the **Contacts** button in the **Navigation** pane.
2. Outlook displays a list of your current contacts. Or
3. Click the **New** down arrow in the **Standard** toolbar then click **New Contact**.
4. The **Contact** window appears.

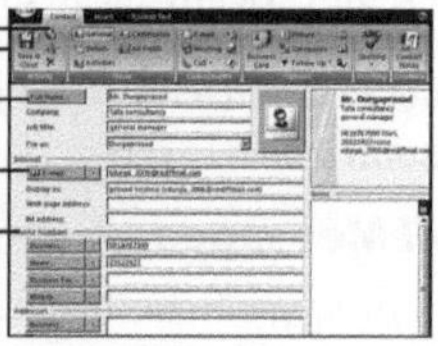

5. Click in the **Full Name** text box and type a person's name.
6. Type any additional information that you want to store about a person, such as additional e-mail addresses, telephone numbers.
7. Click **Save & Close** in the **Actions** group, to save your current contact information or click **Save & New** (to save your current contact information) and open a new Contact window to store another name.

Printing the Contacts List

Printing your Contacts list is no different from printing anything else in Outlook, except for a few unique options. For example, you can select a print style from card, booklet, memo, or phone directory formats, and also select the contacts you want printed.

1. Click the **Contacts** button in the **Navigation** Pane.
2. The **Contacts** list appears.
3. Click the **Print** button on the **Standard** toolbar. Or
4. Click the **File** menu and choose **Print**. Alternatively, press **Ctrl + P** keys together.

Notes:

The shortcut key to open the Contacts window is ***Ctrl + N*** *keys pressed together*

Several of the fields in the Contact item window have buttons and list arrows next to them. The buttons display dialog boxes to assist you with the fields, while the arrows are used if a contact has more than one phone number, e-mail account, or address.

Delete a contact

You can also delete contacts if you no longer need them.

1. Select a contact in the Contacts list and click the ***Delete*** *button on the Standard toolbar.*

2. The contact is moved to the ***Deleted Items*** *in the* ***Mailbox****.*

Notes:

To preview the printed contacts, click the ***Preview*** *button in the* ***Print*** *dialog box.*

To print only selected contacts, hold down the ***Ctrl*** *key as you select contacts in the Contacts list, then select Only selected items in the Print range area of the Print dialog box.*

Day view

Day view gives you an hour-by-hour breakdown of your daily schedule.

1. Click the Day button in the Calendar.

2. Click ***View*** *menu and choose* ***Day****.*

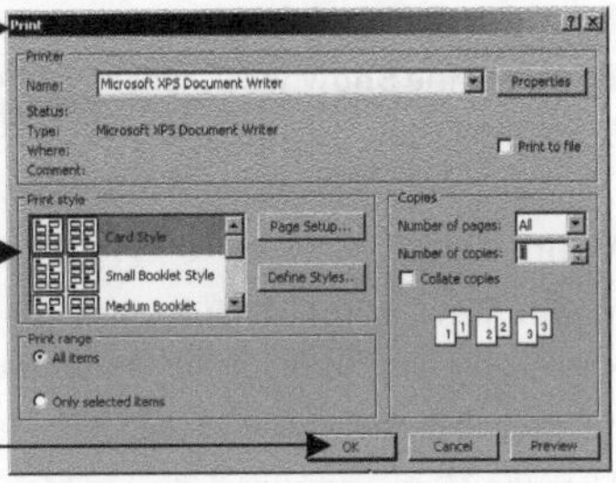

5. The **Print** dialog box appears.

6. Select a Print style from the **Print style** drop-down list.
Scroll down the list to see all the styles.

7. Specify other desired print options and click OK.

Using the Calendar

Calendar is one of the most-used tools in Outlook. The Calendar lets you keep track of appointments, such as a visit to the dentist and events, such as a vacation.

Viewing the Calendar

There are three main Calendar views in Outlook: *Day, Week* and *Month* view. We shall learn about each of these views, and how to navigate within them.

Display the Calendar

First, we need to display the Calendar.

1. Click the **Calendar** button in the **Navigation** pane.
2. The **Calendar** appears.

Navigation buttons Details buttons

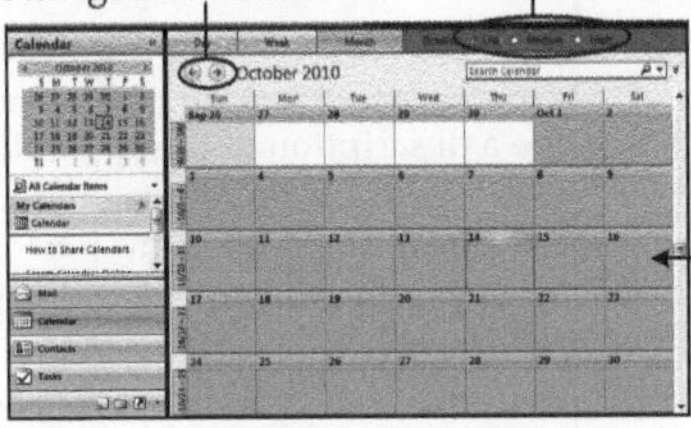

3. The Calendar opens in the month view.

Week view

Week view has two display choices: *Work Week* and *Full Week*. Work Week view displays your schedule *Monday* through *Friday*, while Full Week view displays the full seven-day work week.

Notes:

*The shortcut key to open **Work week** is **Ctrl + Alt + 2** all keys pressed together. and to open **Week** is **Ctrl + Alt + 3** all keys pressed together.*

*The shortcut key to open the Month is **Ctrl +<Alt> + <4>** all keys pressed together.*

*The Keyboard shortcut to create an appointment, press **Ctrl + Shift + A** keys together*

*You can type specific words and phrases in the **Start time** and **End time** boxes instead of dates. For example you can type Today, Tomorrow, New Year's Day, Two Weeks from Tomorrow, Week from Yesterday, Three days before New Year's Day, and most holiday names.*

1. Click the **Week** button in the **Calendar**.
2. Click the **Show work week** or **Show full week** option. Or
3. Click **View** menu and choose the desired option to open either select **Week** or **Work Week**.

Month View

Month view is the default view in the Calendar. Month view shows your schedule for the entire month.

Click the **Month** button in the **Calendar**. Or

Click the **View** menu and choose **Month**.

Scheduling Appointments and Events

Outlook's Calendar is great for keeping track of your appointments and events.

Schedule an appointment

An *appointment* is any scheduled activity that takes place within a one-day time period. When you schedule an appointment, the Calendar blocks off the specified time span—for example, from 10 a.m. to noon.

1. Click the **New Appointment** button on the **Standard** toolbar.
2. An Untitled—Appointment window appears.

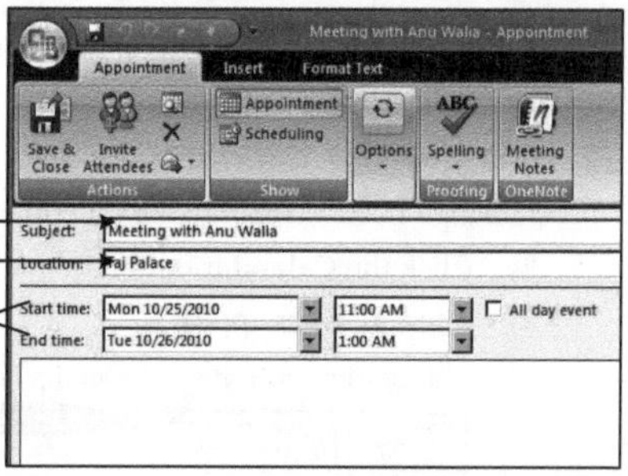

3. Type a description of the appointment in the Subject: field. After you entered the subject it will appear in the title bar.
4. Enter the appointment's location in the Location: field.
5. Specify the date of the appointment and its Start and End time.
   Enter any additional information about the appointment, if desired.
6. Click the **Save & Close** button in the **Actions** group.
   The Appointment window closes and the event appears in your calendar.

Notes:

For existing appointments

1. Open the appointment, or, if the appointment recurs, open the series.

*2. In the **Options** group turn a reminder on or off, on the **Appointment tab**.*

*3. In the **Reminder** list, click **None.***

In Day/Week/ Month view, you can quickly create an event by double-clicking the darker shaded area beneath the date heading of the day of the event.

Working with Recurring Appointments

A *recurring* appointment is an appointment that occurs at regular intervals; for example, every Friday at 11 a.m.

1. Click the New Appointment button on the Standard toolbar.
2. An Untitled—Appointment window appears.
3. Type a description of the appointment in the **Subject Field** (for example, Staff Meeting).
4. Click the **Recurrence** button in the **Options** group.

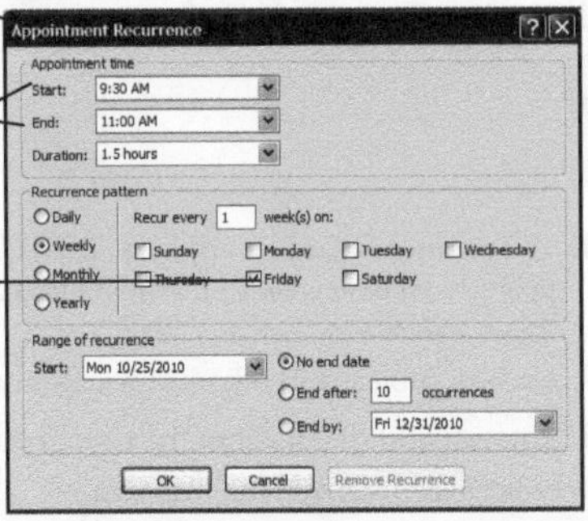

5. The **Appointment Recurrence** dialog box appears. Here you need to specify the time of the appointment, how often the appointment should recur (for example, every Friday), and the start and end date of the recurrence.
6. Make your specifications in the Appointment Recurrence dialog box, and click OK.
7. Click the **Save & Close** button in the **Actions** group.

Creating a Task

Recording your tasks makes them easier to remember and manage. Outlook tasks provide a good way to organize what you need to get done.

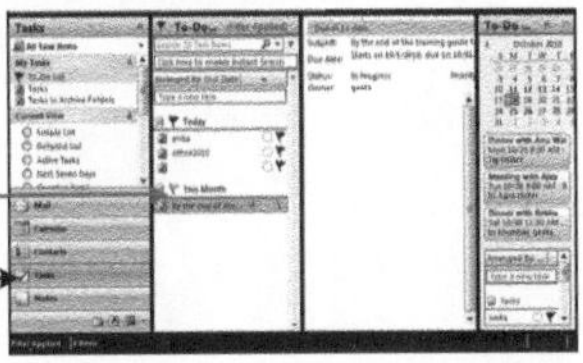

1. Click the **Tasks** button in the **Navigation** Pane.
2. The **To-Do** List appears in Tasks.
3. Click the **New** button on the **Standard** toolbar.

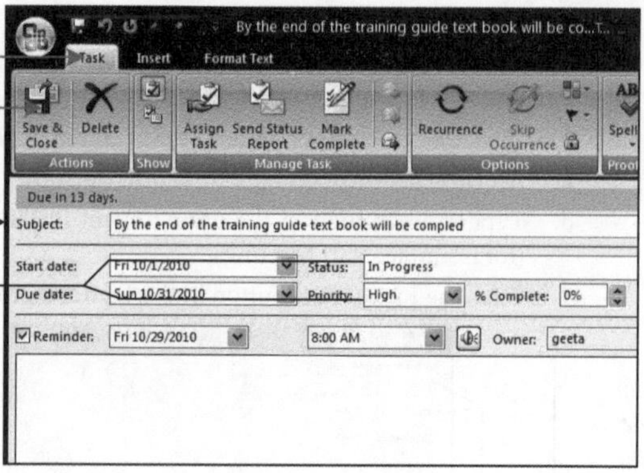

4. A **Task** item window appears. Task Item Window Fields provide an overview of the fields that are available in this window.
5. Enter a subject and other information about the task.
6. You can add detail about the task in the text area.

   Enter task details in the text area.
7. Click the **Save & Close** button in the **Actions** group on the Ribbon.

Index

MS Word 2007

MS Excel 2007

MS Access 2007

MS PowerPoint 2007

MS Outlook 2007